Modern Critical Views

Chinua Achebe
Henry Adams
Aeschylus
S. Y. Agnon
Edward Albee
Raphael Alberti
Louisa May Alcott
A. R. Ammons
Sherwood Anderson
Aristophanes
Matthew Arnold
Antonin Artaud
John Ashbery
Margaret Atwood
W. H. Auden
Jane Austen
Isaac Babel
Sir Francis Bacon
James Baldwin
Honoré de Balzac
John Barth
Donald Barthelme
Charles Baudelaire
Simone de Beauvoir
Samuel Beckett
Saul Bellow
Thomas Berger
John Berryman
The Bible
Elizabeth Bishop
William Blake
Giovanni Boccaccio
Heinrich Böll
Jorge Luis Borges
Elizabeth Bowen
Bertolt Brecht
The Brontës
Charles Brockden Brown
Sterling Brown
Robert Browning
Martin Buber
John Bunyan
Anthony Burgess
Kenneth Burke
Robert Burns
William Burroughs
George Gordon, Lord
    Byron
Pedro Calderón de la Barca
Italo Calvino
Albert Camus
Canadian Poetry: Modern
    and Contemporary
Canadian Poetry through
    E. J. Pratt
Thomas Carlyle
Alejo Carpentier
Lewis Carroll
Willa Cather
Louis-Ferdinand Céline
Miguel de Cervantes

Geoffrey Chaucer
John Cheever
Anton Chekhov
Kate Chopin
Chrétien de Troyes
Agatha Christie
Samuel Taylor Coleridge
Colette
William Congreve & the
    Restoration Dramatists
Joseph Conrad
Contemporary Poets
James Fenimore Cooper
Pierre Corneille
Julio Cortázar
Hart Crane
Stephen Crane
e. e. cummings
Dante
Robertson Davies
Daniel Defoe
Philip K. Dick
Charles Dickens
James Dickey
Emily Dickinson
Denis Diderot
Isak Dinesen
E. L. Doctorow
John Donne & the
    Seventeenth-Century
    Metaphysical Poets
John Dos Passos
Fyodor Dostoevsky
Frederick Douglass
Theodore Dreiser
John Dryden
W. E. B. Du Bois
Lawrence Durrell
George Eliot
T. S. Eliot
Elizabethan Dramatists
Ralph Ellison
Ralph Waldo Emerson
Euripides
William Faulkner
Henry Fielding
F. Scott Fitzgerald
Gustave Flaubert
E. M. Forster
John Fowles
Sigmund Freud
Robert Frost
Northrop Frye
Carlos Fuentes
William Gaddis
Federico García Lorca
Gabriel García Márquez
André Gide
W. S. Gilbert
Allen Ginsberg
J. W. von Goethe

Nikolai Gogol
William Golding
Oliver Goldsmith
Mary Gordon
Günther Grass
Robert Graves
Graham Greene
Thomas Hardy
Nathaniel Hawthorne
William Hazlitt
H. D.
Seamus Heaney
Lillian Hellman
Ernest Hemingway
Hermann Hesse
Geoffrey Hill
Friedrich Hölderlin
Homer
A. D. Hope
Gerard Manley Hopkins
Horace
A. E. Housman
William Dean Howells
Langston Hughes
Ted Hughes
Victor Hugo
Zora Neale Hurston
Aldous Huxley
Henrik Ibsen
Eugène Ionesco
Washington Irving
Henry James
Dr. Samuel Johnson and
    James Boswell
Ben Jonson
James Joyce
Carl Gustav Jung
Franz Kafka
Yasonari Kawabata
John Keats
Søren Kierkegaard
Rudyard Kipling
Melanie Klein
Heinrich von Kleist
Philip Larkin
D. H. Lawrence
John le Carré
Ursula K. Le Guin
Giacomo Leopardi
Doris Lessing
Sinclair Lewis
Jack London
Robert Lowell
Malcolm Lowry
Carson McCullers
Norman Mailer
Bernard Malamud
Stéphane Mallarmé
Sir Thomas Malory
André Malraux
Thomas Mann

Modern Critical Views

Katherine Mansfield
Christopher Marlowe
Andrew Marvell
Herman Melville
George Meredith
James Merrill
John Stuart Mill
Arthur Miller
Henry Miller
John Milton
Yukio Mishima
Molière
Michel de Montaigne
Eugenio Montale
Marianne Moore
Alberto Moravia
Toni Morrison
Alice Munro
Iris Murdoch
Robert Musil
Vladimir Nabokov
V. S. Naipaul
R. K. Narayan
Pablo Neruda
John Henry Newman
Friedrich Nietzsche
Frank Norris
Joyce Carol Oates
Sean O'Casey
Flannery O'Connor
Christopher Okigbo
Charles Olson
Eugene O'Neill
José Ortega y Gasset
Joe Orton
George Orwell
Ovid
Wilfred Owen
Amos Oz
Cynthia Ozick
Grace Paley
Blaise Pascal
Walter Pater
Octavio Paz
Walker Percy
Petrarch
Pindar
Harold Pinter
Luigi Pirandello
Sylvia Plath
Plato

Plautus
Edgar Allan Poe
Poets of Sensibility & the
  Sublime
Poets of the Nineties
Alexander Pope
Katherine Anne Porter
Ezra Pound
Anthony Powell
Pre-Raphaelite Poets
Marcel Proust
Manuel Puig
Alexander Pushkin
Thomas Pynchon
Francisco de Quevedo
François Rabelais
Jean Racine
Ishmael Reed
Adrienne Rich
Samuel Richardson
Mordecai Richler
Rainer Maria Rilke
Arthur Rimbaud
Edwin Arlington Robinson
Theodore Roethke
Philip Roth
Jean-Jacques Rousseau
John Ruskin
J. D. Salinger
Jean-Paul Sartre
Gershom Scholem
Sir Walter Scott
William Shakespeare
  Histories & Poems
  Comedies & Romances
  Tragedies
George Bernard Shaw
Mary Wollstonecraft
  Shelley
Percy Bysshe Shelley
Sam Shepard
Richard Brinsley Sheridan
Sir Philip Sidney
Isaac Bashevis Singer
Tobias Smollett
Alexander Solzhenitsyn
Sophocles
Wole Soyinka
Edmund Spenser
Gertrude Stein
John Steinbeck

Stendhal
Laurence Sterne
Wallace Stevens
Robert Louis Stevenson
Tom Stoppard
August Strindberg
Jonathan Swift
John Millington Synge
Alfred, Lord Tennyson
William Makepeace Thackeray
Dylan Thomas
Henry David Thoreau
James Thurber and S. J.
  Perelman
J. R. R. Tolkien
Leo Tolstoy
Jean Toomer
Lionel Trilling
Anthony Trollope
Ivan Turgenev
Mark Twain
Miguel de Unamuno
John Updike
Paul Valéry
Cesar Vallejo
Lope de Vega
Gore Vidal
Virgil
Voltaire
Kurt Vonnegut
Derek Walcott
Alice Walker
Robert Penn Warren
Evelyn Waugh
H. G. Wells
Eudora Welty
Nathanael West
Edith Wharton
Patrick White
Walt Whitman
Oscar Wilde
Tennessee Williams
William Carlos Williams
Thomas Wolfe
Virginia Woolf
William Wordsworth
Jay Wright
Richard Wright
William Butler Yeats
A. B. Yehoshua
Emile Zola

Modern Critical Views

WALT WHITMAN

Edited with an introduction by

Harold Bloom

Sterling Professor of the Humanities
Yale University

CHELSEA HOUSE PUBLISHERS
New York

PROJECT EDITORS: Emily Bestler, James Uebbing
EDITORIAL COORDINATOR: Karyn Browne
EDITORIAL STAFF: Sally Stepanek, Linda Grossman, Jennifer Caldwell, Lois Lapid
DESIGN: Susan Lusk

Cover illustration by Peterson Design.
Composition provided by Collage Publications, Inc. New York, N.Y.

Printed and bound in the United States of America

10   9   8   7   6   5   4   3   2

Library of Congress Cataloging-in-Publication Data

Walt Whitman, modern critical views.
  Bibliography: p.
  Contents: Introduction: Whitman's "The Real Me"/
Harold Bloom—Whitman/D.H. Lawrence—Policy
made personal/Kenneth Burke—[etc.]
  1. Whitman, Walt, 1819–1892—Criticism and
interpretation—Addresses, essays, lectures.
I. Bloom, Harold.
PS3238.W365   1984   811'.3   84-23828
ISBN 0-87754-603-7

Contents

Introduction . . . . . . *Harold Bloom*   1

Whitman . . . . . . *D. H. Lawrence*   11

Policy Made Personal . . . . . . *Kenneth Burke*   25

The Theory of America . . . . . . *Richard Chase*   55

Whitman Justified: The Poet in 1860 . . . . . . *Roy Harvey Pearce* .   65

The Delicacy of Walt Whitman . . . . . . *James Wright*   87

Always Going Out and Coming In . . . . . . *R. W. B. Lewis*   99

Whitman's Image of Voice: To
      the Tally of My Soul . . . . . . *Harold Bloom* 127

The Wound-Dresser . . . . . . *Paul Zweig* 143

Chronology 159

Contributors 161

Bibliography 163

Acknowledgments 167

Index 169

Editor's Note

The essays in this volume are arranged in the order of their publication. They chronicle the major phases in which an advanced view of Whitman's nature and achievement as a poet has evolved. All of them center upon what is most difficult and vital in Whitman's work, the ambiguity of the self or selves and the curious relation between the Whitmanian self and soul. And all of them emphasize that Whitman's true originality was as much in substance as in form, or rather the trope of form.

What emerges from these essays is a partial portrait of the greatest, most enigmatic and most American of all American poets. "Partial," because Whitman took care to evade all of our categorical modes of representing him, and yet these partial views all seem to me just and valid. They depict a major mythologizer who has become our major American literary myth, our national poet, as Emerson brilliantly first proclaimed him to be.

Introduction

I

As poet and as person, Walt Whitman remains large and evasive. We cannot know, even now, much that he desired us not to know, despite the best efforts of many devoted and scholarly biographers. The relation between his life and his poetry is far more uncertain than most of his readers believe it to be. Yet Whitman is so important to us, so crucial to an American mythology, so absolutely central to our literary culture, that we need to go on trying to bring his life and his work together. Our need might have delighted Whitman, and might have troubled him also. Like his master, Emerson, Whitman prophesied an American religion that is post-Christian, but while Emerson dared to suggest that the Crucifixion was a defeat and that Americans demand victory, Whitman dared further, and suggested that he himself had satisfied the demand. Here is Emerson:

> The history of Christ is the best document of the power of character which we have. A youth who owed nothing to fortune and who was "hanged at Tyburn"—by the pure quality of his nature has shed this epic splendor around the facts of his death which has transfigured every particular into a grand universal symbol for the eyes of all mankind ever since.
>
> He did well. This great Defeat is hitherto the highest fact we have. But he that shall come shall do better. The mind requires a far higher exhibition of character, one which shall make itself good to the senses as well as to the soul; a success to the senses as well as to the soul. This was a great Defeat; we demand Victory. . . .

This grand journal entry concludes, magnificently: "I am *Defeated* all the time; yet to Victory I am born." And here is Whitman, "he that shall come," doing better:

> That I could forget the mockers and insults!
> That I could forget the trickling tears and the blows of the bludgeons and
> hammers!
> That I could look with a separate look on my own crucifixion and bloody
> crowning.
>
> I remember now,
> I resume the overstaid fraction,

> The grave of rock multiplies what has been confided to it, or to any graves,
> Corpses rise, gashes heal, fastenings roll from me.
> I troop forth replenish'd with supreme power, . . .

This is Walt Whitman "singing and chanting the things that are part of him, / The worlds that were and will be, death and day," in the words of his involuntary heir, Wallace Stevens. But which Walt Whitman is it? His central poem is what he finally entitled "Song of Myself," rather than, say, "Song of My Soul." But which self? There are two in the poem, besides his soul, and the true difficulties of reading Whitman begin (or ought to begin) with his unnervingly original psychic cartography which resists assimilation to the Freudian maps of the mind. Freud's later system divides us into the "I" or ego, the "above-I" or superego, and the "it" or id. Whitman divided himself (or recognized himself as divided) into "my self," "my soul," and the "real Me" or "Me myself," where the self is a kind of ego, the soul not quite a superego, and the "real Me" not at all an id. Or to use a vocabulary known to Whitman, and still known to us, the self is personality, the soul is character, and again the "real Me" is a mystery. Lest these difficulties seem merely my own, and not truly Whitman's, I turn to the text of "Song of Myself." Here is Walt Whitman, "My self," the *persona* or mask, the personality of the poet:

> Walt Whitman, a kosmos, of Manhattan the son,
> Turbulent, fleshy, sensual, eating, drinking and breeding,
> No sentimentalist, no stander above men and women or apart from them,
> No more modest than immodest.

That is Walt Whitman, one of the roughs, an American, but hardly Walter Whitman Jr., whose true personality, "real Me" or "Me myself," is presented in the passage I love best in the poem:

> These come to me days and nights and go from me again,
> But they are not the Me myself.
> Apart from the pulling and hauling stands what I am,
> Stands amused, complacent, compassionating, idle, unitary,
> Looks down, is erect, or bends an arm on an impalpable certain rest,
> Looking with side-curved head curious what will come next,
> Both in and out of the game and watching and wondering at it.

This "Me myself" is not exactly "hankering, gross, mystical, nude," nor quite "turbulent, fleshy, sensual, eating, drinking and breeding." Graceful and apart, cunningly balanced, charming beyond measure, this curious "real Me" is boylike and girllike, very American yet not one of the roughs, provocative, at one with itself. Whatever the Whitmanian soul may be, this "Me myself" evidently can have no equal relationship with it. When the Whitmanian "I" addresses the soul, we hear a warning:

I believe in you my soul, the other I am must not abase itself to you,
And you must not be abased to the other.

The "I" here is the "Myself" of "Song of Myself," poetic personality, robust and rough. "The other I am" is the "Me myself," in and out of the game, and clearly not suited for embraces with the soul. Whitman's wariness, his fear of abasement, whether of his soul or of his true, inner personality, one to the other, remains the enigma of his poetry, as of his life, and accounts for his intricate evasions both as poet and as person.

II

Whitman's critics thus commence with a formidable disadvantage as they attempt to receive and comprehend his work. The largest puzzle about the continuing reception of Whitman's poetry is the still prevalent notion that we ought to take him at his word, whether about his self (or selves) or about his art. No other poet insists so vehemently and so continuously that he will tell us all, and tell us all without artifice, and yet tells us so little, and so cunningly. Except for Dickinson (the only American poet comparable to him in magnitude), there is no other nineteenth-century poet as difficult and hermetic as Whitman; not Blake, not Browning, not Mallarmé. Only an elite can read Whitman, despite the poet's insistence that he wrote for the people, for "powerful uneducated persons," as his "By Blue Ontario's Shore" proclaims. His more accurate "Poets to Come" is closer to his readers' experience of him:

I am a man who, sauntering along without fully stopping, turns a casual
look upon you and then averts his face. . . .

Whitman was surely too sly to deceive himself, or at least both of his selves, on this matter of his actual poetic evasiveness and esotericism. Humanly, he had much to evade, in order to keep going, in order to start writing and then to keep writing. His biographers cannot give us a clear image of his childhood which was certainly rather miserable. His numerous siblings had mostly melancholy life histories. Madness, retardation, marriage to a prostitute, depressiveness and hypochondria figure among their fates. The extraordinary obsession with health and cleanliness that oddly marks Whitman's poetry had a poignant origin in his early circumstances. Of his uneasy relationship with his father we know a little, though not much. But we know nothing really of his mother, and how he felt towards her. Perhaps the most crucial fact about Whitman's psyche we know well enough; he needed, quite early, to become the true father of all his siblings, and perhaps of his mother also. Certainly he fathered and mothered as many of his siblings as he could, even as he so beautifully became a surrogate father and mother for thousands of wounded and sick soldiers, Union and Confederate, white and black, in the hospitals of Washington, D.C. throughout the Civil War.

The extraordinary and truthful image of Whitman that haunts our country; the vision of the compassionate, unpaid, volunteer wound-dresser comforting young men in pain and soothing the dying, is the climax of Paul Zweig's book on how the man Walter Whitman Jr. became the poet Walt Whitman. This vision informs the finest pages of Zweig's uneven but moving study; I cannot recall any previous Whitman biographer or critic so vividly and humanely portraying Whitman's hospital service. Searching for the authentic Whitman, as Zweig shows, is a hopeless quest; our greatest poet will always be our most evasive, and perhaps our most self-contradictory. Whitman, at his greatest, has overwhelming pathos as a poet; equal I think to anything in the language. The *Drum-Taps* poem called "The Wound-Dresser" is far from Whitman at his astonishing best, and yet its concluding lines carry the persuasive force of his poetic and human images for once unified:

> Returning, resuming, I thread my way through the hospitals,
> The hurt and wounded I pacify with soothing hand,
> I sit by the restless all the dark night, some are so young,
> Some suffer so much, I recall the experience sweet and sad,
> (Many a soldier's loving arms about this neck have cross'd and rested,
> Many a soldier's kiss dwells on these bearded lips.)

Zweig is admirably sensitive in exploring the ambiguities in Whitman's hospital intensities, and more admirable still in his restraint at not voicing how much all of us are touched by Whitman's pragmatic saintliness during those years of service. I cannot think of a Western writer of anything like Whitman's achievement who ever gave himself or herself up so directly to meeting the agonized needs of the most desperate. There are a handful of American poets comparable to Whitman in stature: Emily Dickinson certainly, Wallace Stevens and Robert Frost perhaps, and maybe one or two others. Our image of them, or of our greatest novelists, or even of Whitman's master, Emerson, can move us sometimes, but not as the image of the wound-dresser Whitman must move us. Like the Lincoln whom he celebrated and lamented, Whitman is American legend, a figure who has a kind of religious aura even for secular intellectuals. If Emerson founded the American literary religion, Whitman alone permanently holds the place most emblematic of the life of the spirit in America.

These religious terms are not Zweig's, yet his book's enterprise usefully traces the winding paths that led Whitman on to his apotheosis as healer and comforter. Whitman's psychosexuality, labyrinthine in its perplexities, may have been the central drive that bewildered the poet into those ways, but it was not the solitary, overwhelming determinant that many readers judge it to have been. Zweig refreshingly is not one of these overdetermined readers. He surmises that Whitman might have experienced little actual homosexual intercourse. I suspect none, though Whitman evidently was intensely in love with some unnamed man in 1859, and rather differently in love again with Peter Doyle about five years later. Zweig accurately observes that: "Few poets have written as erotically as Whitman, while having so little to say about sex. For the most part, his erotic poetry is intransitive, self-delighting." Indeed, it is precisely auto-erotic rather more than it is homo-erotic; Whitman overtly celebrates masturbation, and his most authentic sexual passion is always for himself. One would hardly know this from reading many of Whitman's critics, but one certainly knows it by closely reading Whitman's major poems. Here is part of a crucial crisis-passage from "Song of Myself," resolved through successful masturbation:

> I merely stir, press, feel with my fingers, and am happy,
> To touch my person to some one else's is about as much as I can stand.
> Is this then a touch? quivering me to a new identity,
> Flames and ether making a rush for my veins,
> Treacherous tip of me reaching and crowding to help them,
> My flesh and blood playing out lightning to strike what is hardly different
>   from myself, . . .
> I went myself first to the headland, my own hands carried me there.
> You villain touch! what are you doing? my breath is tight in its throat,
> Unclench your floodgates, you are too much for me.
> Blind loving wrestling touch, sheath'd hooded sharp-tooth'd touch!
> Did it make you ache so, leaving me?
> Parting track'd by arriving, perpetual payment of perpetual loan,
> Rich showering rain, and recompense richer afterward.
> Sprouts take and accumulate, stand by the curb prolific and vital,
> Landscapes projected masculine, full-sized and golden.

I take it that this celebratory mode of masturbation, whether read metaphorically or literally, remains the genuine scandal of Whitman's poetry. This may indeed be one of the kernel passages in Whitman, expanded and elaborated as it is from an early notebook passage that invented the remarkable trope of "I went myself first to the headland," the headland being the psychic place of *extravagance*, of wandering beyond limits, from which you cannot scramble back to the shore, place of the father, and from which you may topple over into the sea, identical with night, death and the fierce old mother. "My own hands carried me there," as they fail to carry Whitman in "When Lilacs Last in the Dooryard Bloom'd":

> O great star disappear'd—O the black murk that hides the star!
> O cruel hands that hold me powerless—O helpless soul of me!

These are Whitman's own hands, pragmatically cruel because they cannot hold him potently, disabled as he is by a return of repressed guilt. Lincoln's death has set going memories of filial guilt, the guilt that the mortal sickness of Walter Whitman Sr. should have liberated his son into the full blood of creativity that ensued in the 1855 first edition of *Leaves of Grass* (the father died a week after the book's publication). What Whitman's poetry does not express are any reservations about auto-eroticism, which more than sado-masochism remains the last Western taboo. It is a peculiar paradox that Whitman, who proclaims his love for all men, women and children, should have been profoundly solipsistic, narcissistic and self-delighting, but that paradox returns us to the Whitmanian self or rather selves, the cosmological *persona* as opposed to the daemonic "real Me."

III

The most vivid manifestation of the "real Me" in Whitman comes in the shattering "Sea-Drift-" poem, "As I Ebb'd with the Ocean of Life":

O baffled, balk'd, bent to the very earth,
Oppress'd with myself that I have dared to open my mouth,
Aware now that amid all that blab whose echoes recoil upon me I have not
    once had the least idea who or what I am,
But that before all my arrogant poems the real Me stands yet untouch'd,
    untold, altogether unreach'd,
Withdrawn far, mocking me with mock-congratulatory signs and bows,
With peals of distant ironical laughter at every word I have written,
Pointing in silence to these songs, and then to the sand beneath.
I perceive I have not really understood any thing, not a single object, and
    that no man ever can,
Nature here in sight of the sea taking advantage of me to dart upon me and
    sting me,
Because I have dared to open my mouth to sing at all.

It is Walt Whitman, Kosmos, American, rough, who is mocked here by his real self, a self that knows itself to be a mystery, because it is neither mother, nor father, nor child; neither quite female nor quite male; neither voice nor voicelessness. Whitman's "real Me" is what is best and oldest in him, and like the faculty Emerson called "Spontaneity," it is no part of the creation, meaning both nature's creation and Whitman's verbal cosmos. It is like a surviving fragment of the original Abyss preceding nature, not Adamic but pre-Adamic. This "real Me" is thus also presexual, and so plays no role either in the homo-erotic "Calamus" poems or in the dubiously heterosexual "Children of Adam" group. Yet it seems to me pervasive in the six long or longer poems that indisputably are Whitman's materpieces: "The Sleepers,"

"Song of Myself," "Crossing Brooklyn Ferry," "As I Ebb'd with the Ocean of Life," "Out of the Cradle Endlessly Rocking," and "When Lilacs Last in the Dooryard Bloom'd." Though only the last of these is overtly an elegy, all six are in covert ways elegies for the "real Me," for that "Me myself" that Whitman could not hope to celebrate as a poet and could not hope to fulfill as a sexual being. This "real Me" is not a spirit that denies, but rather one that always remains out of reach, an autistic spirit. In English Romantic poetry and in later nineteenth-century prose romance there is the parallel being that Shelley called "the Spirit of Solitude," the daemon or shadow of the self-destructive young Poet who is the hero of Shelley's *Alastor*. But Whitman's very American "real Me" is quite unlike a Shelleyan or Blakean Spectre. It does not quest or desire, and it does not want to be wanted.

Though Zweig hints that Whitman has been a bad influence on other writers, I suspect that a larger view of influence would reverse this implicit judgment. Whitman has been an inescapable influence not only for most significant American poets after him (Frost, indebted directly to Emerson, is the largest exception) but also for the most gifted writers of narrative fiction. This influence transcends matters of form, and has everything to do with the Whitmanian split between the *persona* of the rough Walt and the ontological truth of the "real Me." Poets as diverse as Wallace Stevens and T.S. Eliot have in common perhaps only their hidden, partly unconscious reliance upon Whitman as prime precursor. Hemingway's acknowledged debt to *Huckleberry Finn* is real enough, but the deeper legacy came from Whitman. The Hemingway protagonist, split between an empirical self of stoic courage and a "real Me" endlessly evasive of others while finding its freedom only in an inner perfection of loneliness, is directly descended from the dual Whitman of "Song of Myself." American elegiac writing since Whitman (and how surprisingly much of it *is* covertly elegiac) generally revises Whitman's elegies for the self. *The Waste Land* is "When Lilacs Last in the Dooryard Bloom'd" rewritten, and Stevens' "The Rock" is not less Whitmanian than Hart Crane's *The Bridge*.

Zweig's book joins itself to the biographical criticism of Whitman by such scholars as Bliss Perry, Gay Wilson Allen, Joseph Jay Rubin, Justin Kaplan and others whose works are part of a useful tradition that illuminates the American-ism of Whitman and yet cannot do enough with Whitman's many paradoxes. Of these, I judge the most crucial to be expressed by this question: how did someone of Whitman's extraordinarily idiosyncratic nature become so absolutely central to nearly all subsequent American literary high culture? This centrality evidently cannot ebb among us, as can be seen in the most recent poems of John Ashbery in his book, *The Wave*, or in the stories of Harold Brodkey, excerpted from his vast and wholly Whitmanian work-in-progress. Whitman's powerful yet unstable identities were his own inheritance from the Orphic Emerson, who proclaimed the central man or poet-to-come as necessarily metamorphic, Bacchic and yet original, and above all American and not British or European in his cultural vistas. This prescription was and is dangerous, because it asks for pragmatism and yet affirms impossible hopes. The rough Whitman is democratic, "real Me" an elitist, but both selves are equally Emersonian.

Politically, Whitman was a Free Soil Democrat who rebelled against the betrayal by the New York Democratic Party of its Jacksonian tradition, but Zweig rightly emphasizes the survival of Emersonian "Prudence" in Whitman which caused him to oppose labor unions. I suspect that Whitman's politics paralleled his sexual morality: the rough Walt homo-erotic and radical, the "real Me" auto-erotic and individualistically elitist. The true importance of this split emerges neither in Whitman's sexuality nor in his politics, but in the delicacy and beauty of his strongest poems. Under the cover of an apparent rebellion against traditional literary form, they extend the poetic tradition without violating it. Whitman's elegies for the self have much in common with Tennyson's, but are even subtler, more difficult triumphs of High Romanticism. Here I dissent wholly from Zweig, who ends his book with a judgment I find both wrong and puzzling:

> ... *Leaves of Grass* was launched on a collision course with its age. Whitman's work assaulted the institution of literature and language itself and, in so doing, laid the groundwork for the anti-cultural ambition of modernist writing. He is the ancestor not only of Henry Miller and Allen Ginsberg but of Kafka, Beckett, Andre Breton, Borges—of all who have made of their writing an attack on the act of writing and on culture itself.

To associate the subtle artistry, delicate and evasive, of Whitman's greatest poems with Miller and Ginsberg rather than with Hemingway and Stevens and Eliot, is already an error. To say that Kafka, Beckett, and Borges attack, by their writing, the act of writing and culture, is to mistake their assault upon certain interpretive conventions for a war against literary culture. But the gravest misdirection here is to inform readers that Whitman truly attacked the institutions of language and literature. Whitman's "real Me" has more to do with the composition of the great poems than the rough Walt ever did. "Lilacs," which Zweig does not discuss, is as profoundly traditional an elegy as *In Memoriam* or *Adonais*. Indeed, "Lilacs" echoes Tennyson, while "As I Ebb'd" echoes Shelley and "Crossing Brooklyn Ferry" invokes *King Lear*. Zweig is taken in by the prose Whitman who insists he will not employ allusiveness, but the poet Whitman knew better, and is brilliantly allusive, as every strong poet is compelled to be, echoing his precursors and rivals but so stationing the echoes as to triumph with and in some sense over them.

Zweig's study is an honorable and useful account of Whitman's poetic emergence, but it shares in some of the severe limitations of nearly all Whitman criticism so far published. More than most of the biographical critics, Zweig keeps alert to Whitman's duality, and I am grateful to him for his eloquent representations of the poet's war years. Yet Whitman's subtle greatness as a poet seems to me not fully confronted, here or elsewhere. The poetry of the "real Me," intricate and forlorn, is addressed to the "real Me" of the American reader. That it reached what was oldest and best in Eliot and Stevens is testified to by their finest poetry, in contradistinction to their prose remarks upon Whitman. Paradoxically, Whitman's best critic remains, not an American, but D.H. Lawrence, who lamented that, "The Americans are not worthy of their Whitman." Lawrence believed that Whitman had gone further, in actual living expression, than any other poet. The belief was extravagant, certainly, but again the Whitmanian poems of Lawrence's superb final phase show us what Lawrence meant. I give the last word here though, not to Lawrence, but to Emerson, who wrote the first words about Whitman in his celebrated 1855 letter to the poet, words that remain true nearly 130 years further on in our literary culture:

> I am not blind to the worth of the wonderful gift of *Leaves of Grass*. I find it the most extraordinary piece of wit and wisdom that America has yet contributed. . . .

D. H. LAWRENCE

Whitman

Post mortem effects?

But what of Walt Whitman?

The "good grey poet."

Was he a ghost, with all his physicality?

The good grey poet.

Post mortem effects. Ghosts.

A certain ghoulish insistency. A certain horrible pottage of human parts. A certain stridency and portentousness. A luridness about his beatitudes.

DEMOCRACY! THESE STATES! EIDOLONS! LOVERS, ENDLESS LOVERS!

ONE IDENTITY!

ONE IDENTITY!

I AM HE THAT ACHES WITH AMOROUS LOVE.

Do you believe me, when I say post mortem effects?

When the *Pequod* went down, she left many a rank and dirty steamboat still fussing in the seas. The *Pequod* sinks with all her souls, but their bodies rise again to man innumerable tramp steamers, and ocean-crossing liners. Corpses.

What we mean is that people may go on, keep on, and rush on, without souls. They have their ego and their will, that is enough to keep them going.

So that you see, the sinking of the *Pequod* was only a metaphysical tragedy after all. The world goes on just the same. The ship of the *soul* is sunk.

From *Studies in Classic American Literature*. Copyright © 1923 by Thomas Seltzer, Inc., 1951 by Frieda Lawrence.

But the machine-manipulating body works just the same: digests, chews gum, admires Botticelli and aches with amorous love.

I AM HE THAT ACHES WITH AMOROUS LOVE.

What do you make of that? I AM HE THAT ACHES. First generalization. First uncomfortable universalization. WITH AMOROUS LOVE! Oh, God! Better a bellyache. A bellyache is at least specific. But the ACHE OF AMOROUS LOVE!

Think of having that under your skin. All that!

I AM HE THAT ACHES WITH AMOROUS LOVE.

Walter, leave off. You are not HE. You are just a limited Walter. And your ache doesn't include all Amorous Love, by any means. If you ache you only ache with a small bit of amorous love, and there's so much more stays outside the cover of your ache, that you might be a bit milder about it.

I AM HE THAT ACHES WITH AMOROUS LOVE.

CHUFF! CHUFF! CHUFF!

CHU-CHU-CHU-CHU-CHUFF!

Reminds one of a steam-engine. A locomotive. They're the only things that seem to me to ache with amorous love. All that steam inside them. Forty million foot-pounds pressure. The ache of AMOROUS LOVE. Steam-pressure. CHUFF!

An ordinary man aches with love for Belinda, or his Native Land, or the Ocean, or the Stars, or the Oversoul: if he feels that an ache is in the fashion.

It takes a steam-engine to ache with AMOROUS LOVE. All of it.

Walt was really too superhuman. The danger of the superman is that he is mechanical.

They talk of his "splendid animality." Well, he'd got it on the brain, if that's the place for animality.

> I am he that aches with amorous love:
> Does the earth gravitate, does not all matter, aching, attract all matter?
> So the body of me to all I meet or know.

What can be more mechanical? The difference between life and matter is that life, living things, living creatures, have the instinct of turning right away from *some* matter, and of blissfully ignoring the bulk of most matter, and of turning towards only some certain bits of specially selected matter. As for living creatures all helplessly hurtling together into one great snowball, why, most very living creatures spend the greater part of their time getting out of the sight, smell or sound of the rest of living creatures. Even bees only cluster on their own queen. And that is sickening enough. Fancy all white humanity clustering on one another like a lump of bees.

No, Walt, you give yourself away. Matter *does* gravitate, helplessly. But men are tricky-tricksy, and they shy all sorts of ways.

Matter gravitates because it *is* helpless and mechanical.

And if you gravitate the same, if the body of you gravitates to all you meet or know, why, something must have gone seriously wrong with you. You must have broken your mainspring.

You must have fallen also into mechanization.

Your Moby Dick must be really dead. That lonely phallic monster of the individual you. Dead mentalized.

I only know that my body doesn't by any means gravitate to all I meet or know. I find I can shake hands with a few people. But most I wouldn't touch with a long prop.

Your mainspring is broken, Walt Whitman. The mainspring of your own individuality. And so you run down with a great whirr, merging with everything.

You have killed your isolate Moby Dick. You have mentalized your deep sensual body, and that's the death of it.

I am everything and everything is me and so we're all One in One Identity, like the Mundane Egg, which has been addled quite a while.

"Whoever you are, to endless announcements—"
"And of these one and all I weave the song of myself."

Do you? Well, then, it just shows you haven't *got* any self. It's a mush, not a woven thing. A hotch-potch, not a tissue. Your self.

Oh, Walter, Walter, what have you done with it? What have you done with yourself? With your own individual self? For it sounds as if it had all leaked out of you, leaked into the universe.

Post mortem effects. The individuality had leaked out of him.

No, no, don't lay this down to poetry. These are post mortem effects. And Walt's great poems are really huge fat tomb-plants, great rank graveyard growths.

All that false exuberance. All those lists of things boiled in one pudding-cloth! No, no!

I don't want all those things inside me, thank you.

"I reject nothing," says Walt.

If that is so, one must be a pipe open at both ends, so everything runs through.

Post mortem effects.

"I embrace ALL," says Whitman. "I weave all things into myself."

Do you really! There can't be much left of *you* when you've done. When you've cooked the awful pudding of One Identity.

"And whoever walks a furlong without sympathy walks to his own funeral dressed in his own shroud."

Take off your hat then, my funeral procession of one is passing.

This awful Whitman. This post mortem poet. This poet with the private soul leaking out of him all the time. All his privacy leaking out in a sort of dribble, oozing into the universe.

Walt becomes in his own person the whole world, the whole universe, the whole eternity of time. As far as his rather sketchy knowledge of history will carry him, that is. Because to *be* a thing he had to know it. In order to assume the identity of a thing, he had to know that thing. He was not able to assume one identity with Charlie Chaplin, for example, because Walt didn't know Charlie. What a pity! He'd have done poems, paeans and what not, Chants, Songs of Cinematernity.

"Oh, Charlie, my Charlie, another film is done——"

As soon as Walt *knew* a thing, he assumed a One Identity with it. If he knew that an Esquimo sat in a kyak, immediately there was Walt being little and yellow and greasy, sitting in a kyak.

Now will you tell me exactly what a kyak is?

Who is he that demands petty definition? Let him behold me *sitting in a kyak.*

I behold no such thing. I behold a rather fat old man full of a rather senile, self-conscious sensuosity.

DEMOCRACY. EN MASSE. ONE IDENTITY.

The universe, in short, adds up to ONE.

ONE.

1.

Which is Walt.

His poems, *Democracy, En Masse, One Identity*, they are long sums in addition and multiplication, of which the answer is invariably MYSELF.

He reaches the state of ALLNESS.

And what then? It's all empty. Just an empty Allness. An addled egg.

Walt wasn't an esquimo. A little, yellow, sly, cunning, greasy little Esquimo. And when Walt blandly assumed Allness, including Esquimoness, unto himself, he was just sucking the wind out of a blown egg-shell, no more. Esquimos are not minor little Walts. They are something that I am not, I know that. Outside the egg of my Allness chuckles the greasy little Esquimo. Outside the egg of Whitman's Allness too.

But Walt wouldn't have it. He was everything and everything was in him. He drove an automobile with a very fierce headlight, along the track of a fixed idea, through the darkness of this world. And he saw Everything that way. Just as a motorist does in the night.

I, who happen to be asleep under the bushes in the dark, hoping a snake won't crawl into my neck; I, seeing Walt go by in his great fierce poetic machine, think to myself: What a funny world that fellow sees!

ONE DIRECTION! toots Walt in the car, whizzing along it.

Whereas there are myriads of ways in the dark, not to mention trackless wildernesses. As anyone will know who cares to come off the road, even the Open Road.

ONE DIRECTION! whoops America, and sets off also in an automobile.

ALLNESS! shrieks Walt at a cross-road, going whizz over an unwary Red Indian.

ONE IDENTITY! chants democratic En Masse, pelting behind in motorcars, oblivious of the corpses under the wheels.

God save me, I feel like creeping down a rabbit-hole, to get away from all these automobiles rushing down the ONE IDENTITY track to the goal of ALLNESS.

"A woman waits for me——"

He might as well have said: "The femaleness waits for my maleness." Oh, beautiful generalization and abstraction! Oh, biological function.

"Athletic mothers of these States——" Muscles and wombs. They needn't have had faces at all.

> As I see myself reflected in Nature,
> As I see through a mist, One with inexpressible completeness, sanity, beauty,
> See the bent head, and arms folded over the breast, the Female I see.

Everything was female to him: even himself. Nature just one great function.

> This is the nucleus—after the child is born of woman, man is born of woman,
> This is the bath of birth, the merge of small and large, and the outlet again——

"The Female I see——"

If I'd been one of his women, I'd have given him Female. With a flea in his ear.

Always wanting to merge himself into the womb of something or other.

"The Female I see——"

Anything, so long as he could merge himself.

Just a horror. A sort of white flux.

Post mortem effects.

He found, like all men find, that you can't really merge in a woman, though you may go a long way. You can't manage the last bit. So you have to give it up, and try elsewhere. If you *insist* on merging.

In "Calamus" he changes his tune. He doesn't shout and thump and exult any more. He begins to hesitate, reluctant, wistful.

The strange calamus has its pink-tinged root by the pond, and it sends up its leaves of comradeship, comrades from one root, without the intervention of woman, the female.

So he sings of the mystery of manly love, the love of comrades. Over and over he says the same thing: the new world will be built on the love of comrades, the new great dynamic of life will be manly love. Out of this manly love will come the inspiration for the future.

Will it though? Will it?

Comradeship! Comrades! This is to be the new Democracy: of Comrades. This is the new cohering principle in the world: Comradeship.

Is it? Are you sure?

It is the cohering principle of true soldiery, we are told in *Drum Taps*. It is the cohering principle in the new unison for creative activity. And it is extreme and alone, touching the confines of death. Something terrible to bear, terrible to be responsible for. Even Walt Whitman felt it. The soul's last and most poignant responsibility, the responsibility of comradeship, of manly love.

Yet you are beautiful to me, you faint-tinged roots, you make me think of death.
Death is beautiful from you (what indeed is finally beautiful except death and love?)
I think it is not for life I am chanting here my chant of lovers, I think
    it must be for death,
For how calm, how solemn it grows to ascend to the atmosphere of lovers,
Death or life, I am then indifferent, my soul declines to prefer
(I am not sure but the high soul of lovers welcomes death most)
Indeed, O death, I think now these leaves mean precisely the same as you mean——

This is strange, from the exultant Walt.

Death!

Death is now his chant! Death!

Merging! And Death! Which is the final merge.

The great merge into the womb. Woman.

And after that, the merge of comrades: man-for-man love.

And almost immediately with this, death, the final merge of death.

There you have the progression of merging. For the great mergers, woman at last becomes inadequate. For those who love to extremes. Woman is inadequate for the last merging. So the next step is the merging of the man-for-man love. And this is on the brink of death. It slides over into death.

David and Jonathan. And the death of Jonathan.

It always slides into death.

The love of comrades.

Merging.

So that if the new Democracy is to be based on the love of comrades, it will be based on death too. It will slip so soon into death.

The last merging. The last Democracy. The last love. The love of comrades.

Fatality. And fatality.

Whitman would not have been the great poet he is if he had not taken the last steps and looked over into death. Death, the last merging, that was the goal of his manhood.

To the mergers, there remains the brief love of comrades, and then Death.

> Whereto answering, the sea.
> Delaying not, hurrying not
> Whispered me through the night, very plainly before daybreak,
> Lisp'd to me the low and delicious word death,
> And again death, death, death, death.
> Hissing melodious, neither like the bird nor like my arous'd child's heart,
> But edging near as privately for me rustling at my feet,
> Creeping thence steadily up to my ears and laving me softly all over
> Death, death, death, death, death——

Whitman is a very great poet, of the end of life. A very great post mortem poet, of the transitions of the soul as it loses its integrity. The poet of the soul's last shout and shriek, on the confines of death. *Après moi le déluge.*

But we have all got to die, and disintegrate.

We have got to die in life, too, and disintegrate while we live.

But even then the goal is not death.

Something else will come.

"Out of the cradle endlessly rocking."

We've got to die first, anyhow. And disintegrate while we still live.

Only we know this much. Death is not the *goal*. And Love, and merging, are now only part of the death-process. Comradeship—part of the death-process. Democracy—part of the death-process. The new Democracy—the brink of death. One Identity—death itself.

We have died, and we are still disintegrating.

But IT IS FINISHED.

Consummatum est.

Whitman, the great poet, has meant so much to me. Whitman, the one man breaking a way ahead. Whitman, the one pioneer. And only Whitman. No English pioneers, no French. No European pioneer-poets. In Europe the would-be pioneers are mere innovators. The same in America. Ahead of Whitman, nothing. Ahead of all poets, pioneering into the wilderness of unopened life, Whitman. Beyond him, none. His wide, strange camp at the end of the great high-road. And lots of new little poets camping on

Whitman's camping ground now. But none going really beyond. Because Whitman's camp is at the end of the road, and on the edge of a great precipice. Over the precipice, blue distances, and the blue hollow of the future. But there is no way down. It is a dead end.

Pisgah. Pisgah sights. And Death. Whitman like a strange, modern, American Moses. Fearfully mistaken. And yet the great leader.

The essential function of art is moral. Not aesthetic, not decorative, not pastime and recreation. But moral. The essential function of art is moral.

But a passionate, implicit morality, not didactic. A morality which changes the blood, rather than the mind. Changes the blood first. The mind follows later, in the wake.

Now Whitman was a great moralist. He was a great leader. He was a great changer of the blood in the veins of men.

Surely it is especially true of American art, that it is all essentially moral. Hawthorne, Poe, Longfellow, Emerson, Melville: it is the moral issue which engages them. They all feel uneasy about the old morality. Sensuously, passionally, they all attack the old morality. But they know nothing better, mentally. Therefore they give tight mental allegiance to a morality which all their passion goes to destroy. Hence the duplicity which is the fatal flaw in them; most fatal in the most perfect American work of art, *The Scarlet Letter*. Tight mental allegiance given to a morality which the passional self repudiates.

Whitman was the first to break the mental allegiance. He was the first to smash the old moral conception, that the soul of man is something "superior" and "above" the flesh. Even Emerson still maintained this tiresome "superiority" of the soul. Even Melville could not get over it. Whitman was the first heroic seer to seize the soul by the scruff of her neck and plant her down among the potsherds.

"There!" he said to the soul. "Stay there!"

Stay there. Stay in the flesh. Stay in the limbs and lips and in the belly. Stay in the breast and womb. Stay there, O Soul, where you belong.

Stay in the dark limbs of negroes. Stay in the body of the prostitute. Stay in the sick flesh of the syphilitic. Stay in the marsh where the calamus grows. Stay there, Soul, where you belong.

The Open Road. The great home of the Soul is the open road. Not heaven, not paradise. Not "above." Not even "within." The soul is neither "above" nor "within." It is a wayfarer down the open road.

Not by meditating. Not by fasting. Not by exploring heaven after heaven, inwardly, in the manner of the great mystics. Not by exaltation. Not by ecstasy. Not by any of these ways does the soul come into her own.

Only by taking the open road.

Not through charity. Not through sacrifice. Not even through love. Not through good works. Not through these does the soul accomplish herself.

Only through the journey down the open road.

The journey itself, down the open road. Exposed to full contact. On two slow feet. Meeting whatever comes down the open road. In company with those that drift in the same measure along the same way. Towards no goal. Always the open road.

Having no known direction, even. Only the soul remaining true to herself in her going.

Meeting all the other wayfarers along the road. And how? How meet them, and how pass? With sympathy, says Whitman. Sympathy. He does not say love. He says sympathy. Feeling with. Feel with them as they feel with themselves. Catching the vibration of their soul and flesh as we pass.

It is a new great doctrine. A doctrine of life. A new great morality. A morality of actual living, not of salvation. Europe has never got beyond the morality of salvation. America to this day is deathly sick with saviourism. But Whitman, the greatest and the first and the only American teacher, was no Saviour. His morality was no morality of salvation. His was a morality of the soul living her life, not saving herself. Accepting the contact with other souls along the open way, as they lived their lives. Never trying to save them. As leave try to arrest them and throw them in gaol. The soul living her life along the incarnate mystery of the open road.

This was Whitman. And the true rhythm of the American continent speaking out in him. He is the first white aboriginal.

"In my Father's house are many mansions."

"No," said Whitman. "Keep out of mansions. A mansion may be heaven on earth, but you might as well be dead. Strictly avoid mansions. The soul is herself when she is going on foot down the open road."

It is the American heroic message. The soul is not to pile up defenses round herself. She is not to withdraw and seek her heavens inwardly, in mystical ecstasies. She is not to cry to some God beyond, for salvation. She is to go down the open road, as the road opens, into the unknown, keeping company with those whose soul draws them near to her, accomplishing nothing save the journey, and the works incident to the journey, in the long life-travel into the unknown, the soul in her subtle sympathies accomplishing herself by the way.

This is Whitman's essential message. The heroic message of the American future. It is the inspiration of thousands of Americans today, the best souls of today, men and women. And it is a message that only in America can be fully understood, finally accepted.

Then Whitman's mistake. The mistake of his interpretation of his watchword: Sympathy. The mystery of SYMPATHY. He still confounded it with Jesus' LOVE, and with Paul's CHARITY. Whitman, like all the rest of us, was at the end of the great emotional highway of Love. And because he couldn't help himself, he carried on his Open Road as a prolongation of the emotional highway of Love, beyond Calvary. The highway of Love ends at the foot of the Cross. There is no beyond. It was a hopeless attempt, to prolong the highway of Love.

He didn't follow his Sympathy. Try as he might, he kept on automatically interpreting it as Love, as Charity. Merging.

This merging, en masse, One Identity, Myself monomania was a carry-over from the old Love idea. It was carrying the idea of Love to its logical physical conclusion. Like Flaubert and the leper. The decree of unqualified Charity, as the soul's one means of salvation, still in force.

Now Whitman wanted his soul to save itself, *he* didn't want to save it. Therefore he did not need the great Christian receipt for saving the soul. He needed to supersede the Christian Charity, the Christian Love, within himself, in order to give his Soul her last freedom. The highroad of Love is no Open Road. It is a narrow, tight way, where the soul walks hemmed in between compulsions.

Whitman wanted to take his Soul down the open road. And he failed in so far as he failed to get out of the old rut of Salvation. He forced his Soul to the edge of a cliff, and he looked down into death. And there he camped, powerless. He had carried out his Sympathy as an extension of Love and Charity. And it had brought him almost to madness and soul-death. It gave him his forced, unhealthy, post-mortem quality.

His message was really the opposite of Henley's rant:

> I am the master of my fate.
> I am the captain of my soul.

Whitman's essential message was the Open Road. The leaving of the soul free unto herself, the leaving of his fate to her and to the loom of the open road. Which is the bravest doctrine man has ever proposed to himself.

Alas, he didn't quite carry it out. He couldn't quite break the old maddening bond of the love-compulsion, he couldn't quite get out of the rut of the charity habit. For Love and Charity have degenerated now into habit: a bad habit.

Whitman said Sympathy. If only he had stuck to it! Because Sympathy means feeling with, not feeling for. He kept on having a passionate feeling *for* the negro slave, or the prostitute, or the syphilitic. Which is merging. A sinking of Walt Whitman's soul in the souls of these others.

He wasn't keeping to his open road. He was forcing his soul down an old rut. He wasn't leaving her free. He was forcing her into other people's circumstances.

Supposing he had felt true sympathy with the negro slave? He would have felt *with* the negro slave. Sympathy—compassion—which is partaking of the passion which was in the soul of the negro slave.

What was the feeling in the negro's soul?

"Ah, I am a slave! Ah, it is bad to be a slave! I must free myself. My soul will die unless she frees herself. My soul says I must free myself."

Whitman came along, and saw the slave, and said to himself: "That negro slave is a man like myself. We share the same identity. And he is bleeding with wounds. Oh, oh, is it not myself who am also bleeding with wounds?"

This was not *sympathy*. It was merging and self-sacrifice. "Bear ye one another's burdens."—"Love thy neighbour as thyself."—Whatsoever ye do unto him, ye do unto me."

If Whitman had truly *sympathised*, he would have said: "That negro slave suffers from slavery. He wants to free himself. His soul wants to free him. He has wounds, but they are the price of freedom. The soul has a long journey from slavery to freedom. If I can help him I will: I will not take over his wounds and his slavery to myself. But I will help him fight the power that enslaves him when he wants to be free, if he wants my help. Since I see in his face that he needs to be free. But even when he is free, his soul has many journeys down the open road, before it is a free soul."

And of the prostitute Whitman would have said:

"Look at that prostitute! Her nature has turned evil under her mental lust for prostitution. She has lost her soul. She knows it herself. She likes to make men lose their souls. If she tried to make me lose my soul, I would kill her. I wish she may die."

But of another prostitute he would have said:

"Look! She is fascinated by the Priapic mysteries. Look, she will soon be worn to death by the Priapic usage. It is the way of her soul. She wishes it so."

Of the syphilitic he would say:

"Look! She wants to infect all men with syphilis. We ought to kill her."

And of another syphilitic:

"Look! She has a horror of her syphilis. If she looks my way I will help her to get cured."

This is sympathy. The soul judging for herself, and preserving her own integrity.

But when, in Flaubert, the man takes the leper to his naked body;

when Bubu de Montparnasse takes the girl because he knows she's got syphilis; when Whitman embraces an evil prostitute: that is not sympathy. The evil prostitute has no desire to be embraced with love; so if you sympathise with her, you won't try to embrace her with love. The leper loathes his leprosy, so if you sympathise with him, you'll loathe it too. The evil woman who wishes to infect all men with her syphilis hates you if you haven't got syphilis. If you sympathise, you'll feel her hatred, and you'll hate too, you'll hate her. Her feeling is hate, and you'll share it. Only your soul will choose the direction of its own hatred.

The soul is a very perfect judge of her own motions, if your mind doesn't dictate to her. Because the mind says Charity! Charity! you don't have to force your soul into kissing lepers or embracing syphilitics. Your lips are the lips of your soul, your body is the body of your soul; your own single, individual soul. That is Whitman's message. And your soul hates syphilis and leprosy. Because it *is* a soul, it hates these things which are against the soul. And therefore to force the body of your soul into contact with uncleanness is a great violation of your soul. The soul wishes to keep clean and whole. The soul's deepest will is to preserve its own integrity, against the mind and the whole mass of disintegrating forces.

Soul sympathises with soul. And that which tries to kill my soul, my soul hates. My soul and my body are one. Soul and body wish to keep clean and whole. Only the mind is capable of great perversion. Only the mind tries to drive my soul and body into uncleanness and unwholesomeness.

What my soul loves, I love.

What my soul hates, I hate.

When my soul is stirred with compassion, I am compassionate.

What my soul turns away from, I turn away from.

That is the *true* interpretation of Whitman's creed: the true revelation of his Sympathy.

And my soul takes the open road. She meets the souls that are passing, she goes along with the souls that are going her way. And for one and all, she has sympathy. The sympathy of love, the sympathy of hate, the sympathy of simple proximity: all the subtle sympathisings of the incalculable soul, from the bitterest hate to the passionate love.

It is not I who guide my soul to heaven. It is I who am guided by my own soul along the open road, where all men tread. Therefore, I must accept her deep motions of love, or hate, or compassion, or dislike, or indifference. And I must go where she takes me. For my feet and my lips and my body are my soul. It is I who must submit to her.

This is Whitman's message of American democracy.

The true democracy, where soul meets soul, in the open road. Democracy. American democracy where all journey down the open road. And where a soul is known at once in its going. Not by its clothes or appearance. Whitman did away with that. Not by its family name. Not even by its reputation. Whitman and Melville both discounted that. Not by a progression of piety, or by works of Charity. Not by works at all. Not by anything but just itself. The soul passing unenhanced, passing on foot and being no more than itself. And recognized, and passed by or greeted according to the soul's dictate. If it be a great soul, it will be worshipped in the road.

The love of man and woman: a recognition of souls, and a communion of worship. The love of comrades: a recognition of souls, and a communion of worship. Democracy: a recognition of souls, all down the open road, and a great soul seen in its greatness, as it travels on foot among the rest, down the common way of the living. A glad recognition of souls, and a gladder worship of great and greater souls, because they are the only riches.

Love, and Merging, brought Whitman to the Edge of Death! Death! Death!

But the exultance of his message still remains. Purified of MERGING, purified of MYSELF, the exultant message of American Democracy, of souls in the Open Road, full of glad recognition, full of fierce readiness, full of joy of worship, when one soul sees a greater soul.

The only riches, the great souls.

KENNETH BURKE

Policy Made Personal

The plan here is to consider first Whitman's statement of policy in *Democratic Vistas*. Even there his views of history, society, and nature are personalized somewhat. But the full job of personalization is done in his *Leaves of Grass*, which is to be considered in a second section. And finally, since both of these sections are general in their approach, a third section will put the main stress upon one poem, "When Lilacs Last in the Dooryard Bloom'd." Throughout, however, we shall proceed as much as practicable by the inspection and comparison of contexts. Unless otherwise specified, all words or expressions in quotation marks are Whitman's. (Perhaps a better subtitle would be: On Interrelations Among Key Terms in Whitman's Language.)

I. VISTAS

The design of Whitman's essentially idealistic thought is neatly indicated in the three stages of historical unfolding he assigns to "America, type of progress." This alignment seems a handy place to spin from.

The first stage was embodied in the Declaration of Independence, the Constitution, and its Amendments. It "was the planning and putting on record the political foundation rights of immense masses of people . . . not for classes, but for universal man."

The second stage is in the "material prosperity" that resulted after the democratic foundations had been laid: "wealth, labor-saving machines . . . a currency," etc.

A third stage, still to come but "arising out of the previous ones,"

From *Leaves of Grass One Hundred Years After*, edited by Milton Hindus. Stanford University Press, 1955.

would bring about the corresponding "spiritualization" of the nation's sheerly material development.

The first and third stages are in the realm of idea, or spirit. The second stage is in the realm of matter. Writing his essay a few years after the close of the Civil War, he placed himself and his times in stage two, a time marked by "hollowness at heart," lack of honest belief in "the underlying principles of the States," "depravity of the business classes," while all politics were "saturated in corruption" except the judiciary ("and the judiciary is tainted"). "A mob of fashionably dressed speculators and vulgarians . . . crude defective streaks in all the strata of the common people . . . the alarming spectacle of parties usurping the government . . . these savage, wolfish parties . . . delicatesse . . . polite conformity . . . exterior appearance and show, mental and other, built entirely on the idea of caste" . . . in sum: "Pride, competition, segregation, vicious wilfulness, and license beyond example, brood already upon us."

One could cite many other statements of like attitude. But the idealistic design of his thinking permitted him without discouragement to take full note of such contemporary ills, and perhaps even to intensify them as one step in his essay. For against the dissatisfactions of the present, he could set his "planned Idea," a promise for the future. Since "the fruition of democracy, on aught like a grand scale, resides altogether in the future," he would "presume to write, as it were, upon things that exist not, and travel by maps yet unmade, and a blank." Thus, the technically negative nature of the "fervid and tremendous Idea" is made in effect positive, so far as *personal* considerations go. By seeing contemporary conditions in terms of future possibilities, in "vistas" that stressed "results to come," he could treat "America and democracy as convertible terms," while having high hopes for both. He says, "It is useless to deny" that "Democracy grows rankly up the thickest, noxious, deadliest plants and fruits of all—brings worse and worse invaders— needs newer, larger, stronger, keener compensations and compellers"; but, in line with post-Hegelian promises, he saw in any greater challenge the possibility of a correspondingly greater response.

In sum, then, as regards the basic design of his thinking, the *Vistas* found elation in a project for the "spiritualization of our nation's wealth." (He likes words like "richness" and "luxuriance," words that readily suggest both material and spiritual connotations, gaining resonance and persuasiveness from this ambiguity.) "The extreme business energy, and this almost maniacal appetite for wealth prevalent in the United States, are parts of amelioration and progress," he says (in terms that, of all things, suggest Marxist patterns of thought with regard to material development under capitalism); but a different order of motives is manifest in the statement (he would probably have said "promulgation") of his ideal: "Offsetting the material civilization of our race . . . must be its moral civilization."

If, by very definition, one can view all materially acquisitive behavior in terms of ideal future fulfillment, it follows that the poet could contemplate with "joy" the industrious industrial conquest of the continent. Not until late in life (after his paralytic stroke) does this "ecstatic" champion of the "athletic" and "electric" body turn from identification with the feller of trees (as in *Song of the Broad-Axe*) to identification with the fallen tree itself (as in *Song of the Redwood-Tree*), though he always had fervid ways of being sympathetic to child, adult, and the elderly. Our point is simply that the zestfulness of the typical Whitman survey could follow logically from his promissory principle, his idealization of the present in terms of the future.

Halfway between the realm of materials amassed by his countrymen's "oceanic, variegated, intense, practical energy" and the realm of spirit, or idea, we might place his cult of the sturdy human body, its "spinal," "athletic," "magnetic" qualities and the "appetites" that make for "sensuous luxuriance." (As the recipe also called for a male type "somewhat flushed," we dare wonder ironically whether his notion of the perfect "manly" temperament also concealed a syndrome of symptoms, an idealistic recognition, without realistic diagnosis, of the hypertension that must have preceded his paralysis. Surely, prophesying after the event, we might propose that Whitman's headlong style should involve high blood pressure as its nosological counterpart.)

For an "over-arching" term here, Whitman could speak of "nature" in ways that, while clearly referring to the materialistic on one side, also have pontificating aspects leading into a Beyond, along Emersonian lines. (In fact, toward the close of the *Vistas*, one is often strongly reminded of Emerson's earlier and longer transcendentalist essay, *Nature*, first published in 1836.) Democracy was Nature's "younger brother," and Science was "twin, in its field, of Democracy in its." But such equations were idealistically weighted to one side: for while "Dominion strong is the body's; dominion stronger is the mind's."

Somewhere between the grounding of his position in time, and its grounding in eternity, there is its grounding in terms of personality (two of his special words to this end being "identity" and "nativity").

For grounding in time, one obvious resource is a contrast with some previous time (antithesis being one of the three major stylistic resources, as we are informed in Aristotle's *Rhetoric*). But though "democracy" is thus pitted against "feudalism," Whitman admonishes that "feudalism, caste, ecclesiastical traditions . . . still hold essentially, by their spirit, even in this country, entire possession of the more important fields." For "All smells of princes' favors." And "The United States are destined either to surmount the gorgeous history of feudalism, or else prove the most tremendous failure of time." Whereas now we tend to think of Shakespeare as poignantly at the crossing between the feudal and the modern, the antithetical genius of Whitman's scheme led him to say: "The great poems, Shakespeare included, are poisonous to the idea of the pride and dignity of the common people." For though Shakespeare was conceded to be "rich," and "luxuriant as the sun," he was the "artist and singer of feudalism in its sunset." In contrast, Whitman called: "Come forth, sweet democratic despots of the west." And being against "parlors, parasols, piano-songs," he matched his praise of the "divine average" by words against "the mean flat average." Declaring, "We stand, live, move, in the huge flow of our age's materialism," he quickly added, "in its spirituality." And "to offset chivalry," he would seek "a knightlier and more sacred cause today." In so far as the claims of traditional culture were effete and pretentious (and "for a single class alone"), he admonished against "Culture"—and later, apologists of Nazism could take over the tenor of his slogans by the simple device of but half-hearing him.

As for eternity: His attacks upon traditional ecclesiastical forms were stated in terms of an "all penetrating Religiousness" that vigorously proclaimed its scorn of "infidels." He always identified democracy with what he called "the religious element," however that might differ from the norms of conventional churchgoing (and it differed greatly, as regards its relation to his cult of the "body electric").

His notion of "succession" (a eulogistic word that sounds nearly like his very dyslogistic one, "secession") we have already touched upon. It is in line with the typical nineteenth-century doctrine of permanent evolution, into ever higher forms, a design that falls in the realm of time, so far as the manifestations of history are concerned, but that would be above time, in so far as its operation were constant. "The law over all, the law of laws, is the law of successions; that of the superior law, in time, gradually supplanting and overwhelming the inferior one." Fittingly, the essay reverts to this "law" in the paragraph-long closing sentence, where America, "illumined and illuming," is saluted in terms of the ideal future, when she will have "become a full-formed world, and divine Mother, not only of material but spiritual worlds, in ceaseless succession, through time—the main thing being the average, the bodily, the concrete, the democratic, the popular, on which all the superstructures of the future are to permanently rest."

The lines succinctly assemble the main components of his Ideal Matrix, or "divine Mother." (And what better words for an *ending* than "permanently rest"?) But the personalizing of this "Mother" (the democratic creed) will take on attributes not strictly germane to either the politics of democracy or the personality of motherhood.

The logic of his terminology centers in his emphasis upon the individual person ("rich, luxuriant, varied personalism"). In proclaiming that "the ripeness of religion" is to be sought in the "field of individuality," and is "a result that no organization or church can ever achieve," he automatically sets up the dialectical conditions for a principle of division matched by a principle of merger. While his brand of "personalism" will "promulge" the "precious idiocrasy and special nativity and intention that he is, the man's self," all such individual selves are to be joined in democratic union, or "cohesion"; and the result is "ensemble-Individuality," an "idiocrasy of universalism," since the "liberalist of today" seeks "not only to individualize, but to universalize." And while the aim is to formulate "one broad, primary, universal, common platform," he says, "even for the treatment of the universal" it is good "to reduce the whole matter to the consideration of a single self, a man, a woman, on permanent grounds."

In sum: There is "the All, and the idea of All, with the accompanying idea of eternity" (the poems will speak of "the all-mother," and the "Mother of All"). And in silence, in the "solitariness of individuality," one can "enter the pure ether of veneration," to "commune" with the "mysteries" and the "unutterable." Or (as regards the timely), "individuality" and its "unimpeded branchings" will "flourish best under imperial republican forms" (for the grandeur of spiritualized democratic "expansion" will make for an "empire of empires").

So we have the "idea of perfect individualism," of "completeness in separation," with its dialectical counterpart: "the identity of the Union at all hazards." Not only must man become "a law, a series of laws unto himself"; also "the great word Solidarity has arisen." The "individualism, which isolates" is but "half only," and has for its other half the "adhesiveness or love, that fuses." Thus, both of these trends (contradictory or complementary?) are "vitalized by religion," for you in your solitude can "merge yourself" in the "divine." (A sheerly politico-economic variant of this dialectic for fitting the one and the many together is in his statement: "The true gravitation-hold of liberalism in the United States will be a more universal ownership of property, general homesteads, general comfort—a vast, inter-twining reticulation of wealth.")

But if the three stages are handiest as a way into the underlying idealistic *design* of Whitman's thinking, perhaps the most succinct *doctrinal* passage is this:

"Long ere the second centennial arrives, there will be some forty to fifty States, among them Canada and Cuba. When the present century closes, our population will be sixty or seventy millions. The Pacific will be ours, and the Atlantic mainly ours. There will be daily electric communication with every part of the globe. What an age! What a land! Where, elsewhere, one so great? The individuality of one nation must then, as always, lead the world. Can there be any doubt who the leader ought to be? Bear in mind, though, that nothing less than the mightiest original non-subordinated SOUL has ever really, gloriously led, or ever can lead."

Then comes the very important addition, in parentheses: "This SOUL—its other name, in these Vistas, is LITERATURE." Then follows typical talk of "ideals," and of a "richness" and "vigor" that will be in letters "luxuriantly."

The essay's opening reference to "lessons" attains its fulfillment in these views of Whitman on the didactic or moralizing element in his ideal literature, its social service in the training of personalities. By the "mind," which builds "haughtily," the national literature shall be endowed "with grand and archetypal models," as we confront the "momentous spaces" with a "new and greater personalism," aided by the "image-making faculty."

Here, then, is the grand mélange: "Arrived now, definitely, at an apex for these Vistas," Whitman sees in dream "a new and greater literatus order," its members "always one, compact in soul," though "separated . . . by different dates or States." This band would welcome materialistic trends both "for their oceanic practical grandeur" and "for purposes of spiritualization." And by "serving art in its highest," such a "band of brave and true" would also be "serving God, and serving humanity."

Such a literature would affirm the "fervid comradeship," "adhesive love," between man and man that Whitman so strongly associated with his evangel of democracy. And as for woman, the "prophetic literature of these States," inspired by "Idealism," will train toward "the active redemption of woman," and "a race of perfect Mothers."

He offers four portraits of ideal female types: a servant, a business-woman, a housewife, and a fourth that we might call a grand old lady ("a resplendent person . . . known by the name of the Peacemaker"). It is particularly relevant to look more closely at this fourth figure.

Whitman has just been referring to "that indescribable perfume of genuine womanhood . . . which belongs of right to all the sex, and is, or ought to be, the invariable atmosphere and common aureola of old as well as young." The next paragraph begins: "My dear mother once described to me . . . ," etc. Eighty years old, this fourth type of personality that his mother is said to have described was a kind of grandmotherly Whitman. She had lived "down on Long Island." She was called the "Peacemaker" because of her role as "the reconciler in the land." She was "of happy and sunny temperament," was "very neighborly"; and she "possessed a native dignity." "She was a sight to look upon, with her large figure, her profuse snow-white hair (uncoifed by any head-dress or cap) . . . and peculiar personal magnetism"—and when reading the word on which the recital of his four "portraits" ends, might we not fittingly recall that Whitman's poems are dotted with references to the "electric" and "magnetic"?

We consider this all of a piece: the steps from "the indescribable perfume of genuine womanhood," to "My dear mother," to the grand-motherly figure in which this entire set of portraits culminates (and thus toward which the series might be said to have tended from the start). Frankly, we stress the point for use later, when we shall be considering the scent of lilacs, "the perfume strong I love," mentioned in commemoration of the poet's great dead democratic hero. Meanwhile, a few more considerations should be noted, before we turn from his prose statement of policy to its personalizing in his verse.

We should recall his principle of cultural *ascesis* (the notion that "political democracy" is "life's gymnasium . . . fit for freedom's athletes," and that books are "in highest sense, an exercise, a gymnast's struggle"). It is easy to see how thought thus of a *studious athleticism* might, on the one hand, proclaim "health, pride, acuteness, noble aspirations" as the "motive-elements of the grandest style"; on the other hand, given the "appetites" that go with such exercisings and exertions, the poet might find no embarrass-ments in equating democracy with the grandeur of ever expanding empire.

But there is one mild puzzler to be noted with regard to the Whitman cult of democratic expansionism. When saying that the "spine-character of the States will probably run along the Ohio, Missouri and Mississippi rivers, and west and north of them, including Canada," he describes the "giant growth" thus: "From the north, intellect, the sun of things, also the idea of unswayable justice, anchor amid the last, the wildest tempests. From the south the living soul, the animus of good and bad, haughtily admitting no demonstration but its own. While from the west itself comes solid personal-ity, with blood and brawn, and the deep quality of all-accepting fusion."

One automatically waits for some mention of the east here—but there is none. Interestingly enough, one of the poems ("To the Leaven'd Soil They Trod") discusses "vistas" and *ends* on a similar design:

> The prairie draws me close, as the father to bosom broad the son,
> The Northern ice and rain that began me nourish me to the end,
> But the hot sun of the South is to fully ripen my songs.

Presumably, the poet mentions only three points of the compass, since he was born in the *East*, and was so *tendency-minded*. And perhaps, since the *Vistas* contain the equation, "the democratic, the west," the East is, by the dialectical or rhetorical pressures of antithesis, the vestigially and effetely "feudal," except in so far as it is inspirited by the other three sources of motivation. (South, by the way, is in Whitman's idiom the place from which "perfume" comes. As regards North, we must admit to not having fully done our lessons at this time.)

A few further points, before turning from the *Vistas* to the *Leaves*:

In connection with the notion of guidance through literature, Whitman writes: "A strong mastership of the general inferior self by the superior self, is to be aided, secured, indirectly, but surely, by the literatus." And we might remember this word "mastership," to puzzle over it, when in the poem of the "Lilacs" he says: "Yet the lilac with mastering odor holds me," even though we may not quite succeed in fitting the passages to each other.

And we should note Whitman's words in praise of a strong political digestion, since they bear so directly upon the relation between his design and his doctrine: "And as, by virtue of its cosmical, antiseptic power, Nature's stomach is fully strong enough not only to digest the morbific matter always presented . . . but even to change such contributions into nutriment for highest use and life—so American democracy's."

Such faith in the virtues of a healthy appetite is doubtless implied when, on the subject of political corruption, Whitman assures us that "the average man . . . remains immortal owner and boss, deriving good uses, somehow, out of any sort of servant in office." (Or, more generally, here is the encouragement of the sprout-out-of-rot principle.) At every step along the way, whatever tax is levied by their Lordships, Favoritism and Dishonesty, it remains a fact that Democracy does build its roads and schools and courthouses—and the catalogue of its accumulations, when listed under one national head, becomes truly "oceanic" and "over-arching." But at the mention of catalogues, we might well turn to a survey of the verse.

II. LEAVES

No two opening lines of a poet's work ever indicated more clearly the sheer dialetics of a position than in the "Inscription" with which *Leaves of Grass* begins:

> One's-Self I sing, a simple separate person,
> Yet utter the word Democratic, the word En-Masse.

For a poet generally so voluble, this entire poem of eight lines is astoundingly efficient. Note how the second stanza (proclaiming that "physiology" is equally important with "physiognomy" and "brain," and that he sings "The Female equally with the Male") ambiguously translates his code into its corresponding *sexual* terms. Then, in the third stanza, he merges life, work, God's laws, song, and his futuristic cult of the present, all under the sign of strong motives and hopeful attitudes:

> Of Life immense in passion, pulse, and power,
> Cheerful, for freest action form'd under the laws divine,
> The Modern Man I sing.

The main themes that are lacking are: (1) his merging of birth and death in the allness of the mother, and (2) his stress upon perpetual passage (what would Whitman do without the word "pass" or its components: "I come and I depart"?). And, of course, the notable equating of democracy with the love of male for male is manifest here only if we read as a *double-entendre* his words about Male and Female (though most likely they were not so intended).

In his "oceanic" accumulation of details, the catalogues that characterize most of his longer poems (such as *Salut au Monde!*), there is obviously the "spiritualization" of matter. Here is his primary resource for those loosely yet thematically guided associations of ideas which enable him to "chant the chant of dilation or pride." Of such spiritual possessions, he has "stores and plenty to spare." Who was more qualified than Whitman to write a *Song of the Exposition* with its closing apostrophe to the "universal Muse" and maternal Union: "While we rehearse our measureless wealth, it is for thee, dear Mother"? In effect, the Whitman catalogue locates the rhetorical device of amplification in the very nature of things.

It is possible that, after long inspection, we might find some "over-arching" principle of development that "underlies" his typical lists. Always, of course, they can be found to embody some principle of repetitive form, some principle of classification whereby the various items fall under the same head (as with the third stanza of the *Salut*, for instance, which races through a scattering of nationalities, with a scattering of details hastily allotted to each: the Australians "pursuing the wild horse," the Spanish semipleonastically dancing "with castanets in the chestnut shade," "echoes from the Thames," "fierce French liberty songs," and so on, ending with the Hindoo "teaching his favorite pupil the loves, wars, adages, transmitted safely from poets who wrote three thousand years ago"). Some critic might also discern a regular canon of *development* in such "turbulent" heapings. Meanwhile, in any case, there are the many variations by internal contrast (as with varying rhythm and length of line, or as the variations on "out of" that mark the opening lines of "Out of the Cradle Endlessly Rocking": out of, over, down from, up from, out from, from the, from your, from under, from those, from such, borne hither). And even where epanaphora is extreme, there are large tidal changes from stanza to stanza, or rhetorical forms that suggest the shifting of troops in military maneuvers.

"Melange, mine own . . . Omnes! Omnes! . . . the word En-Masse . . . the One formed out of all . . . toward all . . . made ONE IDENTITY . . . they shall flow and unite . . . merge and unite . . . to merge all in the travel they tend to . . . All, all, toward the mystic Ocean tending . . . Song of the Universal . . . O public road . . . to know the universe itself as a road . . . along the grand roads of the universe . . . All, all, for immortality . . . it makes the whole coincide . . . I become part of that, whatever it is . . ."—such lines state the "omnific" principle behind the aggregates of the catalogues.

To such a cult of the "divine average," good will and good cheer sometimes come easy: "I love him, though I do not know him . . . I know not where they go; / But I know they go toward the best . . . surely the drift of them is something grand . . . illustrious every one . . . Great is Wealth— great is Poverty . . . Flaunt away, flags of all nations! . . . I believe material- ism is true, and spiritualism is true—I reject no part . . . I do not see one imperfection in the universe . . . the venerealee is invited." He thinks hap- pily of "easily written, loose-fingered chords," and "the loose drift of charac- ter, the inkling through random types." He assures us, in hale and hearty camaraderie: "I turn the bridegroom out of bed, and stay with the bride myself"—nay more: "My voice is the wife's voice." His gusto suggests some- thing like a cheerleader's at a chess tournament when he proclaims: "Hurrah for positive science! long live exact demonstration!" But the tactics are much subtler when, addressing a locomotive, he says, "Law of thyself complete, thine own track firmly holding."

In a poet capable of maintaining "this is Ocean's poem," a poet "aware of the mighty Niagara," the principle of joyously infused oneness can be centered in various terms of high generalization: "the greatness of Re- ligion . . . the real and permanent grandeur of These States . . . efflux of the Soul . . . great City . . . transcendental Union . . . teeming Nation of na- tions . . . the immortal Idea . . . Sex" (which "contains all" . . . "every hour the semen of centuries")—all such subjects serve as variants on his theme of unified diversity. "Underneath all, Nativity" ("I swear I am charmed with nothing except nativity, / Men, women, cities, nations, are only beautiful from nativity"), by which he meant the individual being's uniqueness of identity ("singleness and normal simplicity and separation"). When he thinks of "Death, merged in the thought of materials," he swears, "there is nothing but immortality!" When he "wander'd, searching among burial places," he "found that every place was a burial place." All "to the Ideal tendest"; "Only the good is universal"; "All swings around us. / I have the idea of all, and am all and believe in all"; "He resolves all tongues into his own."

In his prophetic role as "Chanter of Personality," he can use the Idea of Allness as justification for his claim to act as the spokesman for all: "I act as the tongue of you; / Tied in your mouth, in mine it begins to be loosened." Corresponding to "the great Idea, the idea of perfect and free individuals," an idea for which "the bard walks in advance," there are the many forms of idealized "appetite." These range from thoughts of a gallant and adventurous launching of "all men and women forward with me into the Unknown," to the notion of normal physical sensations programmatically made excessive, an abnormality of super-health: "Urge, and urge, and urge . . . complete abandonment . . . scattering it freely . . . athletic Democracy . . . ecstatic songs . . . the smoke of my own breath . . . the boundless impatience of restraint . . . unmitigated adoration . . . I inhale great draughts of space . . . tumbling on steadily, nothing dreading . . . give me the coarse and rank . . . fond of his sweetheart, relishing well his steak . . . aplomb in the midst of irrational things . . . turbulent, fleshy, sensual, eating, drinking, and breeding." In earlier versions of this last set honorifically describing himself, "turbulent" had been "disorderly." And we glimpse something of his rhetorical tactics when we recall that "I am he who goes through the streets" later became "I am he who walks the States." He gains concreteness in such inventions as "love-juice," "limitless limpid jets of love," and "life-lumps." Or analogies between the physical body and what J.C. Ransom has called the world's body are exploited in such statements as "Through you I drain the pent-up rivers of myself" (elsewhere he similarly speaks of "pent-up, aching rivers").

When we turn from the physical body and the world's body to the body politic, we note how such concretizing of the "democratic" code almost automatically vows the poet to imagery of a homosexual cast. For if Democracy is to be equated with "the manly love of comrades," and if such love is to be conceived *concretely*, in terms of bodily intimacy, such social "adhesiveness" ("the great rondure, the cohesion of all") that he advocates is almost necessarily matched by many expressions of "robust love" that would be alien to the typical heterosexual poet, as conditioned by our mores. And though the sex of his lover is not specified in the startling section 5 of *Song of Myself*, the many similarly motivated poems in *Calamus* give reason enough to assume that he is here writing of a male attachment, as with the "hugging and loving bed-fellow" of section 3 (though this passage may also be complicated by infantile memories of the mother). In any case, we should note, for what little it may be worth, that in *The Sleepers* Whitman associates the "onanist" with the color "gray," the same color with which he associates himself ("gray eyes" and "gray-necked"), while the "hermit thrush" singing in the "swamps" of the "Lilacs" poem is "gray-brown" (though "smoke" and "debris" here are also gray; and there are other grays that are still further afield). The directest association of himself with an onanistic motive is in the last two lines of "Spontaneous Me." Also, he uses a spiritual analogue (frequently encountered in devotional verse) when, concerning his literary motive, he apostrophizes his tongue: "Still uttering—still ejaculating—canst never cease this babble?"

As regards the poetic I, who would "promote brave soldiers," has "voyagers' thoughts," would "strike up for a New World," is "he that aches with amorous love," would "dilate you with tremendous breath," or "buoy you up": here his motives and motifs get their summarization in his title of titles, *Leaves of Grass*. Accordingly, one direct way into his verse is to ask what associations clearly cluster about these two nouns, "leaves" and "grass" (which are related to each other as individuals are to the group, thus being in design like his term in the *Vistas*, "ensemble-Individuality," though in that formula the order is reversed). Here we are at the core of his personalizing tactics. And, typically, it is in his *Song of Myself* that he specifically offers answers to the question, "What is the grass?" (As indication that he would here be the Answerer to a fundamental question, he tells us that it has been asked by a child.) In section 6 of this poem, he offers several definitions:

First, he says of grass: "I guess it must be the flag of my disposition, out of hopeful green stuff woven." Other references to "stuff" in this poem are: "voices . . . of wombs and of the father-stuff"; "This day I am jetting the stuff of far more arrogant republics": "I am . . . / Maternal as well as paternal, a child as well as a man, / Stuff'd with the stuff that is coarse and stuff'd with the stuff that is fine." Elsewhere we have noted "I pour the stuff to start sons and daughters fit for these States," and "these States with veins full of poetical stuff." Interestingly enough, all other three references to "flag" in this poem are in contrast with "hopeful green." There are "flag-tops . . . draped with black muslin" to "guard some corpse"—and twice the word is used as a verb, in the sense of "droop": "Did you fear some scrofula out of the unflagging pregnancy?" and "The hounded slave that flags in the race." (Note that "draped" is an ablaut form of "drooped" and "dropt.")

Second: "Or I guess it is the handkerchief of the Lord, / A scented gift and remembrancer designedly dropt, / Bearing the owner's name . . ." We have noted no other references to handkerchiefs in Whitman, though there is always *Othello* in the offing! But the verb "dropt" recalls the "drooped" and "dropt" of the "Lilacs" poem (which also refers to "inlooped flags with the cities draped in black") and since the matter of *scent* also links these two contexts, we shall wait for further leads here when we specifically deal with this theme. So far as the internal organization is concerned, by the way, we might note that the reference to the "owner's name" attains an enigmatic fulfillment near the end of the poem, when the poet decides that his motive is "without name . . . a word unsaid," though "To it the creation is the friend whose embracing awakes me."

Other meanings he offers are:

"I guess the grass is itself a child"; . . . "Or I guess it is a uniform hieroglyphic, / . . . Growing among black folks as among white." Again, it seems like "the beautiful uncut hair of graves"—and as Whitman frequently shuttles back and forth along the channel of affinity that links love and death or womb and tomb, his next stanza, beginning "Tenderly will I use you curling grass," contrives by quick transitions to go from "the breasts of young men" to "mothers' laps." In the following stanza, grass is related to both "the white heads of old mothers" and "the colorless beards of old men," while a reference to "the faint red roofs of mouths" leads to the specifically poetic motive, in the mention of "uttering tongues."

Near the close of the poem (section 49) the theme of grass as the "hair of graves" is developed further ("O grass of graves"), while the connotations are generally of a maternal, or even obstetrical sort, in the references to the "bitter hug of mortality," the "elder-hand pressing," and the "accoucheur" who helps bring about "the relief and escape" through Death.

The scent theme figures here likewise, thanks to a bit of rhetorical alchemy. For after apostrophizing the "Corpse" as "good manure," the poet assures us: "but that does not offend me, / I smell the white roses sweet-scented and growing," whereat the associations, taking their lead from the vital connotations of the participle "growing," shift into quite a different order: "I reach to the leafy lips, I reach to the polish'd breasts of melons." And do we not find tonal vestiges of "leafy" in the two similar-sounding words of the next line: "And as to you Life I reckon you are the leavings of many deaths"?

To trail down the various uses of the verb "leave," in the light of the possibility that it may secondarily involve motives intrinsic to the noun "leaves," would take us on a longer journey than we could manage now. But let us look at a few. Consider, for instance, in *Song of Myself*, section 3: "As the hugging and loving bed-fellow sleeps at my side through the night... / Leaving me baskets cover'd with white towels swelling the house with their plenty." In this context for "leaving," the hug is not overtly maternal, though the food connotations suggest that it may be secondarily so, quite as the "baskets" in this passage might correspond food-wise to the "polish'd breasts of melons" in the other. And similarly, in *Song of Myself*, section 6, an implicit food motive seems to guide the steps from "curling grass" to "the breasts of young men," and thence finally via "mothers" to "mouths," with a final turn from the nutriently oral to the poetically eloquent, in "uttering tongues." Yet, as regards "swelling the house with their plenty": we might recall that in "I Sing the Body Electric" we find the step from "love-flesh swelling and deliciously aching" to "jets of love hot and enormous," and two pages later: "There swells and jets a heart" (after talk of "blood" that might well bear study in connection with the talk of blood in the poem beginning "Trickle drops! my blue veins leaving! / O drops of me! trickle, slow drops, / Candid from me falling, drip, bleeding drops"). So the "hug" of Death or

bed-fellows seems sometimes maternal, sometimes "democratic," or inde-
terminately something of both.

But our main intention at this point was to consider some more
obvious cases where we might seem justified in adding the verb forms to our
inquiry into the various major meanings of "leaves." Perhaps the perfect
pontificating case is in *Starting from Paumanok*, where the line, "Take my leaves
America" suggests something midway between "receive my offerings" and
"put up with my constant departures." Or in so far as Whitman sometimes
uses "blade" as a synonym for "leaf," there is another kind of bridge between
noun and verb when, in "Scented Herbage of My Breast," in connection with
male love, he says: "Emblematic and capricious blades I leave you." And
before moving on, we'd like to consider one more context where the verb
form seems quite relevant to our concerns. We have in mind the passage on
Death, the "hug of mortality," the "sweet-scented," and Life as "the leavings
of many deaths," a development that is immediately preceded by the lines
(except for fifteen words):

> I find letters from God dropt in the street, and every one is sign'd by God's name,
> And I leave them where they are . . .

This is in section 48 of *Song of Myself*. Though this longest poem is
sometimes entitled "Walt Whitman," we have said that there is in it a *problem
of name* (that is, a problem of *essence*, of *fundamental motivation*; and we would
base our position, naturally, upon the fact that, as the poet nears his windup,
he centers upon the problem of locating a substance "without name"). But,
relevantly reverting to the context where the word "name" first appears, we
find it precisely in that passage (of section 6) where he speaks of the Lord's
"scented" handkerchief, "bearing the owner's name," and "designedly
dropt."

There are the many obvious places where the leaves are the leaves of
books (a usage that fits well with a pun on utterance, in the notion of a tree's
"uttering" leaves). A three-line poem in *Calamus* embodies this usage incidentally, in the course of a somewhat secretive confession:

> Here the frailest leaves of me and yet my strongest lasting,
> Here I shade and hide my thoughts, I myself do not expose them,
> And yet they expose me more than all my other poems.

The word "calamus" itself is apparently within the same orbit, and even
allows us to watch "flag" for signs of similar meaning, since calamus is "sweet
flag," of which our dictionary says: "The root has a pungent, aromatic taste,
and is used in medicine as a stomachic; the leaves have an aromatic odor, and
were formerly used instead of rushes to strew on floors." Thus, we might
assume that "calamus" is one of his "scent" words, though our incomplete

reading has not as yet given us a clear title to this assumption. However, we can cite a one-page poem ("These I Singing in Spring") in which the mention of "calamus-root" accompanies such clearly scent-conscious references as "smelling the earthy smell," "lilac, with a branch of pine," and "aromatic cedar" (calamus-root here being specified as "the token of comrades"). Since "calamus" is the Latin word for "reed," we also dare note inklings of grassiness in the "reedy voice" of the hermit thrush that warbles through the "Lilacs" poem.

"Herbage" clearly belongs here—as in "Scented Herbage of My Breast" (though the subsequent references to "tomb-leaves," "body-leaves," "tall leaves," and "slender leaves . . . blossoms of my blood," while they are clear as radiations from the leaf motif, are somewhat vague in themselves). Herbage for grass is matched by feuillage for leaves; and as judged by the assemblage of details in *Our Old Feuillage*, leaves can be any item that he includes in his surveys and poetic catalogues, here called "bouquets" ("Always . . . All sights . . . All characters . . ."; "Always the free range and diversity—always the continent of Democracy"; and "Encircling all, vast-darting up and wide, the American Soul, with equal hemispheres, one Love, one Dilation or Pride").

Leaves are sometimes called "blades"; and the blade of the broad-axe is called a "gray-blue leaf" (thereby adding the *gray* strand—and since the axe was "to be leaned and to lean on," we recall: "I lean and loafe at my ease observing a spear of summer grass"). Besides adding "spear" to our radiations, we note that "lean and loafe" are here attitudinally identical. But further, lo! not only is "loafe" tonally an ablaut form of "leaf"—change the unvoiced "f" to its voiced cognate, "v," and you have the close tonal proximity between "loafe" and "love."

"Leaves" and "grass" cross over into the scent category, in the reference to roots and leaves as "perfume," or in lines such as "The prairie-grass dividing, its special odor breathing," and "The sniff of green leaves and dry leaves . . . and of hay in the barn"—or the reference to "words simple as grass" that are "wafted with the odor of his body or breath."

Nowhere do we recall encountering such connotations as in the 129th Psalm, "Let them be as the grass upon the housetops, which withereth afore it groweth up"; or in Isaiah 40: "The grass withereth, the flower fadeth: because the spirit of the Lord bloweth upon it: surely the people is grass."

We should note two other major principles of unity:

First, there are the references to the "first," a common poetic and narrative device for the *defining of essence*. Perhaps the central example is his line: "I speak the password primeval, I give the sign of democracy." The more familiar we become with Whitman's vocabulary, the more condensed this line is felt to be. Identity is proclaimed quasi-temporally, in the word "primeval." Such firstness is further established in terms of the poetic I as spokesman for a public cause. But the more closely one examines the word "sign" in Whitman, the more one comes to realize that it has a special significance for him ranging from signs of God ("and every one is sign'd by God's name, / And I leave them where they are") to such signs as figure in a flirtation. (In "Among the Multitude," for instance: "I perceive one picking me out by secret and divine signs / . . . that one knows me. / Ah lover and perfect equal," as per the ambiguously "democratic" kind of equality especially celebrated in the *Calamus* poems.) "Password" is notable for merging one of his major verbs with the term that sums up his own specialty (elsewhere he has "passkey").

When proclaiming "a world primal again," he characteristically identifies it with the "new," the "expanding and swift," and the "turbulent." Another variant of such quasi-temporal firstness is in his term "nativity," as with "Underneath all, Nativity." And often references to the "child" serve the same reductive function (as with "Years looking backward resuming in answer to children").

Lines such as "Unfolded out of the folds of the woman, man comes unfolded," and "Out of the cradle endlessly rocking" reveal how readily such essentializing in terms of the "primal" can lead into the realm of the maternal (which may range from the sheer abstract principle of Union to the personally "electric," "magnetic," or "athletic"). And we might discern a "democratic" variant of the attitude implicit in the German epithet *wohlgeboren*, when he temporally defines his personal essence thus: "Starting from fish-shape Paumanok where I was born, / Well-begotten, and rais'd by a perfect mother."

There is a notable variant of the temporal idiom in "Crossing Brooklyn Ferry." For as the literal crossing of the river becomes symbolically a vision of crossing into the future, so the poet becomes a kind of essentializing past, defining the nature of his future readers. In "With Antecedents," we see how this temporal or narrative mode of defining essence can fit into the dialectics of *logical* priority (priority in the sense that the first premise of a syllogism can be considered prior to the second premise). For while, as his very title indicates, he is concerned with the temporally prior, he reduces his temporal sequence in turn to terms of "all" when he says: "We stand amid time beginningless and endless, we stand amid evil and good, / All swings around us."

In his *Song of the Open Road*, which calls upon us continually to "reach" and "pass," and "to merge all in the travel they tend to," he uses a reverse kind of temporal priority; namely: seniority. "Old age, calm, expanded, broad with the haughty breadth of the universe, / Old age, flowing free with the delicious near-by freedom of death." (The broad-breadth pair here could lead us into his notable breast-breath set.) But with the subject of

Death, we come upon another kind of summing up, since it names the direction in which the "ever-tending" is headed. ("Tend" is as typical a Whitman word as "pass," though it occurs much less frequently.) So, let us consider Whitman's poetizing of Death. But since Death is the Great Positive-Seeming Negative, perhaps we might best consider it with relation to the poet's use of the negative in general.

The incidence of negatives is probably highest in the poems of the *Calamus* period; at least, in many places here they come thick and fast. There is almost an orgy of not's and nor's in "Not Heaving from My Ribb'd Breast Only," as sixteen of the poem's seventeen lines so begin, while one line contains a second. Since the poem is composed of a single periodic sentence about "adhesivenes" (the "pulse of my life"), we should certainly be justified in asking whether there may be a substantive relation in these poems between the negative and the resolve to celebrate democracy with songs of "manly attachment." (See also particularly in this same series: "Not Heat Flames Up and Consumes"; "City of Orgies"; "No Labor-Saving Machine"; or the way in which a flat "no" serves as fulcrum in "What Think You I Take My Pen in Hand?")

It might also be worth noting that the *Calamus* theme of the "subtle electric fire that for your sake is playing within me" produces two significant and quite appealing instances of anacoluthon: "City whom that I have lived and sung in your midst will one day make you illustrious," and "O you whom I often and silently come where you are that I may be with you." (We mention anacoluthon here because, tentatively, though not for certain, we incline to believe that the figure indicates a certain deviousness in thinking, hence may remotely indicate a "problematical" motive.)

A more orthodox strategy of deflection (almost a *diplomacy*) is to be seen in another poem of the *Calamus* series, "Earth, My Likeness." Beginning on the theme of the analogy between the poet's body and the earth as a body, the poet then avows a questionable motive in himself, after figuratively attributing a like motive to the earth:

> I now suspect there is something fierce in you eligible to burst forth,
> For an athlete is enamour'd of me, and I of him,
> But toward him there is something fierce and terrible in me eligible to burst forth,
> I dare not tell it in words, not even in these songs.

In *Song of Myself* (section 44) there is an absolute negative, identified with a "first":

> Afar down I see the huge first Nothing, I know I was even there,
> I waited unseen and always, and slept through the lethargic mist,
> And took my time, and took no hurt from the fetid carbon.
>
> Long I was hugg'd close—long and long.

Immediately after, the thought is developed in terms of the maternal. For instance: "Cycles ferried my cradle," and "Before I was born out of my mother generations guided me," lines that overlap upon even the sheer titles of *Crossing Brooklyn Ferry* and "Out of the Cradle Endlessly Rocking." The word "hugg'd" might remind us of the previously quoted reference to "the hugging and loving bed-fellow . . . / Leaving me baskets," etc. (section 3). Or there was the "hug of mortality" in section 49, and the death-smell that "does not offend me" and was quickly replaced by talk of the "sweet-scented."

Section 12 in *Starting from Paumanok* has some interesting involvements with the negative. First the poet addresses his femme, Democracy. In her name he will make both the "songs of passion" and the "true poem of riches." He will "effuse egotism," and will show that male and female are equal.

We might note that such equality of sex could mean one thing as applied to the body politic, but something quite different if applied to the individual personality. For within the individual personality, an "equality" of "male" and "female" motives could add up to an ambivalence of the *androgynous* sort, as it would not, strictly in the realm of politics. Yet we must also bear in mind the fact that, however close language may be to the persuasions and poetics of sexual courtship, language as such is nonsexual; and in so far as motivational perturbations arising from purely *linguistic* sources become personalized in terms of any real or imagined distinctions between "male" and "female," such sexual-seeming differentiations should be inadequate to the case; hence, any purely linguistic situations that happened to be stated in sexual terms (involving either sexual differentiations or sexual mergers) should have elements that could be but *prophetically glimpsed* beyond a terminology formed by sexual analogies.

For instance, though language necessarily has a realm of dialectical resources wholly extrinsic to sexuality, there is the ironic linguistic fact that concrete bisexual imagery may be inevitable, if a poet, let us say, would give us not at one time the image of *mother* and at another the image of *father*, but would rather seek to localize in concrete imagery the idea of *parent*. At the very least, thinking of such a linguistic embarrassment along psychoanalytic lines, we might expect some kind of merger or amalgam like that in Whitman's exclamation: "Mother! with subtle sense severe, with the naked sword in your hand." (And after the analogy of "spears" of grass, we might well have swords of grass, too, not forgetting the naked broad-axe. Further, a poet given to homosexual imagery might well, when writing of his verbal art, glimpse the wholly nonsexual quandaries that lie in the bed of language, far beyond any and all sociopolitical relations.)

But we were on the subject of the negatives in section 12 of *Starting from Paumanok*. Immediately after the poet has proclaimed the equality of male and female, and has vowed that he will prove "sexual organs and acts" to be "illustrious," the negatives come piling in. He will show that "there is no imperfection in the present, and can be none in the future," and that "nothing can happen more beautiful than death." The next stanza has a negative in four of its five verses, and the positive line is introduced by a disjunctive conjunction:

I will not make poems with reference to parts,
But I will make poems, songs, thoughts, with reference to ensemble,
And I will not sing with reference to a day, but with reference to all days,
And I will not make a poem nor the least part of a poem but has reference to the soul,
Because having look'd at the objects of the universe, I find there is no one
    nor any particle of one but has reference to the soul.

Whereas the Whitman negative, at one extreme, seems to involve the notions of No-No that trouble the scruples of "manly love" (scruples that somehow connect with thoughts of the maternal and, of course, with the problem of his identity, or "nativity," as a poet), in the above quotation we see how such matters fade into purely technical considerations. For if the *particulars* of life are positive, then the "ensemble" or "soul" would be correspondingly negative; or if you considered the "ensemble" positive, then the "parts" would be negative (as with Spinoza's principle: *omnis determinatio est negatio*). Or in a fluctuant medium such as Whitman's, where the issues need not be strictly drawn, the talk of parts and wholes may merely call forth a general aura of negativity. However, once we consider this problem from the standpoint of the distinction between positive and negative, we should note the dialectical resources whereby, above the catalogues of positive details that characteristically make up so many of his poems, there should hover some summarizing principle—and this principle would be "negative," at least in the sense that no single detail could be it, though each such positive detail might partitively stand for it, or be infused with its spirit. (The problem is analogous to that of negative theology.)

When the technical principles of positive and negative are projected into their moralistic counterparts (as good and evil), the poet can assert by the doubling of negatives, as in "I will show that there is no imperfection." And if you will agree that death is negative (in so far as it is the privation of life), then you will note double negativity lurking in the statements that "nothing can happen more beautiful than death," or "Copulation is no more rank to me than death is."

Sometimes the *principle* of negativity is present, but in a positive-seeming statement that is really a denial of a social negative, as with "the bowels sweet and clean," or "perfect and clean the genitals previously jetting." Or here is a line that runs heretically counter to vast sums expended in the advertising of deodorants for people who think that their vague sense of personal guilt is to be eliminated by purely material means: "the scent of these armpits aroma finer than prayer." In keeping with this pattern, he can also celebrate the "joy of death," likening it to the discharging of excrement ("My voided body nothing more to me, returning to the purifications"). Similarly, farther afield, as though boasting of virtues, he can tell of the vices that were "not wanting" in him ("the wolf, the snake, the hog," among others). For he "will make the poem of evil also," for "I am myself just as much evil as good, and my nation is"—whereat, expanding further, "and I say there is in fact no evil." Accordingly, "none can be interdicted, / None but are accepted."

At one point in *Song of the Open Road* he formulates the principle in general terms, in ways suggesting Hegel: "It is provided in the essence of things that from any fruition of success, no matter what, shall come forth something to make a greater struggle necessary," a principle that could provide good grounds for feeling downcast, if one were so inclined. Elsewhere, "after reading Hegel," he avows: "the vast all that is called Evil I saw hastening to merge itself and become lost and dead." And in keeping with the same design, he could praise the earth because "It grows such sweet things out of such corruptions."

In sum, Whitman would programmatically make all days into a kind of permanent Saturnalian revel, though celebrating not a golden age of the past, but rather the present in terms of an ideal future. And, in poetically personalizing his program, he "promulges" democracy in terms of a maternal allness or firstness and fraternal universality ambiguously intermingling in a death hug that presents many central problems for the patient pedestrian analyzer of The Good Gray Poet's terminology.

But when we remind ourselves that the Roman Saturnalia traditionally involved a ritualistic reversal of roles, with the slaves and servants playing as masters for a day while the masters playfully took orders, we wonder whether the ironic bitterness of Whitman's poem, "Respondez! Respondez!" (first published in 1856 as "Poem of the Proposition of Nakedness") might be studied as a kind of Saturnalia-in-reverse.

"Let the slaves be masters! let the masters become slaves!" he exhorts—but this call to the answerer is phrased rather in the accents of outrage. "Let the cow, the horse, the camel, the garden-bee—let the mud-fish, the lobster, the mussel, eel, the sting-ray, and the grunting pig-fish—let these, and the like of these, be put on a perfect equality with man and woman!"

In this almost splutteringly ferocious poem, the nation is surveyed wholly without benefit of his normal "spiritualization":

Stifled, O days, O lands! in every public and private corruption!
Smothered in thievery, impotence, shamelessness, mountain-high;
Brazen effrontery, scheming, rolling like ocean's waves around and upon you,
    O my days! my lands! . . .
—Let the theory of America still be management, caste, comparison!
    (Say! what other theory would you?)

And so on, and so on. "Let there be money, business, imports, exports, custom, authority, precedents, pallor, dyspepsia, smut, ignorance, unbelief!"

As for this sullen poem in which he stylistically turns his usual promulgations upside down, we perhaps have here the equivalent of such reversal as marks the mystic state of "accidie." In any case, of all his negatives, this poem would seem to have been one that carried him quite outside his characteristic literary role. It shows how very harsh things could seem to him, in those days, when for a moment he let himself look upon the conditions of his day without the good aid of his futuristic IDEA.

III. LILACS

Having considered Whitman's political philosophy in general, and the general way in which he personalized his outlook by translation into the rapt editorializing of his verse, we would here narrow our concerns to a close look at one poem, his very moving dirge, "When Lilacs Last in the Dooryard Bloom'd," perhaps the poem of his in which policies and personalizations came most nearly perfectly together.

The programmatic zestfulness that marks Whitman's verse as strongly as Emerson's essays encountered two challenges for which it had not been originally "promulged": the Civil War, and the valetudinarianism forced upon him by his partial paralytic stroke in 1873.

Before these developments, his stylistics of "spiritualization" had provided him with a categorical solution for the problem of evil as he saw it. Except for the outlaw moment of "Respondez! Respondez!" (or its much briefer form, "Reversals") his futuristic idealizing could readily transform all apprehensions into promises, and could discern a unitary democratic spirit behind any aggregate of natural or man-made places or things that added up to national power and prowess. This same principle was embodied in the random samplings that made up his poetic surveys and catalogues (which do impart a note of exhilaration to his text, even though one inclines to skim through them somewhat as when running the eye down the column of a telephone directory). And whatever guilt was left unresolved by his code could be canceled by the accents of perfervid evangelism (notably in his celebrating of "adhesiveness").

But since the entire scheme was based upon an ideal of all-pervasive and almost promiscuous Union, the motives of secession that culminated in the Civil War necessarily filled him with anguish. And even many of the inferior poems in *Drum Taps* become urgent and poignant, if read as the diary of a man whose views necessarily made him most sensitive to the dread of national dismemberment. Here, above all, was the development in history itself which ran harshly counter to the basic promises in which his poetry had invested. He reproaches not himself but "America": "Long, too long . . . / you learned from joys and prosperity only." And, in slightly wavering syntax, he says the need is henceforth "to learn from crises of anguish."

Yet in one notable respect, his doctrines had prepared him for this trial. In contrast with the crudity of mutual revilement and incrimination that marks so many contemporary battles between the advocates of Rightist and Leftist politics, Whitman retained some of the spontaneous gallantry toward the enemy that sometimes (as in *Chevy-Chase*) gives the old English-Scottish border ballads their enlightening moral nobility. And whatever problematical ingredients there may have been in his code of love as celebrated in the *Calamus* poems, these motives were sacrificially transformed in his work and thoughts as wound-dresser ("I have nourished the wounded and soothed many a dying soldier" . . . "Upon this breast has many a dying soldier leaned to breathe his last" . . . "Many a soldier's loving arms about this neck have cross'd and rested, / Many a soldier's kiss dwells on these bearded lips").

Similarly, when ill health beset him, though it went badly with one who had made a particular point of celebrating the body at the height of its physical powers, here too he had a reserve to draw upon. For his cult of death as a kind of all-mother (like the sea) did allow him a place in his system for infirmities. Further, since death was that condition toward which all life *tends*, he could write of old age, "I see in you the estuary that enlarges and spreads itself grandly as it pours in the great sea"—and though this is nearly his briefest poem, it is surely as *expansionist* a view as he ever proclaimed in his times of broad-axe vigor. We have already mentioned his new-found sympathy with the fallen redwood tree. Other identifications of this sort are imagined in his lines about an ox tamer, and about a locomotive in winter (he now wrote "recitatives").

As for the lament on the death of Lincoln: here surely was a kind of Grand Resolution, done at the height of his powers. Embodied in it, there is a notable trinity of sensory images, since the three major interwoven symbolic elements—evening star, singing bird, and lilac—compose a threeness of sight, sound, and scent respectively. Also, perhaps they make a threeness of paternal, filial, and maternal respectively. Clearly, the star stands for the dead hero; and the "hermit" bird, "warbling a song," just as clearly stands for the author's poetizing self. But whereas vicarious aspects of star and bird are thus defined within the poem itself, we believe that the role of the lilac is better understood if approached through an inquiry into the subject of scent in general, as it figures in Whitman's idiom.

In the section on *Vistas*, we put much more store by the passage where, after referring to "that indescribable perfume of geniune woman-hood," Whitman next speaks to his mother, then proceeds to describe an elderly lady, a "resplendent person, down on Long Island." We consider this set of steps strongly indicative, particularly in so far as many other passages can be assembled which point in the same direction. And though Whitman's associations with scent radiate beyond the orbit of the feminine, maternal, and grandmotherly, we believe that his terms for scent have their strongest motivational jurisdiction in this area, with the *Calamus* motive next.

In this Lincoln poem, the lilac is explicitly called "the perfume strong I love." The sprigs from the lilac bushes ("to perfume the grave of him I love") are not just for this one coffin, but for "coffins all." And the Death figured in such lilac-covered coffins is called a "Dark Mother." In "Out of the Cradle Endlessly Rocking," where there is the same identification of the maternal and the deathly, the development is built about the account of a solitary "he-bird . . . warbling" for his lost mate, quite as with the mournful warbling of the hermit thrush—and the incident is said to have taken place "When the lilac-scent was in the air and Fifth-month grass was growing."

The cedars and the pines in the "recesses" of the swamp where the hermit thrush is singing are also explicitly included in the realm of scent, as evidenced by the lines: "From the fragrant cedars and the ghostly pines"; "Clear in the freshness moist and the swamp-perfume"; "There in the fragrant pines and the cedars dusk and dim." See also, in *Starting from Paumanok*, that poem of his origins and of his femme Democracy: having heard "the hermit thrush from the swamp-cedars, / Solitary, singing in the West, I strike up for a New World." But it is the lilac that holds the poet "with mastering odor," as he says in the Lincoln poem.

In another poem, *A Broadway Pageant* (and one should think also of broad-axe and broad breast), there is a passage that clearly brings out the identification between scent and the maternal, though in this case the usage is somewhat ambiguous in attitude, whereas by far the great majority of references to scent in Whitman are decidedly on the favorable side: "The Originatress comes, / The nest of languages, the bequeather of poems, the race of eld, / Florid with blood, pensive, rapt with musings, hot with passion, / Sultry with perfume." (His word "florid" here could be correlated with a reference to "Florida perfumes," in a poem on Columbia, "the Mother of All.") In this same poem, near the end, there is a passage about "the all-mother" and "the long-off mother" which develops from the line: "The box-lid is but perceptibly open'd, nevertheless the perfume pours copiously out of the whole box." Psychoanalytically, the point about identification here could be buttressed by the standard psychoanalytic interpretation of "box," and thus perhaps by extending the same idea to the coffin—but we would prefer to stress merely the sequence of steps in this passage itself, while noting that the terms for derivation ("out of") take us once again back to the "Cradle" poem.

Consider also this passage, near the windup of *Song of Myself*:

> The past and present wilt—I have fill'd them, emptied them,
> And proceed to fill my next fold of the future.
>
> Listen up there! what have you to confide to me?
> Look in my face while I snuff the sidle of evening . . .

Does not "snuff the sidle" here suggest the picture of a youngster nosing against the side of the evening, as were the evening an adult, with a child pressing his face against its breast? In any case, "fold" is a notable word in Whitman, with its maternal connotations obvious in the line where the syllable is repeated almost like an *idée fixe*: "Unfolded out of the folds of the woman, man comes unfolded," an expression that also has the "out of" construction. Another reference, "Endless unfolding of words of ages," leads into talk of acceptance ("I accept Reality and dare not question it, / Materialism first and last imbuing")—and two lines later he speaks of "cedar and branches of lilac." Recall also the traditional association of the feminine with matter (as in Aristotle). In the "Lilacs" poem, immediately before the words "dark mother," death is called "cool-enfolding."

In one of the *Calamus* poems, a reference to "perfume" follows immediately after the line, "Buds to be unfolded on the old terms," and there are other lines that extend the area of the perfume beyond the feminine and maternal to the realm of manly adhesiveness, and to his poetic development in general, as in "In Cabin'd Ships at Sea": "Bear forth to them folded my love, (dear mariners, for you I fold it here in every leaf)."

There are many other references, direct and indirect, which we could offer to establish the maternal as a major element in the lilac theme. But we believe that these should be enough to prove the point.

Imagine, then, a situation of this sort:

A poet has worked out a scheme for identifying his art with the ideal of a democratic "empire" that he thinks of as a matrix, an All-Mother, a principle of unity bestowing its sanctions upon a strong love of man for man, an "adhesiveness" generally "spiritual," but also made concrete in imagery of "athletic" physical attachment. Quite as God is conceived as both efficient cause and final cause, so this poet's unitary principle is identified with both a source from which he was "unfolded" (the maternal origins "out of" which his art derived) and an end toward which he "ever-tended" (death, that will receive him by "enfolding" him, thus completing the state of "manifold ensemble" through which he had continually "passed," by repeatedly "coming" and "departing"). A beloved democratic hero has died—and the lyric commemoration of this tragic death will be the occasion of the poem.

How then would he proceed, within the regular bounds of his methods and terminology, to endow this occasion with the personal and impersonal *dimensions* that give it scope and resonance? (For a good poem will be not just one strand, but the interweaving of strands.)

Note, first, that the poem involves several situations. There is the commemorated situation, the death of the hero, as made specific in the journey of the coffin on its last journey. There is the immediate situation of the commemorating poet, among a set of sensory perceptions that he associates, for us, with the hero's death. There is the national scene that he can review, after the fashion of his catalogues, when charting the journey of the coffin (and when radiating into other details loosely connected with this). Near the end, a national scene that had *preceded* the hero's death will be recalled (the time of civil war, or intestine strife, that had accounted historically for the tragic sacrifice). And in the offing, "over-arching" all, there is the notion of an ultimate scene (life, death, eternity, and a possibility of interrelationships in terms of which immediate sensory images can seem to take on an element of the marvelous, or transcendent, through standing for correspondences beyond their nature as sheerly physical objects). The reader shifts back and forth spontaneously, almost unawares, among these different scenes, with their different orders of motivation, the interpenetration of which adds subtlety and variety to the poem's easy simplicity.

The three major *sensory* images are star, bird, and bush (each with its own special surroundings: the darkening Western sky for the "drooping" star, the "recesses" of the swamp for the "hermit" bird, the dooryard for the lilac, with its loved strong perfume—and for all three, the evening in "ever-returning spring"). As regards their correspondences with things beyond their nature as sheerly sensory images: the star stands for the dead loved hero (in a scheme that, as with so much of the Wagnerian nineteenth century, readily equates love and death). The bird crosses over, to a realm beyond its sheerly sensuous self, by standing for the poet who mourns, or celebrates, the dead hero (while also ambiguously mourning or celebrating himself).

And what of the third image, the scent of lilac? It fits the occasion in the obvious sense that it blooms in the springtime and is a proper offering for coffins. And though it is from a realm more material, more earthy, than sight or sound, it has a strong claim to "spirit" as well, since scent is *breathed*. (Passages elsewhere in Whitman, such as "sweet-breathed," "inhaling the

ripe breath of autumn," and "the shelves are crowded with perfumes, / I
breathe the fragrance," remind us that references to breathing can be secondarily in the scent orbit, and often are in Whitman's idiom.)

Though, in the lore of the Trinity, the Father is equated with power,
the Son with wisdom, and the Holy Spirit with love, it is also said that these
marks of the three persons overlap. And similarly, in this trinity (of star, bird,
and bush) there are confusions atop the distinctions. In so far as the bird
stands for the poet whose art (according to the *Vistas*) was to teach us lessons,
the bird would correspond to the son, and wisdom. The star, in standing for
the dead Lincoln, would surely be an equivalent of the father, implying power
in so far as Lincoln had been a national democratic leader. Yet the nearest
explicit attribution of power, the adjective "strong," is applied only in
connection with the *lilac*, which would be analogous to the third person of the
trinity, the holy spirit (with the notable exception that we would treat it as
maternal, whereas the Sanctus Spiritus is, *grammatically* at least, imagined
after the analogy of the masculine, though often surrounded by imagery that
suggests maternal, quasi-Mariolatrous connotations).

The relation of lilac to love is in the reference to "heart-shaped
leaves." Since the evening star is unquestionably Venus, the love theme is
implicitly figured, though ambiguously, in so far as Venus is feminine, but is
here the sign of a dead *man*. As for the "solitary" thrush, who sings "death's
outlet song of life," his "carol of death" is a love song at least secondarily, in so
far as love and death are convertible terms. Also, in so far as the bird song is
explicitly said to be a "tallying chant" that matches the poet's own "thought
of him I love," the love motif is connected with it by this route.

But the words, "song of the bleeding throat," remind us of another
motive here, more *autistic*, intrinsic to the self, as might be expected of a
"hermit" singer. Implicit in the singing of the thrush, there is the theme most
clearly expressed perhaps in these earlier lines, from *Calamus*:

> Trickle drops! my blue veins leaving!
> O drops of me! trickle, slow drops,
> Candid from me falling, drip, bleeding drops,
> From wounds made to free you whence you were prison'd,
> From my face, from my forehead and lips,
> From my breast, from within where I was conceal'd, press forth red drops,
>   confession drops,
> Stain every page, stain every song I sing, every word I say, bloody drops,
> Let them know your scarlet heat, let them glisten,
> Saturate them with yourself all ashamed and wet,
> Glow upon all I have written or shall write, bleeding drops,
> Let it all be seen in your light, blushing drops.

Do we not here find the theme of utterance proclaimed in and for
itself, yet after the analogy of violence done upon the self?

Regrettably, we cannot pause to appreciate the "Lilacs" poem in detail. But a few terministic considerations might be mentioned. There is the interesting set of modulations, for instance, in the series: night, black murk, gray debris, dark-brown fields, great cloud darkening the land, draped in black, crepe-veiled, dim-lit, netherward black of the night, gray smoke, gray-brown bird out of the dusk, long black trail, swamp in the dimness, shadowy cedars, dark mother, dusk and dim—all in contrast with the "lustrous" star. (If you will turn to *Song of Myself*, section 6, you will find the "dark mother" theme interestingly foreshadowed in the "dark . . . darker . . . dark" stanza that serves as a transition from "mothers' laps" to "uttering tongues.") And noting the absence of Whitman's distance-blue, we find that he has moved into the more solemn area of lilac, purple, and violet. Note also the spring-sprig modulation.

There are many devices for merging the components. At times, for instance, the swampy "recesses" where the bird is singing are described in terms of scent. Or sight and scent are intermingled when "fragrant cedars" are matched with "ghostly pines" at one point, and "fragrant pines" are matched with "cedars dusk and dim" at another. And of course, there is the notable closing merger, "Lilac and star and bird twined with the chant of my soul," a revision of his "trinity" in the opening stanzas, where the bird does not figure at all, the third of the three being the poet's "thought of him I love."

Prophesying after the event, of course, we could say that the bird had figured *implicitly* from the very first, since the bird duplicates the poet, though this duplex element will not begin to emerge until section 4, where the bird is first mentioned. But once the bird has been introduced, much effectiveness derives from the poem's return, at intervals, to this theme, which is thus astutely released and developed. One gets the feel of an almost frenzied or orgiastic outpouring, that has never stopped for one moment, and somehow even now goes unendingly on.

One gets no such clear sense of progression in the poem as when, say, reading *Lycidas*. But if pressed, we could offer grounds for contending that section 13 (the mathematical center of the poem) is the point of maximum internality. For instance, whereas in sections 4 and 9, the thrush is "warbling" *in* the swamp, here the song is said to come *from* the swamps, *from* the bushes, *out of* the dusk, *out of* the cedars and pines (a prepositional form which we, of course, associate with the maternal connotations it has in the opening stanzas of "Out of the Cradle Endlessly Rocking"). Thus, one might argue that there is a crucial change of direction shaping up here. Also, whereas section 4 had featured the sound of the bird's song, and section 9 had added the star along with talk of the bird's song, in section 13 we have bird, star, and lilac, all three (plus a paradox which we may ascribe at least in part to the accidental limitations of English—for whereas we feel positive in associating lilac with the feminine or maternal, the poet writes of the "mastering" odor with which the lilac holds him).

We could say that the theme of the cradle song, or "Death Carol" (that follows, after a brief catalogue passage) had been implicitly introduced in the "from's" and "out of's" that characterize the first stanza of section 13. But in any case, a clear change of direction follows this movement, with its theme of death as "dark mother." And since we would make much of this point, let us pause to get the steps clear:

As regards the purely sensory imagination, the theme (of the "Death Carol" as cradle song) is developed in the spirit of such words as soothe, serenely, undulate, delicate, soft, floating, loved, laved. And whereas there is no sensory experience suggested in the words "praise! praise! praise!" surely they belong here wholly because of the poet's desire to use whatever associations suggest total relaxation, and because of the perfect freedom that goes with the act of genuine, unstinted praise, when given without ulterior purpose, from sheer spontaneous delight.

What next, then, after this moment of farthest yielding? Either the poem must end there (as it doesn't), or it must find some proper aftermath. The remaining stanzas, as we interpret them, have it in their favor that they offer a solution of this problem.

As we see it, a notable duality of adjustment takes place here (along lines somewhat analogous to the biologists' notion of the correspondence between ontogenetic and phylogenetic evolution, with regard to the stages that the individual foetus passes through, in the course of its development).

In brief, there are certain matters of recapitulation to be treated, purely within the conditions of the poem; but if these are to be wholly vital, there must be a kind of *new act* here, even thus late in the poem, so far as the momentum of the poet is concerned. And we believe that something of the following sort takes place:

In imagining death as maternal, the poet has imagined a state of ideal infantile or intra-uterine bliss. Hence, anything experienced *after* that stage will be like the emergence of the child from its state of Eden into the world of conflict. Accordingly, after the "Death Carol," the poet works up to a recital in terms of armies, battle flags, the "torn and bloody," "debris," etc. Strictly within the conditions of the poem, all these details figure as recollections of the Civil War, with its conditions of strife which accounted historically for the hero's death. But from the standpoint of this section's place *after* the imagining of infantile contentment, all such imagery of discord is, in effect, the recapitulation of a human being's emergence into the intestine turmoils of childhood and adolescence.

After this review of discord, there is a recapitulation designed to bring about the final mergings, fittingly introduced by the repetition of Whitman's password, "passing." There had been much merging already. Now, in the gathering of the clan, there is a final assertion of merger, made as strong and comprehensive as possible. The "hermit song" is explicitly related to the "tallying song" of the poet's "own soul." The "gray-brown bird" is subtly matched by the "silver face" of the star. Our previous notion about the possible pun in "leaves" (as noun and verb) comes as near to substantiation as could be, in the line: "Passing, I leave thee lilac with heart-shaped leaves." There is a comradely holding of hands.

So, with the thought of the hero's death, all is joined: "the holders holding my hand"; "lilac and star and bird twined with the chant of my soul"; "and this for his dear sake," a sacrifice that ends on the line, "The fragrant pines and cedars dusk and dim"—nor should we forget that the sounds issuing from there came from the "recesses" of the "swamp-perfume."

The first line of a Whitman poem is usually quite different rhythmically from the lines that follow. The first line generally has the formal rhythm of strict verse, while even as early as the second line he usually turns to his typical free-verse style. (*Song of the Broad-Axe* is an exception to the rule, as it opens with no less than six lines that do not depart far from the pattern: long-short/ long-short/ long-short/ long, as set by the verse: "Weapon, shapely, naked, wan.") We copied out a batch of first lines, just to see how they would look if assembled all in one place, without reference to the kind of line that characterizes most notably the poet's catalogues. When reading them over, we noted that they are so much of a piece, and gravitate so constantly about a few themes, one might make up a kind of Whitman Medley, composed of nothing but first lines, without a single alteration in their wording. Here is one version of such an arrangement. It is offered as a kind of critical satyr-play, to lighten things after the tragic burden of our long analysis:

First O Songs for a Prelude

Lo, the unbounded sea!
Flood-tide below me! I see you face to face!
In cabined ships at sea,
Out of the cradle endlessly rocking,
Over the Western sea hither from Niphon come
As I ebb'd with the ocean of life,
Facing west from California's shore,
Give me the splendid silent sun with all his beams full-dazzling.

O to make the most jubilant song!
A song for occupations!
A song of the rolling earth, and of words according,
I hear America singing, the varied carols I hear.

These I singing in spring collect for lovers,
Trickle drops! my blue veins leaving!
America always! Always our old feuillage!
Come, said the Muse,
Come my tan-faced children.

(Now list to my morning's romanza, I tell the signs of the Answerer.
An old man bending I come upon new faces,
Spirit whose work is done—spirit of dreadful hours!
Rise, O days, from your fathomless deeps, till you loftier, fiercer sweep.)

As I pondered in silence,
Starting from fish-shape Paumanok where I was born,
From pent-up aching rivers;
As I lay with my head in your lap camerado,
Thou who has slept all night upon the storm;
Vigil strange I kept on the field one night,
On the beach at night
By blue Ontario's shore.

I sing the body electric,
Weapon shapely, naked, wan,
Scented herbage of my breast,
Myself and mine gymnastic ever,
Full of life now, compact visible,
I celebrate myself and sing myself;
Me imperturbe, standing at ease in Nature.

On journeys through the States we start,
Among the men and women, the multitude,
In paths untrodden,
The prairie grass dividing, its special odor breathing—
Not heaving from my ribbed breast only,
Afoot and light-hearted I take to the open road.

You who celebrate bygones,
Are you the new person drawn toward me?
Whoever you are, I fear you are walking the walks of dreams.
Behold this swarthy face, these gray eyes;
Passing stranger! you do not know how longingly I look upon you.

Respondez! Respondez!
Here, take this gift—
Come, I will make the continent indissoluble.
O take my hand, Walt Whitman!
As Adam early in the morning
To the garden anew ascending.

RICHARD CHASE

The Theory of America

Like all of Whitman's prophetic utterances, *Democratic Vistas* (1871) is a transcendental version of Jeffersonian-Jacksonian democracy, the credo which Whitman had more literally expressed in his earlier newspaper writings, particularly the editorials in the Brooklyn *Eagle* and *Times*. The idea of progress becomes the principle of the universe—as we look up from our provisional Pisgah we behold the orbic forms of a benevolent, self-purifying cosmos; as we lower our gaze the vistas out over the continent darken somewhat and are populated with villages, rivers, fields of wheat, factories, mechanics, farmers, patient mothers, small property holders, town meetings—a notably if evanescently envisioned myth of social life.

The absence in *Democratic Vistas* of direct political recommendation may be traced to Whitman's lifelong distrust of government. It may also be traced to Whitman's disillusion with practical politics, which he had long since given up in disgust, saying, for example, that the presidents immediately preceding Lincoln had all been "deform'd, mediocre, snivelling, unreliable, false-hearted men." He had always believed that social reform was a matter of individual regeneration, was not a political but a moral and spiritual problem; and all the weakness and strength of this view are in *Democratic Vistas*. One may note, however, the passage where Whitman momentarily fears he has gone too far in rejecting politics and, even though "these savage, wolfish parties alarm me," urges young men to take up a political career.

The individualism Whitman always championed becomes in *Democratic Vistas* his doctrine of "personalism"; his life-long belief in free trade is spiritualized into a vision of international amity. The moral-prophetic office of the poet on which the *Vistas* insists, had, of course, already been insisted on in the 1855 Preface. But although in many ways *Democratic Vistas* is a restatement of old views, Whitman's strong reaction to the spectacle of the Grant Administration and the Gilded Age gives the piece a novel emphasis on the need for "more compaction and more moral identity" in what the author took to be perilously anarchic times, and it also accounts for the intense concern with "personalism" and the unprecedented urgency with which the great function of the "literatus" is asserted.

Democratic Vistas shares some of that indistinctness of outline which many people now seem to find in nineteenth-century social polemic, over-laden as it often was by merely ethical and prophetic tendencies. Doubtless we miss a certain hardheaded but humane pragmatism in listening to the exhortations of Whitman, as we miss also a genuine sense of history. True, Whitman is capable of historical or political realism. He echoes Mill, Arnold, and Tocqueville in saying that no one ought to "debate to-day whether to hold on, attempting to lean back and monarchize, or to look forward and democratize—but *how*, and in what degree or part, most prudently to democratize." This is a simple observation, but it is also a breath of fresh air in an atmosphere that is sometimes oppressively thick. Whitman can even write that "we do not (at least I do not) put it either on the ground that the People, the masses, even the best of them, are, in their latent or exhibited qualities, essentially sensible and good—nor on the ground of their rights; but that good or bad, rights or no rights, the democratic formula is the only safe and preservative one for coming times," and this is gratifyingly free of jargon.

Whitman can say, too, "I hail with joy the oceanic, variegated, intense practical energy, the demand for facts, even the business materialism of the current age, our States. But woe to the age or land in which these things, movements, stopping at themselves, do not tend to ideas." Matthew Arnold himself might almost have written this. And the *Vistas* is in fact much closer to the general run of nineteenth-century Anglo-Saxon social prophecy than it is to the French enlightenment, Hegel, or Marx. It is true that Whitman fancied himself as something of a Hegelian and even wrote to Edward Dowden that in *Democratic Vistas*, he meant to "project . . . an entirely new breed of authors, poets, American, comprehensive, Hegelian, Democratic, religious." But Whitman's second-hand idea of Hegel is indistinguishable from the loose transcendentalist dialectic he had found in Emerson, and perhaps Carlyle, and had "promulged" in "Song of Myself."

The truth is that *Democratic Vistas* is a kind of American version of Arnold's *Culture and Anarchy*, despite the fact that Whitman and Arnold were very little disposed to believe they had anything in common and despite Whitman's attacks, in the *Vistas*, on "culture" and "the grand style," both of which he understood to be mere dilettantism. But do not both authors believe that the present danger in their countries is anarchy, that modern man places too great a faith in the mere machinery of legislation, that lively, elevating ideas should be current, that the middle class is the one to rely on, that aggressive assertions of material progress, including the mass production of vulgar literature may cloak a virulent moral sickness, that poetry has a very broad function, including that of religion? In one important respect Whitman was more "Arnoldian" than Arnold—to the extent, that is, that his sense of things remained rather too exclusively ethical and literary and lacked historical objectivity.

But *Democratic Vistas* is broadly American in spirit, not only in its native idealism, its large hopefulness, its lack of concern with the limitations of life, its disinclination to understand that society is based on contradictions which may be humanly tragic but that nevertheless "freedom," "personalism," "compaction and moral identity" cannot be understood or exist outside of society. Also characteristic of our native mind is the swinging back and forth from minute realism to the most ultimate and ideal of considerations. Whitman finds it perfectly natural on one page to imply that democracy may turn out to be unworkable but that history has stuck us with it and we must face the fact and, on another page, to say that democracy should not be confined to the political sphere but should be extended, like a redemptive spirit, to every part of life including manners, religion, and literature, as well as the Army and Navy. Again, Whitman can be exact and particular in his denunciation of the social scene but the closest he gets to describing what an admirable American society might be is his pleasing but impalpable vision of "some pleasant western settlement or town, where a couple of hundred best men and women, of ordinary worldly status, have by luck been drawn together."

The fundamental contradiction of *Democratic Vistas* is, of course, one of which Whitman is intensely aware: "This idea of perfect individualism it is indeed that deepest tinges and gives character to the idea of the aggregate. For it is mainly or altogether to serve independent separation that we favor a strong generalization, consolidation." Just how the claims of the individual and those of the aggregate are to be harmoniously reconciled without destroying either is certainly a basic political question. More strongly than anywhere else in his writings, Whitman urges the importance of national unity. But like most Americans of his time Whitman, although capable of understanding unity as consisting in a commonalty of tradition and experience, could not understand that this felt unity must express itself in laws and institutions evolving in history, that it must be made practicable by the social intelligence. Doubtless the Grant Administration exhibited few enough of these unifying political forces. But Whitman's mind was incapable of supplying them. Instead he offered his old solution: the ideal of "perfect comradeship."

It would surely have outraged Whitman to have been told that *Democratic Vistas* shows less knowledge of political realities and a weaker sense of history than *Culture and Anarchy* (to take up again the comparison), or that in so far as he is political at all he is, in an important sense, more conservative than Arnold. Yet both these propositions are true. As for the relative conservatism of these two writers, we have only to ask what, in the *Vistas* and in *Culture and Anarchy*, is taken to be the central and determining fact about the societies to which they refer. The given fact in Arnold's book is historical change of the most portentous sort, for Arnold is as impressed as Tocqueville by the historic forward march of the democratization of the Western world. This change entails a radical departure from all past experience. Arnold's conservatism is confined to his attempt to modify the course of democratization in accordance with the traditional values he cherishes. But he is clearly committed to basic changes.

The given fact in *Democratic Vistas* is a set of American beliefs and attitudes—"the American programme"—which was "put on record" once and for all in "the compacts of the Declaration of Independence" and "the Federal Constitution." The business of poets is not to "criticize life" but to reveal the given "compacts," to furnish the "archetypes" of thought and experience implied by what providence has decreed America to be. From this point of view, Whitman will not even admit that historical change is possible. For despite all his appeals to the future greatness of America there is nothing in this future which is not merely a further revelation of the totally adequate dispensation vouchsafed to Americans at the birth of the Republic. Change is understood as a progressive discovery of something already given, though not at first correctly or clearly perceived in its entirety. If Arnold tends to think of England as hastening perilously into the problematical future, Whitman thinks of America as exploring her "exhaustless mines of the richest ore" and as furnishing out the future with that which has already been given—a future which cannot help being better than the present because it will be a fuller, a more valid realization of what providence decreed America to be in 1776, Whitman seems to think, when to all intents and purposes history stopped, its final purpose of outdating "feudalism" and announcing democracy having been accomplished. History is, as it were, a kind of great mother whose divine duty it was to bear a democratic son to succeed a tyrannical father. Thus the true prophet (says Whitman in *Specimen Days*) does not so much "predict" as "reveal and outpour" the "inner, divine spontaneities" of the soul. One of the paradoxes of Whitman's work is that prophecy as a wild, spontaneous poetic outflowing is the source both of the radical, utopian indeterminacy of "Song of Myself" and the fundamentally conservative political ideas of *Democratic Vistas*. And this paradox is, of course, not only Whitman's. Probably more often than not it is the function of prophecy itself to be emotionally and poetically wild, rhapsodic, and visionary while maintaining conservative political or religious views. At any rate, this paradox is native to the democratic mind. Most Americans, certainly most of our great writers past and present, can see themselves in one form or another in that "conservative Christian anarchist" Henry Adams declared himself to be.

Democratic Vistas is not the great piece of radical social ideology it has sometimes been called. Like most American social thinking, it is conservative, individualistic, and unhistorical. But if this native habit of mind, together with the author's too exclusive preoccupation with moral, spiritual, and literary values, weakened his grasp of political reality, his appraisal of the individual is acute and persuasive, and his account of literature as the force which must reconcile individual and aggregate, though absurd to the extent that it is taken as a direct political recommendation, has its relevance to social actualities.

That celebration of the "simple separate person" which Whitman had come to call "personalism" is the glory of *Democratic Vistas*. "Personalism" is merely Whitman's new word for "identity," but in *Democratic Vistas* the idea is insisted on with a new urgency and beheld with a new clarity. Whitman's greatness had always rested in his ability to describe the plight and career of the self in all of its "singleness and normal simplicity and separation," as he says in the *Vistas*, as well as in the astonishing and ever novel modes of its entanglement with the world in which it exists. In "Song of Myself" we have the comic dance of the self becoming alternately entangled in and extricated from the complicated web of human life and the universe. Here the self was conceived as a kind of coy, elusive, democratic Pan. In "Out of the Cradle" and "As I Ebb'd with the Ocean of Life" the poet had chanted his great dirges on the separation of the self, the plight and pathos of singleness. Here the self had been conceived psychologically and metaphysically. In *Democratic Vistas* the self is intuitively perceived as an irreducible fact of personal and social experience, not immediately as a *political* fact, but as a fact without which there can be no humane politics:

> There is, in sanest hours, a consciousness, a thought that rises independent, lifted out from all else, calm, like the stars, shining eternal. This is the thought of identity—yours for you, whoever you are, as mine for me. Miracle of miracles, beyond statement, most spiritual and vaguest of earth's dreams, yet hardest basic fact, and only entrance to all facts. In such devout hours, in the midst of the significant wonders of heaven and earth (significant only because of the Me in the center), creeds, conventions, fall away

and become of no account before this simple idea. Under the luminousness of real vision, it alone takes possession, takes value. Like the shadowy dwarf in the fable, once liberated and look'd upon, it expands over the whole earth, and spreads to the roof of heaven.

It is hardly possible to imagine a more vital and necessary intuition than this. For surely one may judge whether or not a nation can be called civilized by the extent to which it is able to keep this "most spiritual and vaguest of earth's dreams, yet hardest basic fact" vitally operative. The conditions of the modern world are not conducive to sustaining in the mind "the quality of Being, in the object's self." Fewer and fewer people either have or know how to value Whitman's sense of how the sources of our being pour ever novel forms of vitality into the self and of how the self can be sustained in a hostile world.

Without at all discounting the incalculable value of Whitman's "personalism," one must nevertheless note that he characteristically tries to make it do too much. Not having anything like so clear an intuition of society or of history as he has of the self, he believes only in the self and asks it to do what society ought at least assist in doing. Thus "personalism" not only discovers and asserts the personal; it also, in some unspecified realm of being, "fuses" men into "solidarity."

This is where literature comes in. The "literatuses" of the future will create the kind of instinctive national mind necessary to the resolution of the contradictions of democracy, the purification of its evils, the toughening of its moral and physical being, and the final establishment of the comradely ideal. Whitman believes that so far America has no "real literature" and has produced no literatuses. Apparently not even Emerson is a literatus, not to mention Cooper, Hawthorne, Poe, Thoreau, and Melville. What kind of literature is it that Whitman finds at once not existent and desirable?

The coming American literature must have native roots—art forms "touch a man closest (perhaps only actually touch him) . . . in their expression through autochthonic lights and shades." American poetry must be "bold, modern, and all-surrounding and kosmical"; it must illustrate the people and respond to the slang, the folkways, the vast spectacle of the expanding country; it should not respond to the "covert, the lurid, the maleficent, the devil, the grim estimates inherited from the Puritans, hell, natural depravity, and the like"; it must be morally sound (not, of course, prudish) and appeal to the "absolute Conscience"; it must treat of nature in her universal, cosmical aspect and as the manifestation of the All; it must culminate in "metaphysics"—that is, in an inquiry into "the mysteries of the spiritual world, the soul itself, and the question of the immortal continuation of our identity"; finally it should possess "great poems of death."

In these prescriptions for American literature Whitman is very far from reality. Although his literary ideal corresponds to his own worst poems, it corresponds only partly to his best. Although it is a fair description of much of our second-rate literature, it has little relation to the first-rate either before Whitman or after. If American writing at its best was to be seen in such works as *Huckleberry Finn*, *The Red Badge of Courage*, *The Sound and the Fury*, *The Sun Also Rises*, or the poems of Frost, Eliot, and Stevens, the recommendations of *Democratic Vistas* are clearly out of touch with the American literary spirit. It is only such a work as Frank Norris' *The Octopus* that fulfills Whitman's specifications, and it is a pretty piece of irony that in that novel Presley, the would-be bard who speaks for Norris and wants to celebrate the expanding West in a rhapsodic poem, has apparently never heard of Whitman and delights in the idea that he may be known as the greatest American poet since Bryant.

One must notice that although Whitman speaks of "real literature" and wants a literary response to the realities of American life, he is certainly not demanding what since Stephen Crane and Howells we have been calling "realism" and "naturalism." And although there is a vigorous reforming note in his prophecy and although a connection is made between the People and literature, he is very far from urging "social realism," let alone "socialist realism" or "proletarian literature." At one point he actually urges writers to confront and oppose "the growing excess and arrogance of realism"; to be sure, he is not speaking technically of "literary realism," but the remark is encompassing enough to be relevant. And elsewhere he urges "no useless attempt to repeat the material creation, by daguerreotyping the exact likeness." It is thus only by example and in the limited ways we have noted above, in speaking of *Drum-Taps*, that Whitman is a genuine precursor of modern realism.

Whitman of course asks too much of literature, as he does of "personalism," when he seems to hope that it can resolve the contradictions of democracy by furnishing archetypal images of perfect democratic persons and exploring the modes of human community. The literatus of democratic times, he says, has an even higher calling than the epic poet and prophet of "feudal" times. His task is harder because not only must he create the mythic archetypes of democracy—to take the place of Adam and Eve, Moses, Achilles, Prometheus, Arthur, Milton's Satan, Don Quixote, Shakespeare's Hamlet, Richard II, and Lear; he must also furnish all the spiritual guidance formerly provided by priests. We do know, to be sure, that Shelley's idea about poets being the unacknowledged legislators of the world is not mere illusion. Literature, even when it is abstruse and difficult, as Whitman's poetry often is, has its ways of entering into the national mind, a national mind like our own—at once so unformed and so Alexandrian—not excepted. And we know that the shape and emphasis of political institutions are determined by shared, unconscious patterns of thought. The great writer has his effect on these, even if he is so little read as Walt Whitman. But the fact remains that the "literatus" who creates democratic archetypes as Whitman speaks of them has turned out to be someone like Stephen Vincent Benét—whose archetypes are synthetic products unhappily similar to the other products of our merchandising culture.

The most that can be said in defense of Whitman's program for literature is that literature does in truth deal with and exhibit modes of human community other than the mere idea of equality, which had always been the theoretical basis of Whitman's "adhesive" love of comrades. In *Democratic Vistas*, he had come to fear that equality was producing vulgarity and timidity, and that "a sort of dry and flat Sahara" was appearing in the midst of what ideally should be a various and energetic society. It is to Whitman's credit first, that he saw this to be true and, second, that he was not content merely to urge, as a cure, a more exalted equality. He does not, of course, abandon his faith in equality. He turns elsewhere in an attempt to understand how human experience may be shared and community formed without reducing life to a faceless uniformity. If we wish he had posited a vigorous, various, but harmonious political order, we must nevertheless observe that he was not entirely amiss in looking to literature, part of whose special prowess it is to seek out the difficult grounds of human commonalty.

Democratic Vistas impresses the reader with its many defects before it convinces him that it overcomes them. The piece is ill organized and sometimes otiose. The language burgeons outrageously. One can decipher and accept a reference to nature's "kosmical, antiseptic power" or to history as a series of "idiocratic transfers." But there isn't much excuse for saying of "the third stage" of American history (the first is the laying of the political foundations, the second the consolidation of material progress) that "rising out of the previous ones, to make them and all illustrious, I, now, for one, promulge, announcing a native expression-spirit, getting into form, adult, and through mentality, for these States, self-contain'd, different from others, more expansive," and so on. There is less positively brilliant writing in *Democratic Vistas* than there is in the Preface of 1855, less that is in its way immediately authentic and final. At the same time the *Vistas* makes a more extensive use of the specific virtues of prose than does the Preface, and it has consequently a sustained polemical eloquence and the amplitude of effect and incident which are proper to a meditative and summary as well as a prophetic piece in which the author is reflecting on problems that have occupied a lifetime. There is great eloquence in the passages deploring America's "hollowness of heart"; a sharp satirical pleasure in the author's attacks on "flip-pancy, tepid amours, weak infidelism, small aims"; the old ability to catalogue the multifarious aspects of the city in such a way that the catalogue becomes a vision. And there is spiritedness and clairvoyance in what is doubtless the most valuable function of *Democratic Vistas*—its assertion of "the fresh, eternal qualities of Being."

There is much surface disorder in the loose and impassioned argument of Whitman's essay. Yet this seems a minor fault. Indeed, from a modern point of view, one may feel that a graver fault is the lack of an adequate sense of disorder. Like much amateur philosophy and much nineteenth-century social polemic *Democratic Vistas* strikes the modern reader as being too simply and schematically reasoned, as having underneath its surface sense of wild-ness, indeterminacy, and doubt a too simple, even a complacent, faith in the rational unities of democratic society, which in practice meant a too simple faith in the status quo. History, in so far as it is present at all, is regarded as maternal and beneficent. It therefore has no hazards and can be counted on to foster democracy. "The distinguishing event of my time," as Whitman called the Civil War, conspired to turn his mind too exclusively to modes of reconciliation, comradeship, and unity, and partly as a consequence of the one supreme tragic crisis of our civilization, he failed, like most of his contemporaries, to conceive of radically disastrous historical crises and dilem-mas. He knew that the life of the self, of the individual, might involve such crises. But he did not believe that the same might be true of the history of nations, at least not of America and the nations of the future.

Still *Democratic Vistas* is an admirable and characteristic diatribe. And if one is sorry that in it Whitman is unable to conceive the extreme crises of society, one is certain that no society would be tolerable whose citizens could not find refreshment in its buoyant democratic idealism.

ROY HARVEY PEARCE

Whitman Justified: The Poet in 1860

Where are we going, Walt Whitman? The doors close in an hour.
Which way does your beard point tonight?
                    —ALLEN GINSBERG, "A Supermarket in California"

My title comes from the fourteenth of the "Chants Democratic" in the 1860 *Leaves of Grass*. (This is the poem which finally became "Poets to Come.") The first two stanzas read:

Poets to come!
Not to-day is to justify me, and Democracy, and what we are for,
But you, a new brood, native, athletic, continental, greater than before known,
You must justify me.

Indeed, if it were not for you, what would I be?
What is the little I have done, except to arouse you?

Whitman is, he concludes, "the bard" of a "future" for which he writes only "one or two indicative words."

The vision is utopian, of course—and became increasingly so in the 1870's and 80's, when he was calling for, even guaranteeing, a state of things whereby poems would work so as eventually to make for the withering away of poetry. In a preface of 1872 he could claim:

The people, especially the young men and women of America, must begin to learn that Religion, (like Poetry,) is something far, far different from what they supposed. It is, indeed, too important to the power and perpetuity of the New World to be consigned any longer to the churches, old or new, Catholic or Protestant—Saint this, or Saint that.... It must be consigned

From *The Minnesota Review*, I. Copyright © 1961 by *The Minnesota Review*.

henceforth to Democracy *en masse*, and to Literature. It must enter into the Poems of the Nation. It must make the Nation.

And by 1888 (in "A Backward Glance O'er Travel'd Roads") he could claim that, contrary to European critical opinion, verse was not a dying technique.

> Only a firmer, vastly broader, new area begins to exist—nay, is already form'd—to which the poetic genius must emigrate. Whatever may have been the case in years gone by, the true use for the imaginative faculty of modern times is to give ultimate vivification to facts, to science, and to common lives, endowing them with glows and glories and final illustriousness which belongs to every real thing, and to real things only. Without that ultimate vivification—which the poet or other artist alone can give— reality would seem to be incomplete, and science, democracy, and life itself, finally in vain.

These two statements (and they are quite typical) sum up Whitman's growing sense of the power of poetry, and thus of the poet: Religion, operating as poetry—and *only* as poetry—can make the nation, vivify it: or, in the language of a late poem like "Passage to India," "eclaircise" it.

"In the prophetic literature of these states," he had written in 1871 (in *Democratic Vistas*), ". . . Nature, true Nature, and the true idea of Nature, long absent, must, above all, become fully restored, enlarged, and must furnish the pervading atmosphere to poems . . ." And later in the same essay: "The poems of life are great, but there must be poems of the purports of life, not only in itself, but beyond itself." Life beyond life, poetry beyond poetry: This idea came to count for more and more in Whitman's conception of his vocation, and accordingly, of that of the poets who were to come. The last edition (1892) of *Leaves of Grass* is surely the testament of the sort of "divine literatus" whom he had earlier prophesied. Indeed, he had not only prophesied himself but made the prophecy come true. But, as he acknowledged, this was not the only form of his testament. For, when he wrote of the last edition, "I am determined to have the world know what *I* was pleased to do," he yet recognized: "In the long run the world will do as it pleases with the book." The question remains: How may we use the book so as to know what we please to do with it? And more: What does the book, in its structure and function, in its growth, teach us about the vocation of poet in the modern world? And more: How may it help the poets who yet are to come discover, and so define, their vocation?

The hard fact—so it seems to me—is that Whitman fails as prophetic poet, precisely because he was such a powerfully *humane* poet. The adjective makes us flinch, perhaps: but only because, like Whitman, we have found the beliefs it implies so difficult to hold to that we have come—if not to seek for the prophetic utterances which will offer us something in their stead, then to discount them as disruptive of the high sense of our private selves on which we ground our hopes for the lives we live. Still, it might be that a close reading of Whitman, the poet of 1860—for it is he whom I suggest we must recover—will teach us what it might be like once more to hold to them. Be that as it may, the record of Whitman's life would suggest that his own power, his own humanity, was at the end too much for him. In any case, when he tried to write prophetic poetry, he came eventually to sacrifice man—that finite creature, locked in time and history, at once agonized and exalted by his humanity—for what he has encouraged some of his advocates again to call cosmic man—the cosmic man of, say, these lines from "Passage to India":

Passage, immediate passage! the blood burns in my veins!
Away O soul! hoist instantly the anchor!
Cut the hawsers—haul out—shake every sail!
Have we not stood here like trees in the ground long enough?
Have we not grovel'd here long enough, eating and drinking like mere brutes?
Have we not darken'd and dazed ourselves with books long enough?

Sail forth—steer for the deep waters only,
Reckless O soul, exploring, I with thee, and thou with me,
For we are bound where mariner has not yet dared to go,
And we will risk the ship, ourselves and all.

O my brave soul!
O farther farther sail!
O daring joy, but safe! are they not all the seas of God?
O farther, farther, farther sail!

It is the idea of that "daring joy, but safe"—everywhere in the poem—which prevents one from assenting to this passage and all that comes before it. The passage of a soul, whether it is everyman's or a saint's, is not "safe," however "joyful." So that Whitman cannot focus the poem on the sort of *human* experience to which one might assent, because one could acknowledge its essential humanity. The figures in the passage proliferate farther and farther out from whatever center in which they have originated, until one wonders if there ever was a center. Probably not, because the experience of the pro-tagonist in this poem is that of cosmic man, who, because he is everywhere, is nowhere; who, because he can be everything, is nothing. *This* Whitman, I believe, is he who mistakes vivification for creation, the ecstasy of cadence for the ecstasy of belief, efficient cause for final cause, poet for prophet. Which is not, I emphasize, the same as conceiving of the poet *as* prophet.

Whitman's genius was such as to render him incapable of the kind of discipline of the imagination which would make for the genuine sort of prophetic poetry we find in, say, Blake and Yeats: of whom we *can* say that they were poets *as* prophets; for whom we can observe that poetry is the vehicle for prophecy, not its tenor. Whitman is at best, at *his* best, *visionary*, and sees beyond his world to what it might be—thus, what, failing to be, it is. Blake and Yeats are at best, at *their* best, *prophetic*, and see through their world to what it really is—thus, what, pretending not to be, it might be. Visionary poetry projects a world which the poet would teach us to learn to acknowledge as our own; it comes to have the uncanniness of the terribly familiar. Prophetic poetry projects a world which the poet would teach us is alien to our own yet central to our seeing it as it really is—a world built upon truths we have hoped in vain to forget. We say of the visionary world that we could have made it—at least in dream—work. We say of the prophetic world that we could not possibly have made it, for it was there already. The ground of visionary poetry is indeed dream—work and magical thought; the ground of prophetic poetry, revelation and mythical thought. Thus the special language of prophetic poetry—one of its most marked formal characteristics—must, by the definition of its purpose, be foreign to us (for it reveals a world, and the strange things in it, hidden from us); yet, by the paradox of prophecy, it is a language native to us (for the things it reveals, being universal—out of the realm of day to day time, space, and conception—put all of us, all of our "actual" world, under their aegis). We can "understand" that language because its grammar and syntax are analogous to our own; understanding it, we assent to—and perhaps believe in—the metaphysical system which its structure and vocabulary entail; trying to account for its origin, we agree with the poet that he has been, in some quite literal sense, "inspired."

Now, when the mood came over him—as it did increasingly—perhaps Whitman did claim to have been "inspired" in this literal sense. But even so, his later work fails as prophetic poetry (for that is what it is meant to be) precisely because, like the earlier work, it projects not a world to which the poet stands as witness, but one to which he stands as maker. Yet he asks of the world projected in the later work that, in accordance with the requirements of prophetic poetry, it have the effect of revelation; that its language be at once of and not of our workaday world; that it imply what in *Democratic Vistas* he called a "New World metaphysics." Yet the editions of *Leaves of Grass* from 1867 on fail of the centrality and integrity of properly prophetic poetry: fail, I think, because the poet mistakenly assumes that poetry, when it is made to deal with the universe at large, *becomes* prophecy. For all his revisions and manipulations of his text, for all his enlargement of his themes, the later Whitman is but a visionary poet. And, since he asks more of it than it can properly yield, the vision, and consequently the poetry, even the conception of the poet, get increasingly tenuous. A certain strength is there, of course. But it is the strength of an earlier Whitman, who perhaps prophesied, but could not bring about, his own metamorphosis from poet to prophet. His genius was too great to let him forget that, after all, it was *poets* who were to come.

True enough, he wrote, toward the end of "A Backward Glance O'er Travel'd Roads":

> But it is not on "Leaves of Grass" distinctively as *literature*, or a specimen therefor, that I feel to dwell, or advance claims. No one will get at my verses who insists upon viewing them as a literary performance, or attempt at such performance, or as aiming mainly toward art or aestheticism.

One says: How right, how sad, how wasteful! For, ironically enough, Whitman's words characterize the *failure* of the 1892 *Leaves of Grass*. And one turns to the earlier Whitman, I daresay the authentic Whitman, whose verses did aim mainly toward art and aestheticism: toward a definition of the vocation of the poet in that part of the modern world which was the United States.

For me, then, the most important edition of *Leaves of Grass* is the 1860 edition; and its most important poem is "A Word out of the Sea" (which, of course, became "Out of the Cradle Endlessly Rocking" in later editions.) Here Whitman may be best justified: as a poet. The burden of this essay will be to justify Whitman's way with poetry in the 1860 volume; to show how the structure and movement of this volume and of some of the principal poems in it (above all, "A Word out of the Sea") are such as to furnish a valid and integral way for a poet dedicated to saving poetry for the modern world, thus—as poet, and only as poet—dedicated to saving the modern world for poetry. The Whitman of the 1860 *Leaves of Grass* would be a sage, a seer, a sayer. But he speaks of only what he knows directly and he asks of his speech only that it report fully and honestly and frankly, only that it evoke other speeches, other poems, of its kind. The poems in this volume do justify Whitman's claims for poetry in general—but in terms of what he may in fact give us, not of what he would like, or even need, to give us. The strength of the major poems in the volume is that they somehow resist *our* need for more than they present, and make us rest satisfied—or as satisfied as we ever can be—with what they give. Above all, this is true of "A Word out of the Sea"—as it is less true, and so characteristic of the later Whitman, the poet of "Out of the Cradle Endlessly Rocking."

The 1855, 1856, and 1860 *Leaves of Grass* make a complete sequence—one in which the poet invents modern poetry, explores its possibility as an instrument for studying the world at large and himself as somehow vitally constitutive of it, and comes finally to define, expound, and exemplify the poet's vocation in the modern world. The sequence, in brief, is from language to argument; and it is controlled at all points by a powerful sense of the ego which is struggling to move from language to argument and which must come to realize the limits of its own humanity, which are the limits of argument. If, as we well know, the poet as envisaged in the 1855 and 1856

Leaves of Grass is the counterpart of him of whom Emerson wrote in "The Poet" (1844), the poet envisaged in the 1860 *Leaves of Grass* is the counterpart of him of whom Emerson wrote in his essay on Goethe in *Representative Men* (1850): Not Shakespeare, not Plato, not Swedenberg would do for the modern world, which yet "wants its poet-priest, a reconciler . . ." Goethe was one such: "the writer, or secretary, who is to report the doings of the miraculous spirit of life that everywhere throbs and works. His office is a reception of the facts into the mind, and then a selection of the eminent and characteristic experiences." Note: just a "writer"—(what John Holloway in an important book of a few years ago called the *Victorian Sage*: a philosopher of a kind, but one who constructs his argument according to a grammar of assent). Emerson had concluded:

> The world is young: the former great men call to us affectionately. We too must write Bibles, to unite again the heavens and the earthly world. The secret of genius is to suffer no fiction to exist for us; to realize all that we know; in the high refinement of modern life, in arts, in sciences, in books, in men, to exact good faith, reality and a purpose; and first, last, midst and without end, to honor every truth by use.

The 1860 *Leaves of Grass*, as one of Whitman's notebook entries indicates, was to be a Bible too: "The Great Construction of the New Bible. . . . It ought to be ready in 1859." It was to offer a "third religion," Whitman wrote. And in a way it does; but, for well and for ill, that religion is a religion of man—man as he is, locked in his humanity and needing a religion, yet not claiming to have it by virtue of needing it; not hypnotizing himself into declaring that he has it. (For Whitman a little cadence was a dangerous, if exciting, thing, much cadence, disastrous.) The Whitman of the 1860 *Leaves of Grass* is, *par excellence*, Emerson's "secretary," reporting "the doings of the miraculous spirit of life that everywhere throbs and works." To accept a miracle, to live in its presence, even to try to comprehend it—this is not the same as trying to work one, even claiming to have worked one. And—as the poets who have come after him have variously testified in their puzzled, ambiguous relation to him—Whitman's way with the language of poetry, going against the grain of mass communications and "positivism," may well teach us how to recognize and acknowledge miracles. It cannot teach us how to work them; or even how to earn them. One can well imagine how hard it must be for a poet to go so far with language, only to discover that he can go no farther. Such a discovery constitutes the principal element of greatness in the 1860 *Leaves of Grass*, perhaps the principal element of greatness in Whitman's poetry as a whole.

I have said that in 1855 Whitman "invented" modern poetry. By this I mean only that, along with other major poets of the middle of the century, he participated—but in a strangely isolated way—in the development of romanticist poetics toward and beyond its symbolist phase. (*To invent* may mean, among other things, "to stumble upon.") I do not mean to claim too much for the word *symbolist* here; I use it only generally to indicate that Whitman too came to realize that a poet's vocation was fatefully tied to the state of the language which constituted his medium. He discovered with Baudelaire—although without Baudelaire's (and incidentally Emerson's) overwhelming sense of the problem of "correspondences," that, as regards language, "tout vit, tout agit, tout se correspond." The medium thus had a "life" of its own, and so might generate "life"—the "life" of poetry. Poetry, on this view, thus became *sui generis*, a unique mode of discourse; and the role of the poet became more and more explicitly to be that of the creator: one who might "free" language to "mean"—a creator in a medium, pure and simple. We have in Whitman's early work a version of that conception of poet and poetry with which we are now so familiar: To whom was the poet responsible? Not to whom, the reply ran, but to what? And the answer: to language. And language as such was seen to be the sole, overriding means to establish, or reestablish community. The perhaps inevitable drift—not only in Whitman's work but of that of his contemporaries and of the poets who have come—was toward an idea of poetry as a means of communion, perhaps modern man's sole means of communion, his religion. Professor Abrams (in *The Mirror and the Lamp*) concludes his account of these developments thus:

> It was only in the early Victorian period, when all discourse was explicitly or tacitly thrown into the two exhaustive modes of imaginative and rational, expressive and assertive, that religion fell together with poetry in opposition to science, and that religion, as a consequence, was converted into poetry, and poetry into a kind of religion.

Professor Abrams is speaking about developments in England. In the United States, conditions were somewhat simpler and, withal, more extreme. From the beginning, that is to say, Whitman was sure that the imaginative and rational might well be subsumed under a "higher" category, which was poetry. So that—as I have indicated in my remarks on Whitman and prophetic poetry—for him there was eventually entailed the idea that the New Bible might be just that, a total and inclusive account of cosmic man, of man as one of an infinitude of gods bound up in Nature. It is a nice question whether or not the "symbolist" dedication to the idea of language-as-communion must *inevitably* lead to a search for a metalinguistic structure of analogies and correspondences and then to an idea of poetry as religion and religion as poetry. And it is a nicer question whether or not "symbolist" poetics—with its emphasis on medium as against matrix, language per se as against language-in-culture—is characterized by a certain weakness in linguistic theory. Whitman's work raises these questions; and a full critique of his work would entail a critique of his theory of poetry, thus of his theory of language, thus of his theory of culture. But this is not the place to speak of critics to come, much less to prophesy them.

In any case, we must grant Whitman his special kind of "unmediated vision." But we are not by that token obliged to grant, or claim for him a "mysticism"—or for that matter, "an inverted mysticism"; or to declare that, *ecce*, his poetry is at once "*mystical and irreligious*"; or to see in the Whitman of 1855 a good (prematurely) grey *guru*. (I cite here the recent claims for this Whitman of James Miller, Karl Shapiro, and Malcolm Cowley—who confuse, or conflate, this poet with the one who presided at Camden. And I think of the question, put with such sweet craziness, by Allen Ginsberg in the line I have used as epigraph.) At its most telling, Whitman's earlier poetry manifests what has been called (by Erich Kahler) an "existential consciousness," but of a mid-nineteenth-century American sort—its key term, its center of strength and weakness, being not anguish but joy. Or rather, the key term is triumph—as suffering, the poet endures, and rejoices: seeing that it is his vocation as poet to teach men that they can endure. The freedom which ensues is wonderful, not dreadful.

Thus I take the 1855 and 1856 editions of *Leaves of Grass*, which most freshly project this mode of consciousness, as stages on the way to the 1860 edition. In 1855 and 1856 Whitman shows that he has learned to report truthfully what he has seen; in 1860, that he has learned to measure its significance for the poet taken as the "secretary"—the archetypal man. He strove to go beyond this, but in vain. The movement from the 1855 to the 1856 editions is the movement from the first "Song of Myself" and the first "The Sleepers" (both originally untitled) to the first "Crossing Brooklyn Ferry" (called, in 1856, "Sun-Down Poem"): the poet first learns to discipline himself into regressing deeply into his own pre-conscious; then, with his new-found sense of himself as at once subject and object in his world, he learns to conceive in a new way of the world at large; he is, as though for the first time, "in" the world. The crucial factor is a restoration of the poet's vital relationship to language. A good, powerfully naïve account of this discovery is that in Whitman's prose *American Primer*, written in the 1850's, but not published until after his death:

> What do you think words are? Do you think words are positive and original things in themselves? No: Words are not original and arbitrary in themselves.—Words are a result—they are the progeny of what has been or is in vogue.—If iron architecture comes in vogue, as it seems to be coming, words are wanted to stand for all about iron architecture, for all the work it causes, for the different branches of work and of the workman. . . .
>
> A perfect user of words uses things—they exude in power and beauty from him—miracles in his hands—miracles from his mouth. . . .

> A perfect writer would make words sing, dance, do the male and female act, bear children, weep, bleed, rage, stab, steal, fire cannon, steer ships, sack cities, charge with cavalry or infantry, or do anything, that man or woman or the natural powers can do.
>
> [Note the insistence on "natural"—not "supernatural" powers.]
>
> Likely there are other words wanted.—Of words wanted, the matter is summed up in this: When the time comes for them to represent any thing or state of things, the words will surely follow. The lack of any words, I say again, is as historical as the existence of words. As for me, I feel a hundred realities, clearly determined in me, that words are not yet formed to represent. . . .

These sentiments generally, and some of these phrasings particularly, got into Whitman's prose meditations. More important, from the beginning they inform the poems. They derive much from Emerson's "The Poet," of course; but they are not tied to even Emerson's modestly transcendental balloon. The power which Whitman discovers is the power of language, fueled by the imagination, to break through the categories of time, space, and matter and to "vivify" (a word, as I have said, he used late in his life—so close to Pound's "Make it new") the persons, places, and things of his world, and so make them available to his readers. In the process—since the readers would, as it were, be using words for the first time—he would make them available to themselves; as poets in spite of themselves.

It is as regards this last claim—that the reader is a poet in spite of himself—that the 1860 *Leaves of Grass* is all-important. For there Whitman most clearly saw that the poet's power to break through the limiting categories of day-to-day existence is just that: a poet's power, obtaining only insofar as the poem obtains, and limited as the poem is limited. In 1860, that is to say, Whitman saw that his Bible was to be a poet's Bible, and had to be built around a conception of the poet's life: his origins, experience, and end; his relation with the persons, places, and things of his world. The 1855 and 1856 *Leaves of Grass* volumes are but *collections* of poems—their organization as rushed and chaotic as is the sensibility of the writer of the *American Primer*. *Within* individual poems, there is form, a form which centers on the moment in the poet's life which they project. But the 1860 *Leaves of Grass* is an articulated whole, with an *argument*. The argument is that of the poet's life as it furnishes a beginning, middle, and end to an account of his vocation. The 1860 volume is, for all its imperfections, one of the great works in that romantic mode, the autobiography. Or, let us give the genre to which it belongs a more specific name: archetypal autobiography. The 1860 volume is autobiographical as, say, *Moby Dick* and *Walden* are autobiographical; for its hero is a man in the process of writing a book, of writing himself, of making himself, of discovering that the powers of the self are the stronger for being limited. The hero who can say No! in thunder discovers that he can say Yes! in thunder too—but that the thunderation is his own and no one else's.

Now, to say that the 1860 *Leaves of Grass* is quintessentially auto-biographical is to say what has been said before: most notably by Schyberg, Asselineau, and Allen. But I mean to say it somewhat differently than they do. For they see in the volume a sign of a crisis in Whitman's personal life; and this is most likely so. Yet I think it is wrong to read the volume as, in this *literal* sense, personal—that is, "private." (The Bowers edition of the surviving manuscript of the 1860 edition clearly shows that Whitman—naturally enough, most often in the "Calamus" poems—wanted to keep the book clear of too insistently and privately personal allusions. He was, I think, not trying to "conceal"—much less "mask"—his private personality but to transmute it into an archetypal personality. I think that it is a mistake to look so hard, as some critics do, for the "private" I.) Thus I should read the volume as not a personal but archetypal autobiography: yet another version of that compulsively brought-forth nineteenth-century poem which dealt with the growth of the poet's mind. (Well instructed by our forebears, we now have a variety of names for the form—all demonstrating how deeply, and from what a variety of non-literary perspectives, we have had to deal with the issues which it raises for us: *rite de passage*, quest for identity, search for community, and the like.) Whitman's problem, the poet's problem, was to show that integral to the poet's vocation was his life cycle; that the poet, having discovered his gifts, might now use them to discover the relevance of his life, his *lived* life, his *Erlebnis*, his *career*, to the lives of his fellows. It is the fact that his newly discovered use of poetry is grounded in his sense of a life lived-through: it is this fact that evidences Whitman's ability here, more than in any version of *Leaves of Grass*, to contain his gift and use it, rather than be used by it. Of *this* volume Whitman said: "I am satisfied with *Leaves of Grass* (by far the most of it), as expressing what was intended, namely, to express by sharp-cut self assertion, One's Self and also, or maybe still more, to map out, to throw together for American use, a gigantic embryo or skeleton of Personality,—fit for the West, for native models." Later, of course, he wanted more. But he never had the means beyond those in the 1860 edition to get what he wanted. And that has made all the difference.

The 1860 *Leaves of Grass* opens with "Proto-Leaf" (later, much revised, as "Starting from Paumanok.") Here Whitman announces his themes and, as he had done before, calls for his new religion; but he gives no indication that it is to be a religion of anything else but the poet's universalized vocation. (My misuse of the word *religion* is his. I mean neither to be victimized nor saved by following him here.) It might yet, on this account, be a precursor to a religion, in the more usual (and I think proper) sense, as well as a substitute for it. "Whoever you are! to you endless announcements," he says. There follows "Walt Whitman," a somewhat modified version of the 1855 poem which became "Song of Myself." It is still close to the fluid version of 1855; strangely enough, it is so over-articulated (with some 372 sections) that it does not have the rather massive, and therefore relatively dogmatic, articulation of the final version. In all, it gives us an account of the poet's overwhelming discovery of his native powers. Then in the numbered (but not separately titled) series of poems called "Chants Democratic," the poet—after an apostrophic salutation to his fellows (it ends "O poets to come, I depend on you!")—celebrates himself again, but now as he conceives of himself in the act of celebrating his world. The chief among these poems—as usual, much modified later—became "By Blue Ontario's Shore," "Song of the Broad Axe," "Song for Occupations," "Me Imperturbe," "I Was Looking a Long While," and "I Hear America Singing." Following upon "Walt Whitman," the "Chants Democratic" sequence successfully establishes the dialectical tension between the poet and his world—the tension being sustained as one is made to realize again and again that out of the discovery of his power for "making words do the male and female act" in "Walt Whitman," has come his power to "vivify" his world in the "Chants Democratic."

The transition to "Leaves of Grass," the next sequence—again the poems are numbered, but not separately titled—is natural and necessary. For the poet now asks what it is to make poems in the language which has been precipitated out of the communal experience of his age. The mood throughout is one of a mixture of hope and doubt, and at the end it reaches a certitude strengthened by a sense of the very limitations which initially gave rise to the doubt. The first poem opens—and I shall presently say more about this—with two lines expressing doubt; later—when the prophetic Whitman couldn't conceive of doubting—the lines were dropped in the poem, which became "As I Ebb'd with the Ocean of Life." The second poem is a version of an 1855 poem, "Great Are the Myths"; and it was finally rejected by Whitman as being, one guesses, too certain in its rejection of the mythic mode toward which he later found himself aspiring. The third poem, which, combined with the sixth later became "Song of the Answerer," opens up the issue of communication as such. The fourth, a version of an 1856 poem which eventually became "This Compost," conceives of poetry as a kind of naturalistic resurrection. It moves from "Something startles me where I thought I was safest"—that is, in the poet's relation to the materials of poetry—to a simple acknowledgment at the end that the earth "gives such divine materials to men, and accepts such leavings from them at last." The fifth (later "Song of Prudence") considers the insight central to the poet's vocation. To the categories of "time, space, reality," the poet would add that of "prudence"—which teaches that the "consummations" of poetry are such as to envisage the necessary relationship of all other "consummations": the imagination's law of the conservation of energy. The sixth (which, as I have said, later became part of "Song of the Answerer") develops an aspect of the theme of the fourth and fifth; but now that theme is interpreted as it is bound up in the problem of language: "The words of poems give you more than poems, They give you to form for yourself poems, religions, politics, war, peace, behavior, histories, essays, romances, and everything else." At this depth of discovery there is no possibility of any kind of logically continuous catalogue of what words "give you to form for yourself." Poetry is a means of exhausting man's powers to know the world, and himself in it, as it is. Beyond this, poems

> . . . prepare for death—yet they are not the finish, but rather the onset,
> They bring none to his or her terminus, or to be content and full;
> Whom they take, they take into space, to behold the birth of stars,
>   to learn one of the meanings,
> To launch off with absolute faith—to sweep through the ceaseless rings,
>   and never to be quiet again.

In the seventh poem (later "Faith Poem"), the poet discovers that he "needs no assurance"; for he is (as he says in the eighth poem, later "Miracles") a "realist" and for him the real (by which he means *realia*) constitutes "miracles." The poet is led, in the ninth poem (later "There Was a Child Went Forth"), to a recollection of his first discovery of the miraculousness of the real: a discovery he only now understands; this poem, taken in relation to the rest of the sequence, properly anticipates "A Word out of the Sea." The tenth poem opens, in a passage dropped from the later version, "Myself and Mine,"—but one which is essential as a transition in the sequence:

> It is ended—I dally no more,
> After today I inure myself to run, leap, swim, wrestle, fight . . .

Simply enough: the poet, having accepted his vocation and its constraints, is now free—free *through* it; and he must now teach this freedom to others:

> I charge that there be no theory or school founded out of me,
> I charge you to leave all free, as I have left all free.

The rest of the sequence, some fourteen more poems, celebrates aspects of the poet's new freedom as it might be the freedom of all men. (I forebear giving their later titles.) It is the freedom to rejoice in the miraculousness of the real, and has its own costs. The greatest is a terrible passivity, as though in order to achieve his freedom, man had to offer himself up as the victim of his own newly vivified sensibility. Being as he is, the poet sees (in 12) "the vast similitude/which/interlocks all . . ."; yet he must admit (in 15) "that life cannot exhibit all to me—" and "that I am to wait for what will be exhibited by death." He is (in 17) the man who must "sit and look out upon all the sorrows of the world, and upon all oppression and shame"; and he must

"See, hear,/be/silent," only then to speak. He declares (in 20); ". . . whether I continue beyond this book, to maturity/ . . . /Depends . . . upon you/ . . . you, contemporary America." Poem 24, wherein the poet completes his archetypal act, and gives himself over to his readers, reads:

> Lift me close to your face till I whisper,
> What you are holding is in reality no book, nor part of a book,
> It is a man, flushed and full-blooded—it is I—So long!
> We must separate—Here! take from my lips this kiss,
> Whoever you are, I give it especially to you;
> *So long*—and I hope we shall meet again.

I quote this last poem entire, because I want to make it clear that the lapses into desperate sentimentality—and this poem is a prime example—are intrinsically a part of Whitman's autobiographical mode in the 1860 *Leaves of Grass*, as they are of the mode, or genre, which they represent. It will not do to explain them away by putting them in a larger context, or considering them somehow as masked verses—evidences of Whitman the shape-shifter. (Speaking through a *persona*, the poet perforce hides behind it.) Confronting the agonies and ambiguities of his conception of the poet, Whitman too often fell into bathos or sentimentalism. Yet bathos and sentimentalism, I would suggest, are but unsuccessful means—to be set against evidence of successful means—of solving the archetypal autobiographer's central problem: at once being himself and seeing himself; of bearing witness to his own deeds. If what he is, as he sees it, is too much to bear; if he is incapable of bearing it; if his genius is such as not to have prepared him to bear it—why then, his miraculism will fail him precisely because he cannot stand too much reality.

Bathos and sentimentalism—and also anxious, premonitory yearnings for something beyond mere poetry—inevitably mar the rest of the 1860 *Leaves of Grass*, but not fatally, since they are the by-products of its total argument. At some point, most foxes want to be hedgehogs. Whitman is a poet who must be read at large. And I am claiming that Whitman can be best read at large in the 1860 *Leaves of Grass*. When he can be read in smaller compass—as in "A Word out of the Sea"—it is because in a single poem he manages to recapitulate in little what he was developing at large. I should guess—as I shall presently try to show—that the large poem, the 1860 volume, is a necessary setting for the little poem, "A Word out of the Sea." That poem (later, I remind my reader, "Out of the Cradle . . .") is one of Whitman's greatest. And I shall want to show that it is even greater than we think. So I must carry through, however cursorily, my glance o'er the 1860 *Leaves of Grass*. There comes next a series of poems ("A Word out of the Sea" is one of them) in which the poet meditates the sheer givenness of the world his poems reveal; he is even capable of seeing himself as one of the givens. But then he must specify in detail the nature of his kind of givenness, which includes the power to give, to bring the given to a new life. Here—after "Salut au Monde," "Poem of Joys," "A Word out of the Sea," "A Leaf of Faces," and "Europe"—there is first the "Enfants d'Adam" sequence, and then, after an interlude of generally celebrative poems, the "Calamus" sequence. I want to say of these two sequences only that they are passionate in a curiously objective fashion; I have suggested that the proper word for their mood and tone is neither personal nor impersonal, but archetypal. In contrast, they furnish analogues—directly libidinal analogues, as it were—for the poet's role, seen now not (as in the earlier sequences) from the point of view of a man telling us how he has discovered his gift, put it to use, and measured the cost of using it properly, but seen rather from the point of view of the reader. The *I* of these poems, I suggest, is meant to include the reader—as at once potential poet and reader of poems. So that the "Enfants d'Adam" sequence tells us how it is—what it means, what it costs—to be a maker of poems and the "Calamus" sequence how it is to be a reader of poems—in the first instance the analogue is procreation; in the second it is community. And if Whitman's own homosexuality led him to write more powerfully in the second vein than in the first, we should be mindful of the fact that, in his times as in ours, it seems to be easier to make poems, good poems, even to publish them, than to get readers for them.

Indeed, Whitman announces in the next-to-last of the "Calamus" sequence that we are to be ready for his most "baffling" words, which come in the last poem of the sequence, later "Full of Life Now":

> When you read these, I, that was visible, am become invisible;
> Now it is you, compact, visible, realizing my poems, seeking me,
> Fancying how happy you were, if I could be with you, and become your lover;
> Be it as if I were with you. Be not too certain but I am with you now.

Later Whitman changed *lover* to *comrade*—mistakenly, I think; for, as their function in the 1860 volume shows, the "Calamus" poems were to carry through to completion the poet's conception of his painfully loving relation with his readers.

Having, in the "Enfants d'Adam" and "Calamus" sequences, defined the poetic process itself, as he had earlier defined the poet's discovery of that process, Whitman proceeds variously to celebrate himself and his readers at once under the aegis of the "Enfants d'Adam" and the "Calamus" analogue. (As Lorca said in his "Oda," "Este es el mundo, amigo . . .") Much of the power of the poems, new and old, derives from their place in the sequences. In "Crossing Brooklyn Ferry" and the series of "Messenger Leaves" there are addresses to all and sundry who inhabit Whitman's world, assurances to them that now he can love them for what they are, because now he knows them for what they are. There is then an address to Manahatta—which returns to the problem of naming, but now with an assurance that the problem has disappeared in the solving: "I was asking for something specific and perfect for my city, and behold! here is the aboriginal name!" Then there is an address in "Kosmos" to the simple, separate persons—to each of his readers who is "constructing the house of himself or herself." Then there is "Sleep Chasings" (a version of the 1855 "The Sleepers"), now a sublime poem, in which the poet can freely acknowledge that the source of his strength is in the relation of his night- to his day-time life, the unconscious and the conscious:

> I will stop only a time with the night, and rise betimes
> I will duly pass the day, O my mother, and duly return to you.

And "Sleep Chasings" is the more telling for being followed by "Burial" (originally an 1855 poem which eventually became "To Think of Time"). For in his incessant moving between night and day, the poet manages to make poems and so proves immortal. He makes men immortal in his poems, as he teaches them to make themselves immortal in their acts:

> To think that you and I did not see, feel, think, nor bear our part!
> To think that we are now here, and bear our part!

This poem comes nearly at the end of the 1860 volume. Only an address to his soul—immortal, but in a strictly "poetic" sense—and "So Long!" follow. In the latter we are reminded once again:

> This is no book,
> Who touches this book, touches a man,
> (Is it night? Are we done?)
> It is I you hold, and who holds you,
> I spring from the pages into your arms—decease calls me forth.

We are reminded thus, to paraphrase a recent Whitmanian, that in the flesh of art we are immortal: which is a commonplace. We are reminded also that in our age, the role of art, of poetry, is to keep us alive enough to be capable of this kind of immortality: which is not quite a commonplace.

The central terms in the argument of the 1860 *Leaves of Grass*, I suggest, run something like this: first, in the poems which lead up to "A Word out of the Sea"—self-discovery, self-love, rebirth, diffusion-of-self, art; and second, in the poems which follow "A Word out of the Sea"—love-of-others, death, rebirth, reintegration-of-self, art, immortality. The sequence is that of an ordinary life, extraordinarily lived through; the claims are strictly humanistic. The child manages somehow to achieve adulthood; the movement is from a poetry of diffusion to a poetry of integration. Immortality is the *result* of art, not its origin, nor its cause. The humanism is painful, because one of its crucial elements (centering on "death" as a "clew" in "A Word out of the

Sea") is an acknowledgment of all-too-human limitations and constraints. So long as Whitman lived with that acknowledgment, lived *in* that acknowledgment—even when living with it drove him (as it too often did) toward bathos and sentimentalism—he managed to be a poet, a "secretary," a "sage," a seer, a visionary. His religion was the religion of humanity: the only religion that a work of art can *directly* express, whatever other religion it may confront and acknowledge. *Indirectly*, it can confront religion in the more usual and more proper sense; for it can treat of man in his aspiration for something beyond manhood, even if it cannot claim—since its materials are ineluctably those of manhood—to treat directly of that something-beyond. The burden—someone has called it the burden of incertitude; Keats called it "negative capability"—is a hard one to bear. Whitman, I am suggesting, bore it most successfully, bore it most successfully for us, in the 1860 *Leaves of Grass*.

Which brings me to the most important of the poems first collected in this volume, "A Word out of the Sea." It was originally published separately in 1859, as *A Child's Reminiscence*. Thus far, I have tried to suggest the proper context in which the poem should be read: as part of the volume for which it was originally written; as a turning-point in the argument of that book. Note that "A Word out of the Sea" comes about mid-way in the book after "Walt Whitman," the "Chants Democratic," "Leaves of Grass," "Salut au Monde," and "Poem of Joys"—that is, after those poems which tell us of the poet's discovery of his powers as poet and of his ability to use those powers so to "vivify" his world, and himself in it; after his discovery that it is man's special delight and his special agony to be at once the subject and object of his meditations; after his discovery that consciousness inevitably entails self-consciousness and a sense of the strengths and weaknesses of self-consciousness. Moreover, "A Word out of the Sea" comes shortly before the "Enfants d'Adam" and "Calamus" sequences—that is, shortly before those poems which work out the dialectic of the subject-object relationship under the analogue of the sexuality of man as creator of his world and of persons, places, and things as its creatures. I cannot but think that Whitman knew what he was doing when he placed "A Word out of the Sea" thus. For he was obligated, in all his autobiographical honesty, to treat directly of man's fallibilities as well as his powers, to try to discover the binding relationship between fallibilities and powers: to estimate the capacity of man to be himself and the cost he would have to pay. The poems which came before "A Word out of the Sea" have little to do with fallibilities; they develop the central terms of the whole argument only this far: self-discovery, self-love, rebirth, art. Theirs is the polymorph perverse world of the child. In them, death only threatens, does not promise; power is what counts. The turning-point in the poet's life can come only with the "adult" sense of love and death, the beginning and the end of things, out of which issues art, now a mode of immortality. In "A Word out of the Sea" the 1860 volume has its turning-point. Beyond this poem, we must remember, are the "Enfants d'Adam" and "Calamus" sequences, and also "Crossing Brooklyn Ferry" and the "Messenger Leaves" sequence.

The 1860 poem begins harshly: "Out of the rocked cradle." The past participle, unlike the present participle in the later versions, implies no continuing agent for the rocking; the sea here is too inclusive to be a symbol; it is just a fact of life—life's factuality. Then comes the melange of elements associated with the "sea." They are among the realities whose miraculousness the poet is on his way to understanding. Note the third line (omitted in later versions) which clearly establishes the autobiographical tone and makes the boy at once the product of nature at large and a particular nature: "Out of the boy's mother's womb, from the nipples of her breasts." All this leads to a clear split in point of view, so that we know that the poet-as-adult is making a poem which will be his means to understanding a childhood experience. Initially we are told of the range of experiences out of which this poem comes: the sea as rocked cradle seems at once literally (to the boy) and metaphorically (to the poet) to "contain" the song of the bird, the boy's mother, the place, the time, the memory of the brother, and the as yet unnamed "word stronger and more delicious than any" which marks a limit to the meaning of the whole. This is quite explicitly an introduction. For what follows is given a separate title, "Reminiscence," as though the poet wanted to make quite plain the division between his sense of himself as child and as adult. Then we are presented with the story of the birds, the loss of the beloved, and the song sung (as only *now* the poet knows it) to objectify this loss, so make it bearable, so assure that it can, in *this* life, be transcended. Always we are aware that the poet-as-adult, the creative center of the poem, seeks that "word stronger and more delicious" which will be his means finally to understand his reminiscences and—in the context of this volume (I emphasize: in the context of *this* volume)—serve to define his vocation as poet, at once powerful and fallible. The points of view of bird, child, and adult are kept separate until the passage which reads:

> Bird! (then said the boy's Soul,)
> Is it indeed toward your mate you sing? or is it mostly to me?
> For I that was a child, my tongue's use sleeping,
> Now that I have heard you,
> Now in a moment I know what I am for—I awake,
> And already a thousand singers—a thousand songs, clearer louder, more
> sorrowful than yours,
> A thousand warbling echoes have started to life within me,
> Never to die.

The boy, even as a man recalling his boyhood, does not, as in later versions, at first address the bird as "Demon." He is at this stage incapable of that "or"—in the latter reading "Demon or bird." Even though his soul speaks, he is to discover—some lines later—his special "poetic" relation to the bird. Moreover, as "boy," he holds toward death an attitude half-way between that of the bird—who is merely "instinctive" and that of the man— who is "reflective," capable of "reminiscence." Yet the points of view begin to be hypnotically merged—*after* the fact. In the boy's "soul" the poet discovers a child's potentiality for adult knowledge; but he keeps it as a potentiality, and he never assigns it to the bird, who (or which) is an occasion merely. Yet having seen that potentiality as such, he can "now," in the adult present, work toward its realization, confident that the one will follow necessarily in due course from the other. Now, in the adult present, he can ask for "the clew," "The word final, superior to all," the word which "now" he can "conquer." I cannot emphasize too much that it is a *"word"*—that the poet is translating the sea (and all it embodies) as prelinguistic fact into a word, knowledge of which will signify his coming to maturity. "Out of," in the original title, is meant quite literally to indicate a linguistic transformation. In the record of the growth of his mind, he sees *now* that the word will once and for all precipitate the meaning he has willed himself to create, and in the creating to discover. And it comes as he recalls that time when the sea, manifesting the rhythm of life and death itself,

> Delaying not, hurrying not,
> Whisper'd me through the night, and very plainly before daybreak,
> Lisp'd to me the low and delicious word DEATH,
> And again Death—ever Death, Death, Death

(Not *Death*, merely repeated four times as in later versions—but *ever*, beyond counting. The prophetic Whitman was bound to drop that *ever*, since for him nothing was beyond counting.)

The merging of the points of view occurs as not only past and present, child and adult, but subject and object (i.e., "The sea . . . whisper'd me"— not "*to* me") are fused. The poet now knows the word, because he has contrived a situation in which he can control its use; he has discovered (to recall the language of the *American Primer* notes) another reality, one that words until *now* had not been formed to represent. He has, as only a poet can, *made* a word out of the sea—for the duration of the poem understood *"sea"* as it may be into *"death"*—*"ever death."* His genius is such as to have enabled us to put those quotation marks around the word—guided by him, to have "bracketed" this portion of our experience with language; and we discover that as language binds in the poet's time, so it is bound in human time.

If the end of the poem is to understand cosmic process as a continual loss of the beloved through death and a consequent gain of death-in-life and life-in-death—if this is the end of the poem, nonetheless it is gained through a creative act, an assertion of life in the face of death, and a discovery and acknowledgment of the limits of such an assertion. And this act is that of the very person, the poet, whom death would deprive of all that is beloved in life. Moreover, the deprivation is quite literally that and shows the poet moving, in high honesty, from the "Enfants d'Adam" sequence to "Calamus." In the 1860 volume, "A Word out of the Sea" entails the "Calamus" sequence. (What if Whitman had, in "A Word out of the Sea," written *comrade* instead of *brother*?)

In any case, at this stage of his career, Whitman would not yield to his longing for such comfort as would scant the facts of life and death. There is, I repeat, that opening *rocked*, not *rocking* cradle; there is the quite naturalistic acknowledgment of the "boy's mother's womb." And there is stanza 31 (the stanzas in the 1860 poem are numbered, as the stanzas of the final version are not):

> O give me some clew!
> O if I am to have so much, let me have more!
> O a word! O what is my destination?
> O I fear it is henceforth chaos!
> O how joys, dreads, convolutions, human shapes, and all shapes, spring as
>   from graves around me!
> O phantoms! you cover all the land, and all the sea!
> O I cannot see in the dimness whether you smile or frown upon me;
> O vapor, a look, a word! O well-beloved!
> O you dear women's and men's phantoms!

In the final version, the equivalent stanza reads only:

> O give me the clew (it lurks in the night here somewhere,)
> Or if I am to have so much, let me have more!

The difference between "some clew" and "the clew" marks the difference between a poet for whom questions are real and one for whom questions are rhetorical. The later Whitman was convinced that the lurking clew would find him—and to that degree, whatever else he was, was not a poet. The earlier Whitman, in all humility, feared that what might issue out of this experience was "phantoms"—a good enough word for aborted poems. And often—but not too often—he was right.

Finally, there is not in "A Word out of the Sea" the falsely (and, in the context of the poem, undeservedly) comforting note of "Or like some old crone rocking the cradle swathed in sweet garments, bending aside." Indeed, the sentimentality and bathos of this too-much celebrated line, as I think, is given away by the fact that it is the only simile, the only *like* clause, in the poem. And, in relation to the total effect of the poem, the strategic withdrawal of the *Or* which introduces the line is at least unfortunate, at most disastrous.

I make so much of the kind of disaster, as I think it is, because it became increasingly characteristic of Whitman's way with poetry after the 1860 *Leaves of Grass*. Probably there are poems, written later, which show him at his best; and probably some of his revisions and rejections are for the best. But I more and more doubt it, as I doubt that he had reached his best in 1855 and 1856. I do not mean to take the part of Cassandra; but I think it as inadvisable to take the part of Pollyanna. The facts, as I see them, show that Whitman, for whatever reason, after 1860 moved away from the mode of archetypal autobiography toward that of prophecy. He worked hard to make, as he said, a cathedral out of *Leaves of Grass*. He broke up the beautifully wrought sequence of the 1860 volume; so that, even when he let poems stand unrevised, they appear in contexts which take from them their life-giving mixture of tentativeness and assurance, of aspiration, and render them dogmatic, tendentious, and overweening.

In Lawrence's word, Whitman "mentalized" his poems. To give a few examples of "mentalizing" revisions of 1860 poems: the opening of the third "Enfants d'Adam" poem reads in the 1860 text:

> O my children! O mates!
> O the bodies of you, and of all men and women, engirth
>   me, and I engirth them.

In the 1867 version the lines read:

> I sing the body electric,
> The Armies of those I love engirth me and I engirth them.

Another example: the opening line of the fourteenth poem of the same sequence—reads in the 1860 version: "I am he that aches with love"; and becomes in 1867: "I am he that aches with amorous love." (This is the *amorous* which so infuriated Lawrence.) And another example: the opening lines of the fifteenth poem in the sequence—reads in the 1860 version: "Early in the morning,/ Walking . . ."; and became in 1867: "As Adam early in the morning,/ Walking . . . ." Small examples surely. But note the unsupported and unsupportable claims of "body electric," "armies," "amorous," and the Old Testament "Adam."

A larger—but still characteristic—example is Whitman's revision of the first of the 1860 "Leaves of Grass" sequence, which became "As I Ebb'd with the Ocean of Life." The 1860 poem opens thus:

> Elemental drifts!
> O I wish I could impress others as you and the waves have just been impressing me.

As I ebbed with an ebb of the ocean of life,
As I wended the shores I know.

In the poem as it appears in the 1892 edition of *Leaves of Grass*, the first two lines—expressing doubt, as I have pointed out—are missing; the third has been simplified to "As I ebb'd with the ocean of life"—so that the poet is no longer conceived as part of an "ebb." And the fourth line stands as we have it now. Later in the seventh line of the 1892 version, the poet says that he is "Held by the electric self out of the pride of which I utter poems." In the 1860 version he says that he is "Alone, held by the eternal self of me that threatens to get the better of me, and stifle me." And so it goes—all passion beyond spending (unless vivified by a kind of cosmic electroshock), all poetry beyond the mere writing, all life beyond the mere living—since the poet's tactic, however unconscious, is to claim to have transcended that which must have been hard to live with: his extraordinarily ordinary self and the ordinarily extraordinary death that awaits him. Granting the mood and movement of the later editions of *Leaves of Grass*, it is only proper that Whitman would have rejected the eighth poem in the 1860 "Calamus" sequence—which begins "Long I thought that knowledge alone would suffice me—O if I could but obtain knowledge!" and ends, as the poet is brought to confront the readers to whom he would offer his poems, "I am indifferent to my own songs—I will go with him I love . . . ."

One more example: this one not of a revision but of an addition to a sequence originating in the 1860 volume. In the 1871 *Leaves of Grass*, Whitman, now wholly committed to making of his poem a series of prophetic books, placed in the "Calamus" sequence the woolly "Base of All Metaphysics," the last stanza of which reads:

> Having studied the new and antique, the Greek and Germanic systems,
> Kant having studied and stated, Fichte and Schelling and Hegel,
> Stated the lore of Plato, and Socrates greater than Plato,
> And greater than Socrates sought and stated, Christ divine having studied
> long.
> I see reminiscent to-day those Greek and Germanic systems,
> See the philosophies of all, Christian churches and tenets see,
> Yet underneath Socrates clearly see, and underneath Christ the divine I see,
> The dear love of man for his comrade, the attraction of friend to friend,
> Of the well-married husband and wife, of children and parents,
> Of city for city and land for land.

Whitman stuck by this poem until the end, and it went unchanged into the 1892 edition of *Leaves of Grass*, contributing its bit to the "mentalizing" of the whole. And it is only too typical of additions to the book made from 1867 on.

This Whitman begins to take over *Leaves of Grass* in the 1867 edition and is fully in command by the time of the 1871 edition. It is, unhappily, he whom he knew best and he with whom our poets have tried to make their pacts and truces—but, as I think, so that during the uneasy peace they might come to know another (and, as I have tried to show, earlier) Whitman, whose way with the poetry they seem to sense but can never quite get to. The way to that Whitman is not impassable, although working with the Inclusive Edition of *Leaves of Grass* (upon whose variant readings I have depended) is tedious. But there is yet a more direct way: reading the 1860 *Leaves of Grass*.

Meantime we must bring ourselves to say of the Whitman of 1892, the literatus, that he was driven to claim prophetic powers, not to put poetry to their service. Nothing could hold this Whitman back, not even the facts of a poet's life. Indeed, life—his own and life in general—became less "factual," less "real" for him. And—since justification consists in deriving the necessary from the real, of tracing the necessary back to its roots in the real, of showing that the real is necessary—he no longer had a need to justify himself. Well: In this our world, where we too find it increasingly hard to assent to the factually real, where we have got so far as to call the factually real the "absurd," we find it increasingly difficult to hold ourselves back: as do our poets, acting on our behalf. Thus I daresay we need to recover the Whitman of 1860—with his heroic sense of grounding the necessary in the real. He gave us permission to. I am suggesting that we *need* the poet of 1860, the poet of "A Word out of the Sea." I mean to say thereby that our poets need him too. And justifying the need, we must justify him who contrived that his need be archetypal of ours.

JAMES A. WRIGHT

The Delicacy of Walt Whitman

The public mask, the coarse Whit-
man, is false. Then what is true? Is there a private Whitman who is delicate,
and if there *is* a delicate Whitman, what is his poetry like? Where can we find
it? And what does it have to do with those of us who want to read it? Is
Whitman's delicacy a power that is alive in American poetry at the present
moment? If so, who is displaying it? And is it capable of growth?

The *delicacy* of Walt Whitman. I do not mean to imply that Whitman
was delicate as Nietzsche, for example, was in delicate health. Whitman
really does seem to have been a strong man, in spite of the public mask's
strident insistence on his own vigor. His actions were often modest and yet
they demonstrate a physical condition astonishingly robust. When the war
began, Whitman was forty-two years old. He went into the war. He did not
have to go. I am not concerned with arguing the ethical significance of his
relation to the war. I point only to the fact. In an essay recently published in
the *Sewane Review*, Mr. James M. Cox eloquently describes Whitman's
exploit in terms which reveal the abundant physical strength of the man:

> Whitman's role in the Civil War stands as one of the triumphs of our
> culture. That this figure should have emerged from an almost illiterate
> background to become a national poet, that he should have at the age of
> forty-two gone down into the wilderness of Virginia to walk across the
> bloody battlefields ministering to the sick and wounded, that he should
> have paced through the hospitals and kept a vigil over the mutilated victims
> on both sides, that he should have created the war in prose and poetry of an
> extraordinarily high order—that he should have done these deeds shows
> how truly he had cast himself in the heroic mould.

From *The Presence of Walt Whitman*, edited by R. W. B. Lewis. Copyright © 1962 by Columbia
University Press.

So the delicacy I have in mind is not an empty gentility, nor the physical frailty that sometimes slithers behind arrogance. It is the delicacy of his *poetry* that concerns me. It has its source in the character of Whitman himself, and it is, I believe, available to American poetry at the present time.

Whitman's poetry has delicacy of music, of diction, and of form. The word "delicacy" can do without a rhetorically formal definition; but I mean it to suggest powers of restraint, clarity, and wholeness, all of which taken together embody that deep spiritual inwardness, that fertile strength, which I take to be the most beautiful power of Whitman's poetry, and the most readily available to the poetry, and indeed the civilization, of our own moment in American history.

If what I say is true, then we are almost miraculously fortunate to have Whitman available to us. For some time the features of American poetry most in evidence have been very different from Whitman's: in short, recent American poetry has often been flaccid, obtuse and muddied, and fragmentary, crippled almost. Yet there is great talent alive in our country today, and if the spirit of Whitman can help to rescue that talent from the fate of so many things in America, that begin nobly and end meanly, then we ought to study him as carefully as we can. What is his poetry like?

Let us consider first the delicacy of his music. And since I want to listen to the music closely, a few notes on traditional prosody are in order. At this point Whitman himself is ready to help us. As a stylist, he did not begin as a solitary barbarian (in Ortega's sense of that word). He is many things that are perhaps discomforting and even awkward, but he is not a smug fool—he is not an imitation Dead End Kid pretending that no poet or man of any kind ever existed before he was born upon the earth. Whitman realizes that the past has existed.

He also understands how the past continues to exist: it exists in the present, and comes into living form only when some individual man is willing to challenge it. Whitman dares, like Nietzsche, to challenge not only what he dislikes but also what he *values*. "The power to destroy or remould," writes Whitman in the 1855 Preface to *Leaves of Grass*, "is freely used by him [the greatest poet] but never the power of attack. What is past is past. If he does not expose superior models and prove himself by every step he takes he is not what is wanted."

It seems to me of the gravest importance that Whitman's relation to established traditional forms of poetry and of society itself be clarified, so that we may free him from the tone of pretentious ignorance that has been associated with his mere name, from time to time, by fools. He knows that the past exists, and he knows that, as a poet and as a man, he has a right to live. His duty to the past is precisely this: to have the courage to live and to create his own poetry.

This is the great way of learning from the noble spirits of the past. And the most difficultly courageous way of asserting the shape and meaning of one's own poetry and one's life is to challenge and surpass those very traditions and masters whom one can honestly respect. This deep spiritual kinship between a truly original man and the nobility of the past is formulated thus by Goethe: "People always talk of the study of the ancients; but what does that mean, except that it says, turn your attention to the real world, and try to express it, for that is what the ancients did when they were alive" (*Conversations with Eckermann*). And so in Whitman's music we find him turning away from one masterfully delicate verbal musician, Longfellow, toward the real world. Whitman respected Longfellow for his true gifts, as we ought to do. Our own scorn of Longfellow is cant. It is like the scorn of the great Victorian Englishmen that prevailed until recently under the influence of Lytton Strachey; we scurry forth like insects to deface them as soon as a serious, honorable man like Strachey assures us that Dickens, Tennyson, and Florence Nightingale are safely dead. So let us turn, for just a moment, to Longfellow, whose lovely poetry, even in his own time, was in the strict sense a musical embodiment of the European past. In *Specimen Days* ("My Tribute to Four Poets"), Whitman records a visit to Longfellow which unmistakably reveals his true respect for the poet who was almost universally celebrated as the great poet whom Whitman himself would like to be: "I shall not soon forget his lit-up face," says Whitman, "and glowing warmth and courtesy in the modes of what is called the old school." And then Whitman suddenly, and rather startlingly, remarks on his own poetic relation to Longfellow and others (Emerson, Whittier, and Bryant):

> In a late magazine one of my reviewers, who ought to know better, speaks of my "attitude of contempt and scorn and intolerance" toward the leading poets—of my "deriding" them, and preaching their "uselessness." If anybody cares to know what I think—and have long thought and avow'd—about them, I am entirely willing to propound. I can't imagine any better luck befalling these States for a poetical beginning and initiation than has come from Emerson, Longfellow, Bryant, and Whittier.... Longfellow for rich color, graceful forms and incidents—all that makes life beautiful and love refined—competing with the singers of Europe on their own ground, and with one exception, better and finer work than that of any of them.

Furthermore, Whitman's deep humility (an intellectual as well as a moral virtue) appears in his note on the "Death of Longfellow" (*Specimen Days*). There, in the very act of praising Longfellow for his best gift ("verbal melody") he speaks of his radical inadequacy; and thus Whitman inadvertently, almost as an afterthought, identifies his own great strength:

> Longfellow in his voluminous works seems to me to be eminent in the style and forms of poetical expression that mark the present age, (an idiosyncrasy,

almost a sickness, of verbal melody,). . . . He is certainly the sort of bard and counter-actant most needed for our materialistic, self-assertive, money-worshipping, Anglo-Saxon races, and especially for the present age in America—an age tyrannically regulated with reference to the manufacturer, the merchant, the financier, the politician and the day workman—for whom and among whom he comes as the poet of melody, courtesy, deference—*poet of the mellow twilight of the past* in Italy, Germany, Spain, and Northern Europe. . . . He strikes a splendid average, and does not sing exceptional passions, or humanity's jagged escapades. He is not revolutionary, brings nothing offensive or new, does not deal hard blows. . . . His very anger is gentle, is at second hand, (as in the "Quadroon Girl" and the "Witnesses.") . . . To the ungracious complaint-charge of his want of racy nativity and special originality, I shall only say that America and the world may well be reverently thankful—can never be thankful enough—for any such singing-bird vouchsafed out of the centuries, without asking that the notes be different from those of other songsters; adding what I have heard Longfellow himself say, that ere the New World can be worthily original, and announce herself and her own heroes, she must be well saturated with the originality of others, and respectfully consider the heroes that lived before Agamemnon.

The whole passage is moved by an impulse to pass beyond. Not merely to pass beyond what one hates—the phoniness, the counterfeit poetry which is always among us in its thousand blind, mean, sly forms. But to pass beyond what one loves, to open one's ears, to know what one is doing and why. It is a noble statement by a delicate and reverent man.

Let us apply the statement to Whitman's own music. In effect, he tunes his verses toward those very crass and difficult subjects which Longfellow (for whatever reason) avoided. And yet, even so, Whitman's music is not "jagged" like the escapades of that American humanity he often sings of. It is a *delicate* music, a deeper sound than that of Longfellow; it is alive, and it hurts, as men are hurt on the jagged edges of their own lives.

So Whitman respected Longfellow, a traditional prosodist. In spite of his poems like "Evangeline," which we are told to read as though they were written in the classical dactylic hexameter, Longfellow is predominantly an iambic writer. Moreover, he writes the iambic meter with a masterful grasp of its permissive variations: the elisions, the trochaic substitutions, the spondaic effects and their euphonious combination within regular iambic patterns. But Longfellow does not write about American life. He does not write about its externals. And, shunning its externals, he does not penetrate to its spirit. Whitman notices these radical limits in the very act of praising Longfellow for his mastery—mastery of a kind which forces him to turn away from the living world and to sing either of Europe or of the American past.

Whitman also brings a rare technical understanding of prosody to bear on the living American present. But in his concern to surpass tradition, he deliberately shuns the iambic measure and all its variations, except in a very few instances (like the notorious "O Captain! My Captain!" and the less frequently quoted "Ethopia Saluting the Colors") which offer a helpful contrast to the inventive delicacy of music in Whitman's greater poems.

He shuns the iambic measure. He says, in the 1855 Preface, "The rhythm and uniformity of perfect poems show the free growth of metrical laws, and bud from them as unerringly and loosely as lilacs and roses on a bush, and take shapes as compact as the shapes of chestnuts and oranges." Does Whitman mean that "free growth" is aimless? No, he speaks of "metrical laws." Listen to his poem "Reconciliation":

Word over all, beautiful as the sky,
Beautiful that war and all its deeds of carnage must in time be utterly lost,
That the hands of the sisters Death and Night incessantly softly wash again,
    and ever again, this soil'd world;
For my enemy is dead, a man divine as myself is dead,
I look where he lies white-faced and still in the coffin—I draw near,
Bend down and touch lightly with my lips the white face in the coffin.

We cannot understand this poem's music in traditional prosodic terms. Still, it's fun to note that Whitman did not write non-iambic verse out of pique at his inability to control its rules. Listen again to Whitman's opening line: "Word over all, beautiful as the sky." The line is a flawless iambic pentameter; he uses a trochaic substitution in the first foot, a hovering spondaic echo between the second and third feet, a daring and yet perfectly traditional inversion; and he successfully runs two light stresses before the final strong stress.

It seems to me wonderful that Whitman should have written that line, which is not only iambic, but as bold in its exploitation of the iambic possibilities as the masters themselves: Campion, Herrick, Wyatt, even Milton. And that is not so strange. In a note on "British Literature" (Collect: Notes Left Over), Whitman writes the following: "To avoid mistake, I would say that I not only commend the study of this literature, but wish our sources of supply and comparison vastly enlarged." The trouble is that "the British element these states hold, and have always held, enormously beyond its fit proportions . . . its products are no models for us." So he does not hate traditional British prosody, which is of course predominantly iambic. He loves its great craft, and he shows his ability to emulate it. But he is an adventurer; he wants to listen beyond the admittedly rich music of iambic, and to report what he hears.

In prosody, then, Whitman is sometimes a destroyer, but we must see that he knows exactly what he is destroying. He is both theoretically and practically ready to replace it with a new prosody of his own. He begins with a supremely sensitive ear for the music of language; he moves beyond the permissive variations of iambic; and he is not afraid of the new musical possibilities out there, so he brings some of them back with him. Perhaps they were there all the time; perhaps they are the quantitative possibilities of the classical languages that have drifted around in English. In any case, the iambic conventions do not seem to make much provision for them; and yet they can be incredibly beautiful in Whitman. We need only listen:

> Come lovely and soothing death,
> Undulate round the world, serenely arriving, arriving,
> In the day, in the night, to all, to each,
> Sooner or later delicate death.

Whitman really does have something to teach current American poets, in spite of his entering American poetry once again, in Mr. Randall Jarrell's wicked phrase, as "the hero of a de Mille movie about Whitman"—a movie, one might add, which co-stars the Dead End Kids.

To summarize, Whitman can teach us about some possibilities of musical delicacy in our language. He sympathetically understood iambic forms (exemplified by Longfellow) which in his own poems he is trying to break and surpass. He can also teach courage, for he has great rhythmical daring; he seeks constantly for a music which really echoes and fulfills his imaginative vision.

He becomes a great artist by the ways of growth which Nietzsche magnificently describes in the first speech of *Thus Spake Zarathustra*: the Three Metamorphoses of the Spirit. The spirit that truly grows, says Nietzsche, will first be a camel, a beast of burden, who labors to bear the forms of the past, whether in morality or art or anything else; then he will change into a lion, and destroy not merely what he hates but even what he loves and understands; and the result of this concerned and accurate destruction will be the spirit's emergence as a child, who is at last able to create clearly and powerfully from within his own imagination.

Whitman says of the great poet, "He swears to his art, I will not be meddlesome, I will not have in my writings any elegance, or effect, or originality, to hang in the way between me and the rest like curtains. I will have nothing hang in the way, not the richest curtains" (Preface, 1855). And Whitman is well aware of the many curtains that can hang in the way. There is not only the old-world elegance of Longfellow—which may stand for the prosodic traditions of England, beautiful in themselves—but there is also the curtain of aimless destructiveness, which is eventually not even destructive but just trivial. In "After Trying a Certain Book" (*Specimen Days*), Whitman says that the difficulty of explaining what a poem means is not to be taken as evidence that the poem means nothing: "Common teachers or critics are always asking 'What does it mean?' Symphony of fine musician, or sunset, or sea-waves rolling up the beach—what do they mean? Undoubtedly in the most subtle-elusive sense they mean something—but who shall fathom and define those meanings? (*I do not intend this as a warrant for wildness and frantic escapades. . . .)*" (My italics.) Every scholar and every Beat who mentions Whitman ought to read that salutary note beforehand.

Now I want to speculate on the delicacy of Whitman's diction, his choice of words. What is remarkable is not merely his attempt to include new things—objects, persons, places, and events—in his poems. Something more interesting and complex goes on: in the face of this sometimes difficult and prosaic material ("humanity's jagged escapades"), he is able to retain his delicacy, which is a power of mind as well as a quality of kindness. In a crisis, he keeps his head and his feelings alert. He can be as precise as Henry James, as Mr. Jarrell rightly says; but he is sensitively precise about things that are often in themselves harsh, even brutal.

Mr. Jarrell has written one of the liveliest accounts of Whitman's delicacy of diction, and I refer the reader to that essay. Perhaps Mr. Jarrell does not sufficiently emphasize the enormous strength and courage it required even to face some of the horrible things Whitman faced, much less to claim them for the imagination by means of a diction that is as delicate as that of Keats.

One of my favorite poems in Whitman is "A March in the Ranks Hard-prest, and the Road Unknown" from *Drum-Taps*. It reveals perfectly what I mean about Whitman's delicate diction: his power of retaining his sensitivity right in the face of realities that would certainly excuse coarseness, for the sake of self-defense if for no other reason. But Whitman does not defend himself. As he had told us in a Virgilian line, one of the noblest lines of poetry ever written, "I was the man, I suffered, I was there." The line is great because it is not a boast but a modest bit of information, almost as unobtrusive as a stage-direction or perhaps a whispered aside to the reader. (Whitman is always whispering to us—that is another of his musical delicacies.) There he certainly is, gathering the horror into his delicate words, soothing it if possible, always looking at it and in the deepest sense imagining it:

A march in the ranks hard-prest, and the road unknown,
A route through a heavy wood with muffled steps in the darkness,
Our army foil'd with loss severe, and the sullen remnant retreating,
Till after midnight glimmer upon us the lights of a dim-lighted building,
We come to an open space in the woods, and halt by the dim-lighted building,
'Tis a large old church at the crossing roads, now an impromptu hospital,
Entering but for a minute I see a sight beyond all the pictures and poems ever made,
Shadows of deepest, deepest black, just lit by moving candles and lamps,

And by one great pitchy torch stationary with wild red flame and clouds of smoke,
By these, crowds, groups of forms vaguely I see on the floor,
     some in the pews laid down,
At my feet more distinctly a soldier, a mere lad, in danger of bleeding
     to death, (he is shot in the abdomen,)
I stanch the blood temporarily, (the youngster's face is white as a lily,)
Then before I depart I sweep my eyes o'er the scene fain to absorb it all,
Faces, varieties, postures beyond description, most in obscurity,
     some of them dead,
Surgeons operating, attendants holding lights, the smell of ether,
     the odor of blood,
The crowd, O the crowd of the bloody forms, the yard outside also fill'd,
Some on the bare ground, some on planks or stretchers,
     some in the death-spasm sweating,
An occasional scream or cry, the doctor's shouted orders or calls,
The glisten of the little steel instruments catching the glint of the torches,
These I resume as I chant, I see again the forms, I smell the odor,
Then hear outside the orders given, *Fall in, my men, fall in;*
But first I bend to the dying lad, his eyes open, a half-smile gives he me,
Then the eyes close, calmly close, and I speed forth to the darkness,
Resuming, marching, ever in darkness marching, on in the ranks,
The unknown road still marching.

I want to draw attention to a single small detail of diction, which becomes huge because of its delicacy. I mean the phrase about the wounded young man's face. He suddenly looms up out of the confusion and darkness; he has been shot in the abdomen; and his face, buffaloed by shock, is "white as a lily."

There have been many poets in America who would compare a white face with a lily. There are also many poets who attempt to deal with a subject matter that is, like Whitman's, very far from the traditional materials of poesy as Longfellow understood them. Moreover, I know that there are many brave American men who write about painful experiences. But what is special about Whitman, what makes his diction remarkable in itself and fertile for us today, is that he does all three of these things at once, and in him they become a single act of creation. Unless we can see the nobility of his courage, then we have neither the right nor the intelligence to talk about the delicacy of his style.

Whitman's diction contains a lesson that can actually be learned, and it does not require the vain imitation of his personal appearance and stylistic mannerisms. It is more spiritually inward than any external accident can suggest. It is this: he deliberately seeks in American life the occasions and persons who are central to that life; he sometimes finds them harsh and violent, as in the war; and he responds to the harshness with a huge effort of imagination: to be delicate, precise, sensitive.

I realize that it is difficult to distinguish between the delicacy of Whitman's diction and his sensitivity as a man. But that is just the point. When a certain kind of diction, like a certain kind of meter, is employed by a coarse man, it automatically becomes a mannerism, or perhaps a stock device, detachable from the body of the poem, like a false eyelash, or a shapely artificial breast. Any concentration upon Whitman's stylistic mannerisms alone betrays an obsession with external, accidental things. Perhaps that is why so many bad poets have claimed Whitman as an ancestor.

I want also to say something about the delicacy of form in Whitman's poems. I think at once of the sentence in the 1855 Preface about rhythm and what he calls "uniformity." Here is the sentence again: "The rhythm and uniformity of perfect poems shows the free growth of metrical laws, and bud from them as unerringly and loosely as lilacs and roses on a bush, and take shapes as compact as the shapes of chestnuts and oranges."

This sentence can help us to understand what "form" meant to Whitman and also what it might mean to contemporary poets in America and elsewhere, if they have truly learned from Whitman and still wish to learn from him. The word "form" itself, however, may be ambiguous. So I will shun rhetorical definitions, which often threaten to mislead or oversimplify; and I will discuss a single short poem that, I believe, is a great poem because of the almost perfect delicacy of its form:

> I heard you solemn-sweet pipes of the organ as last Sunday morn I pass'd
>   the church,
> Winds of autumn, as I walk'd the woods at dusk I heard your
>   long-stretch'd sighs up above so mournful, I heard the
> perfect Italian tenor singing at the opera, I heard the soprano in
>   the midst of the quartet singing;
> Heart of my love! you too I heard murmuring low through one of the wrists
>   around my head,
> Heard the pulse of you when all was still ringing little bells last night under
>   my ear.

Does this poem have a form? If so, how can I describe it without losing in a general classification the very details that give the poem its life? I can think of at least two possibly helpful ways of answering these questions. First, Mr. Gay Wilson Allen (in his definitive biography of Whitman) supplies us with a crucial bit of textual information. The version of "I heard you solemn-sweet pipes" which I just quoted is not the only one. An earlier version, one of three poems which Whitman published in 1861, is quoted and discussed by Mr. Allen. The revisions are almost all deletions. The earlier version (printed in the New York *Leader*, October 12, 1861) contained apostrophes to "war-suggesting trumpets," to "you round-lipp'd cannons." In the version which Whitman apparently considered final (printed in the

"Deathbed" edition of 1892), the references to war are deleted. Whitman also deleted a whole single line, in which he addresses a lady who played "delicious music on the harp."

What is left? A simple poem of five lines. Whitman addresses four different sounds. In these apostrophes and in his arrangement of them we can find the form of his poem.

The form is that of parallelism. But immediately we have to distinguish between the grammatical signification of "parallelism" and Whitman's actual use of it. A grammatical parallelism is primarily concerned with sentence-structure: noun balances noun, verb balances verb, either as repetition or as antithesis. But in Whitman's poem, the appearance of grammatical parallelism is so rare as to be almost accidental. In fact, he almost seems to avoid it. For he uses parallelism not as a device of repetition but as an occasion for development. For this reason, we take a certain risk when we read "I heard you solemn-sweet pipes." After the first two lines, we can know only two things: first, we cannot hope to rest on mere parallel sentence-structure; second, the poet is probably going to sing about another sound, but it might be the sound of anything. (The possibility is a little scary in a country where, for example, President Coolidge's taciturnity is automatically considered a joke, instead of a great civic virtue. Behind the uneasy joke lies the dreadful suspicion that we talk too much.) There is no way to read Whitman's poem at all unless we yield ourselves to its principle of growth, a principle that reveals itself only in this particular poem, stage by stage.

Whitman first tries to make sure that we will not confuse his poetic forms with the rules of grammar; and then he lets his images grow, one out of another; and finally, we discover the form of the poem as we read it, and we know what it is only after we have finished.

It is this kind of formal growth that, I believe, gives special appropriateness to Whitman's mention of "shapes as compact as the shapes of chestnuts and oranges." These fruits do indeed have "shapes"—delicate shapes indeed. And they are compact, not diffuse. Their life depends on their form, which grows out of the forms of blossoms, which in turn grew out of the forms of trees, which in turn grew out of the forms of seeds. If I followed the changes that overwhelm an orange seed, I should be startled at the unexpected form of each stage of growth; but the form would be there nevertheless, however unexpected: at once undreamed-of and inevitable.

I have avoided the term "organic unity" because I wanted to read Whitman's poem afresh; and I am afraid that we might confuse the philosophical definition of a term in aesthetics with our empirical attempt to pay attention to the form of a poem. Just as bad poets tend to substitute the external accidents of Whitman's personal mannerisms and habits of dress for his poetry, so we readers might tend to substitute a general term for our reading of poetry—any poetry. If you mention the name of Laforgue, for example, it is a rare graduate student who will not immediately say, or think, the phrase "romantic irony," just as certain famous dogs helplessly salivated when a bell was rung. That's a good simile, as W.C. Fields once observed in another connection. Moreover, the simile is horrible; I wish I could make it even more so.

What is "form"? It is not simply the rules of grammar. And it cannot simply be equated with certain conventions of iambic verse. When reviewers of current American verse say that a certain poem is written "in form," they usually mean it is predominantly iambic, either skillful or clumsy. But the form in Whitman's poems is not iambic. Form, in Whitman, is a principle of growth: one image or scene or sound *grows* out of another. The general device is parallelism, not of grammar but of action or some other meaning. Here is a further example of the parallel form, which is delicate and precise and therefore very powerful but which is not based on the repetition of the sentence-structure:

The little one sleeps in its cradle,
I lift the gauze and look a long time, and silently brush away flies with my hand.

The youngster and the red-faced girl turn aside up the bushy hill,
I peeringly view them from the top.

The suicide sprawls on the bloody floor of the bedroom,
I witness the corpse with its dabbled hair, I note where the pistol has fallen.

Form in Whitman is a principle of imagination: the proliferating of images out of one unifying vision. Every real poem has its own form, which cannot be discovered through rhetoric, but only through imagination. Whitman can teach current American poets to destroy their own rhetoric and trust their own imagination. I shudder to think what would happen if every current versifier in America were to do that. (Is it a shudder of joy? A risky question.)

R. W. B. LEWIS

Always Going Out and Coming In

Walt Whitman is the most blurred, even contradictory figure in the classical or mid-nineteenth-century period of American Literature. Recent scholarship and criticism have been clearing things up a good deal; but both the poet and his work remain something of a jumble. For a number of decades, Whitman was the most misrepresented of our major poets; and the misrepresentation began with Whitman himself, in the last twenty-five years of his life. It was during those years, from 1867 onward, that Whitman—initially a very self-exposed and self-absorbed poet—became willfully self-concealing, while at the same time he asserted in various ways an entity, a being, a persona radically other than the being that lay at the heart of his best poetry.

The chief mode of such concealment and assertion was not creative; it was editorial. Whitman wrote little poetry of lasting value after "Passage to India" (1871); what he did do in those later years was constantly to reshuffle the contents of his expanding book: to disperse the poems out of their original and effective order, to arrange them in new and fundamentally misleading groups, to suppress some of the more telling and suggestive of the items, and to revise or delete a series of key passages. The result of this process was a serious shift of emphasis whereby the authentic Whitman was gradually dismembered and replaced by a synthetic entity that was more posture than poet, more mere representative than sovereign person. It, or he, was the representative—in nearly the conventional political sense—of a rather shallowly and narrowly conceived democratic culture: a hearty voice at the center of a bustling and progressive republic, a voice that saluted the pioneers, echoed the sound of America singing, itself sang songs of joy that foretold the

From *Trials of the Word*. Copyright © 1965 by R. W. B. Lewis. Harcourt-Brace.

future union of the nation and the world and the cosmos, chanted the square deific, and wept over the country's captain lying cold and dead on the deck of the ship of state. Other and truer aspects of Whitman continued to exert an appeal, especially in certain lively corners of Europe. But in the English-speaking world, it was primarily the bombastic, or, as his disciples sometimes said, the "cosmic" Whitman that was better known; and it was this Whitman that was either revered or—in most literary circles after the advent of T.S. Eliot—dismissed or simply disregarded.

So much needs to be said: for our first task is to disentangle Whitman, to separate the real from the unpersuasive, to separate the poet from the posture. To do that, we have, first of all, to put Whitman's poems back into their original and chronological order. It might be argued that we have no right to tamper with the poet's own editorial judgment; that *Leaves of Grass* is, after all, Whitman's book and that we are bound to take it in the order and the form he eventually decided on. The answer to this proposition is that there is no satisfactory way around the critical necessity of discriminating among Whitman's successive revisions of his own work, of appealing from the Whitman of 1867 and 1871 and later to the earlier Whitman of 1855 and 1856 and 1860. The dates just named are all dates of various editions of *Leaves of Grass*; and the latter three, the ones we appeal to, are those of the editions in which most (not all) of the real Whitman is to be found. This Whitman is a great and unique figure who is also the recognizable ancestor of many significant poetic developments since his creative prime—from *symboliste* poetry to imagism to more recent neoromantic and, less interestingly, "beat" writing; a chief, though by no means the only, American begetter of Wallace Stevens and Hart Crane, to some extent of Ezra Pound (as he once reluctantly confessed), and to an obscure but genuine degree of T.S. Eliot.

The importance of chronology, in Whitman's case, cannot be exaggerated. Without it, we can have no clear sense of Whitman's development as a consciousness and as a craftsman: an affair of far graver concern with Whitman than with many other poets of his stature. For, as I shall propose, the development of his consciousness and his craft, from moment to moment and year to year, is the very root of his poetic subject matter. It is what his best poems are mainly about, or what they re-enact: the thrust and withdrawal, the heightening and declining, the flowing and ebbing of his psychic and creative energy. Whitman's poetry has to do with the drama of the psyche or "self" in its mobile and complex relation *to* itself, to the world of nature and human objects, and to the creative act. What is attempted here, consequently, is a sort of chart of Whitman's development—in the belief that such a chart is not simply a required preliminary for getting at Whitman, but, rather, that it is the proper way to identify the poetic achievement, and to evaluate it. And in a case like Whitman's, the chart of the development is not finally separable from the graph of the life, or biography; the biographical material, therefore, has likewise been distributed among the successive commentaries on the editions of Whitman's single lifelong book.

I: 1855

When *Leaves of Grass* was published on July 4, 1855, Walt Whitman, now thirty-six years old, was living in Brooklyn, with his parents and brothers, earning an occasional dollar by carpentering. Both his family and his carpentry served as sources of allusion and metaphor in the poetry; but neither—that is, neither his heredity nor his temporary employment—help much to explain how a relatively indolent odd-jobber and sometime journalist named Walter Whitman developed into Walt Whitman the poet. His mother, whom he salutes in "There Was a Child Went Forth" for having "conceiv'd him in her womb and birth'd him" (the birthday being the last day in May 1819; the place, rural Long Island), was of Dutch and Quaker descent, not especially cultivated, and remembered by her son, in the same poem of 1855, as quiet and mild and clean. His father was a farmer of deteriorating fortunes, temper, and health: "manly, mean, anger'd, unjust" in his son's account; and it is a psychological curiosity that the father died within a week of the son's first public appearance, or birth, as a poet. Other members of the family were sources of that compassionate intimacy with the wretched and the depraved reflected, for example, in "Song of Myself":

> The lunatic is carried at last to the asylum a confirm'd case...
> The prostitute draggles her shawl, her bonnet bobs on her tipsy
>   and pimpled neck...
> Voices of the diseas'd and despairing and of thieves and dwarfs.

Two of Whitman's brothers were diseased, one of them dying eventually in an insane asylum and the other (who was also a drunkard) married to a woman who became a prostitute. Yet another brother was a congenital idiot; and one of Whitman's sisters suffered from severe nervous melancholy. From these surroundings emerged the figure who, in the carpentering imagery of "Song of Myself," felt "sure as the most certain sure, plumb in the uprights, well entretied, braced in the beams"; a figure who not only felt like that but could write like that.

So remarkable and indeed so sudden has the appearance of Whitman the poet seemed, and out of so unlikely and artistically inhospitable a background, that literary historians have been driven to making spectacular guesses about the miraculous cause of it: an intense love affair, for instance, with a Creole lady of high degree; an intense love affair with an unidentified young man; a mystical seizure; the explosive impact of Emerson or of Carlyle or of

George Sand. The literary influences can be documented, though they can scarcely be measured; with the other guesses, evidence is inadequate either to support or altogether to discount them. But perhaps the problem itself has not been quite properly shaped. Whitman's poetic emergence was remarkable enough; but it was not in fact particularly sudden. Nor was the career, seen retrospectively, as haphazard and aimless as one might suppose. Looked at from a sufficient distance, Whitman's life shows the same pattern of thrust and withdrawal, advance and retreat, that pulsates so regularly in the very metrics as well as the emotional attitudes of his verses; and to much the same effect. Up to about 1850, when he was thirty-one, Whitman—like the child in the autobiographical poem already quoted—was always going forth, always brushing up against the numberless persons and things of his world, and always *becoming* the elements he touched, as they became part of him. After 1850, he withdrew for a while into the privacies not only of his family but, more importantly, of his own imagination, in touch now with what he called the "Me myself"—his genius, or muse. It was this latter union between man and muse that, by 1855, produced the most extraordinary first volume of poems this country has so far seen.

One of the things Whitman did not become was a scholar, or even a college graduate. His school days, all spent in the Brooklyn to which his family moved in 1823, ended when he was eleven. Thereafter he was apprenticed as a typesetter for a Long Island newspaper; and characteristically, the boy not only worked at the job, he *became* a typesetter, and typesetting became a part of his imagination. The look of a printed page and the rhetoric of punctuation were integral elements in his poetry—the printing of which he actually set with his own hands or carefully supervised. Between 1831 and 1836, Whitman occasionally wrote articles as well as set type for the paper; and he continued to compose fugitive little pieces from time to time during the five years following, from 1836 to 1841, while he was teaching in a variety of schools in a variety of Long Island villages. Writing, too, became part of him; and Whitman became a writer—at least by intention, announcing very firmly in a newspaper article of 1840, that he "would compose a wonderful and ponderous book . . . [treating] the nature and peculiarities of men, the diversities of their characters. . . . Yes: I *would* write a book! And who shall say that it might not be a very pretty book?"

In 1841, Whitman moved into New York City, where he was absorbed especially by what he called "the fascinating chaos" of lower Broadway, and by the life of saloons and theaters, of operas and art museums. Operatic techniques and museum lore went into his later verses; but what Whitman became at this stage was that elegant stroller, or *boulevardier*, known as a dandy. This role persisted during the five years passed as reporter for a number of New York newspapers: and even after he returned to Brooklyn in 1846 and became editor of the *Eagle*, he came back by ferry to stroll Manhattan on most afternoons. But he was a dandy much caught up in public and political affairs. Among the personae he took on was that of the political activist, an ardent Freesoiler in fact, arguing the exclusion of Negro slavery from the territories with such editorial vehemence that the newspaper's owner fired him in February 1848. Within a matter of days, however, Whitman left for what turned out to be a three-month stay in New Orleans, where he served as assistant editor to that city's *Crescent*. It was there that rumor once assigned him the affair with the Creole lady, that soul-turning initiation into love that is said to have made a poet of him. The legend is almost certainly baseless; but something did happen to Whitman nonetheless. During the long weeks of travel, passing over the vast stretches of land and along the great rivers and lakes (all that "geography and natural life" he catalogues so lavishly in the 1855 Preface), Whitman had his first encounter with the national landscape, and became (it may be hazarded) another of the personalities announced in *Leaves of Grass*: an American.

Back in Brooklyn, Whitman accepted the post of editor-in-chief on the liberal *Freeman* and stayed with it till he resigned in political outrage the following year. He had clearly "become" a journalist, an uncommonly able and effective one; his best poetry sprang in good part from a journalistic imagination—"I witness the corpse with its dabbled hair, I note where the pistol has fallen." At the same time, the forthgoing impulse was nearly—for the moment—exhausted. After expressing his sense of both national and personal betrayal by the Fugitive Slave Law in 1850, Whitman withdrew from the political arena; withdrew from active or regular journalism, and from the life of the city. He moved back to his family and commenced a leisurely existence in which, according to his brother George, "he would lie abed late, and after getting up would write a few hours if he took the notion"—or work at "house-building" for a bit, with his father and brothers, if he took that notion. Now he became a workman; and it was in the role of working-class artisan that he presented himself both in the verses of the 1855 *Leaves of Grass* and in the portrait which appeared as substitute for the author's name in the front of the volume.

For Whitman, I am suggesting, the act of becoming a poet was not a sudden or an unpredictable one. He had always been in the process of becoming a poet, and the figures he successively became, from his school days onward, were not false starts or diversions, but moments in the major process. Typesetter, reporter, dandy, stroller in the city, political activist, surveyor of the national scenery, skilled editor, representative American workman: none of these was ever fully replaced by any other, nor were all at last replaced by the poet. They were absorbed into the poet; and if they do not explain the appearance of genius (nothing can explain that), they explain to some real degree the kind of writing—observant, ambulatory, varied, politically aware, job-conscious—in which *this* particular genius expressed itself.

Signs and symptoms of the poet proper, however, can also be isolated over a good many years. The determination to write a "wonderful" book, in 1840, has already been mentioned; but that was presumably to be a philosophical disquisition in prose. In the early 1840s, the writer-in-general became a writer of fiction, and Whitman contributed a number of moralistic short stories to different New York periodicals, all signed by "Walter Whitman" and none worth remembering. Not much later than that, certainly not later than 1847, Whitman's aspiration turned toward poetry. He began to carry a pocket-size notebook about with him; in this he would jot down topics for poems as they occurred, experimental lines, and trial workings of new metrical techniques. The process was stepped up from 1850 onward. In June 1850, the New York *Tribune* published two free-verse poems by Whitman, the second—later called "Europe: The 72d and 73d Year of These States," on the uprisings of 1848—to be included as the eighth item in the 1855 *Leaves of Grass*. It was probably in 1852 that he composed, though he did not publish, a fairly long poem called "Pictures," which had everything characteristic of his genuine poetry except its maritime movement. And in 1854, the repeal of the Missouri Compromise, and the arrest in Boston of a runaway slave named Anthony Burns, drew from Whitman a forty-line satiric exclamation that would comprise the ninth poem in the first edition—later called "A Boston Ballad."

These creative forays were increasingly stimulated by Whitman's reading, which was not only wide but, as evidence shows, surprisingly careful. He had reviewed works by Carlyle, George Sand, Emerson, Goethe, and others for the Brooklyn *Eagle*. He had known Greek and Roman literature, in translation, for years. "I have wonder'd since," he remarked in A *Backward Glance* (1888), "why I was not overwhelm'd by these mighty masters. Likely because I read them . . . in the full presence of Nature, under the sun . . . [with] the sea rolling in." (The comment suggests much of the quality of Whitman's poetry, wherein a natural atmosphere and sea rhythms help provide fresh versions of ancient and traditional archetypes.) It should be stressed that Whitman's literary education at this time, though it was by no means skimpy, was fairly conventional. It included the major English poets, Shakespeare and Milton especially, but it did not include Oriental writing or the literature of the mystical tradition or that of German idealism—except as those sources reached him faintly through his occasional readings in the essays of Emerson. This is probably to be reckoned fortunate: Whitman's mystical instinct, during his best creative years, was held effectively in check by a passion for the concrete, a commitment to the actual; and discussion of his "mysticism" is well advised to follow his example. Whitman became acquainted, too, with such American writers as Longfellow and Bryant, both of whom he came later to know personally. In addition, he took to making extensive notes and summaries of a long list of periodical essays, mostly dealing with art and artists.

"Art and Artists," in fact, was the title of an essay which Whitman himself read to the Brooklyn Art Union in 1851. And it was here that he first developed his large notion of the artist as hero—of the artist, indeed, as savior or redeemer of the community to which he offers his whole being as champion (sacrificial, if necessary) of freedom and humanity and spiritual health. "Read well the death of Socrates," he said portentously, "and of greater than Socrates." The image of the modern poet as godlike—even Christlike ("greater than Socrates")—was to run through and beneath Whitman's poetry from "Song of Myself" to "Passage to India"; and often, as here, it drew added intensity from Whitman's disillusion with other possible sources for that miraculous national transformation scene he seems to have waited for during most of his life. It was an extravagant notion; but it was one that anticipated several not much less extravagant images, in the twentieth century, of the artist as hero. It was this image, anyhow, that Whitman sought to bring into play in the whole body of the 1855 *Leaves of Grass* and particularly in "Song of Myself."

The first edition contained a long Preface introducing the poet-hero, who is then imaginatively created in the poems that follow. There were twelve of the latter, unnumbered and untitled and of varying length, with unconventional but effective typography—for example:

> The atmosphere is not a perfume . . . . it has no taste of the distillation . . . .
>   it is odorless,
> It is for my mouth forever . . . . I am in love with it.

The first and by far the longest entry was, of course, the poem that in 1881 was labeled "Song of Myself." It is in part genuine though highly original autobiography; in part, it is a form of wish projection. We may think of it, among many other things, as a free-flowing recapitulation of the two processes I have been describing—the process by which a man of many roles becomes a poet, and the process by which the poet becomes a sort of god. There are as many significant aspects to "Song of Myself" as there are critical discussions and analyses of it; if the comment here is mainly limited to the enlargement of its central figure—that is, to the question of its structure—it is because the structure tends to confirm one's sense of Whitman's characteristic movement both in life and in poetry. For if, again, this strange, sometimes baffling, stream-of-consciousness poem does have a discernible structure, an "action" with a beginning, middle, and end, it is almost certainly one that involves the two events or processes just named.

More than one astute reader, while acknowledging a typical pulse or rhythm in the poem, a tidal ebb and flow, has nonetheless denied to it any sustained and completed design. But it may be ventured, perhaps, that "Song of Myself" has not so much a single structure as a number of provisional structures—partly because Whitman, like Melville, believed in a deliberate absence of finish in a work of art; more importantly because of what we may call Whitman's democratic aesthetic. Just as the political activist was absorbed into the poet at some time after 1850, so, and at the same moment, a practical concern with the workings of a democratic society was carried over into the aesthetic realm and applied to the workings of poetry, to the writing and the reading of it. The shape of "Song of Myself" depended, in Whitman's view, on the creative participation of each reader—"I round and finish little," he remarked in A Backward Glance, "the reader will always have his or her part to do, just as much as I have had mine." In a real sense, the poem was intended to have as many structures as there were readers; and the reason was that Whitman aimed not simply to create a poet and then a god, but to assist at the creation of the poetic and godlike in every reader.

Like Emerson, Whitman was here giving a democratic twist to the European Romantic notion of the poet as mankind's loftiest figure. For both Emerson and Whitman the poet's superiority lay exactly in his representativeness. "The poet is representative," Emerson had said, in his essay "The Poet." "He stands among partial men for the complete man, and apprises us not of his wealth, but of the common wealth." This is what Whitman meant when he spoke of "the great poet" as "the equable man"; and it is what he asserted in the opening lines of "Song of Myself":

> I celebrate myself and sing myself
> And what I assume you shall assume.

As one or two commentators—notably Roy Harvey Pearce—have rightly suggested, "Song of Myself" is the first recognizable American epic; but, if so, it is an epic of this peculiar and modern sort. It does not celebrate a hero and an action of ancient days; it creates (and its action is creative) a hero of future days—trusting thereby to summon the heroism implicit in each individual.

Considered in these terms, as the epic consequence of a democratic aesthetic, "Song of Myself" shows a variable number of structural parts. This reader discovers but does not insist upon the following. The invocation leads, in Sections 1 and 2, into a transition from the artificial to the natural—from perfume in houses to the atmosphere of the woods; uncontaminated nature is the first scene of the drama. Next comes the recollection of the union—

mystical in kind, sexual in idiom—between the two dimensions of the poet's being: the limited, conditioned Whitman and the "Me, myself," his creative genius, what Emerson might have called the Over-Soul. This was the union that was consummated somehow and sometime in the early 1850s, and out of which there issued the poem in which the union was itself reenacted.

There follows a long portion, continuing at least through Section 17, where—as a result of union—the *man* becomes a *poet*, and by the very act of creation. What is created is a world, an abundant world of persons and places and things—all sprung into existence by the action of seeing and naming:

> The little one sleeps in its cradle,
> I lift the gauze and look a long time . . .
> The suicide sprawls on the bloody floor of the bedroom,
> I witness the corpse with its dabbled hair . . .
> Where are you off to, lady? for I see you.

The democratic aesthetic is most palpably at work here. What we take at first to be sheer disorder, what some early reviewers regarded as simple slovenliness and lack of form, is in fact something rather different. It is the representation of moral and spiritual and aesthetic equality; of a world carefully devoid of rank or hierarchy. In "Song of Myself," this principle of moral equivalence is not so much stated as "suggested" (one of Whitman's favorite words), and suggested by "indirection" (another favorite word)—by the artfully casual juxtaposition of normally unrelated and unrelatable elements, a controlled flow of associations. Thus:

> The prostitute draggles her shawl, her bonnet bobs on her tipsy and
>   pimpled neck . . .
> The President holding a cabinet council is surrounded by the
>   great Secretaries,
> On the piazza walk three matrons stately and friendly with twined arms,
> The crew of the fish-smack pack repeated layers of halibut in the hold,
> The Missourian crosses the plains toting his wares and his cattle

and so on. In the 1855 Preface, Whitman was willing to make the case explicit: "Each precise object or condition or combination or process exhibits a beauty." And he there illustrated the idea in a succession of still more surprising incongruities: "the multiplication table . . . . old age . . . . the carpenter's trade . . . . the grand-opera."

When, therefore, toward the end of this phase of the poem, the speaker begins to claim for himself the gradually achieved role of poet, it is as the poet of every mode of equality that he particularly wishes to be acknowledged. The announcement runs through Section 25:

> I play not marches for accepted victors only, I play marches for conquer'd
>   and slain persons . . .

> I am the poet of the Body, and I am the poet of the Soul. . . .
> I am the poet of the woman the same as the man . . .
> I am not the poet of goodness only, I do not decline to be the poet
>   of wickedness also.

The *poet* now makes ready for the second great adventure, the long journey, as we may say, toward *godhood*. By way of preparation, he undergoes a second ecstatic experience in Sections 26 and following: an experience of an almost overpoweringly sensuous kind, with the sense of touch so keen as to endanger his health or his sanity: "You villain touch! . . . . you are too much for me." The poet survives, and in Section 33 he is "afoot with [his] vision." In the visionary flight across the universe that is then recounted, the poet enlarges into a divine being by *becoming* each and every element within the totality that he experiences; while the universe in turn is drawn together into a single and harmonious whole since each element in it is invested in common with a portion of the poet's emergent divinity. It is no longer the prostitute who draggles her shawl, the President who holds a cabinet council, the Missourian who crosses the plain: it is "I" who does all that:

> I anchor my ship for a little while only . . .
> I go hunting polar furs and the seal . . .
> I am the man, I suffer'd, I was there . . .
> I am the hounded slave, I wince at the bite of dogs.

And the "I" is itself no longer the individual man-poet; it is the very force or *élan vital* of all humanity.

The journey lasts through Section 33; and in its later moments, as will be noticed, the traveler associates especially with the defeated, the wretched, the wicked, the slaughtered. Whitman's poetic pores were oddly open, as were Melville's, to the grand or archetypal patterns common to the human imagination—so psychologists such as Carl Jung tell us—in all times and places; and the journey of "Song of Myself" requires, at this point, the familiar descent into darkness and hell—until (Section 33) "corpses rise, gashes heal, fastenings roll from me," and an enormous resurrection is accomplished. But what gets reborn, what "troop[s] forth" from the grave is not the poet simply; it is the poet "replenish'd with supreme power," the poet become a divine figure. Just as, by the poetic act of creating a world, the man had previously grown into a poet; so now, by experiencing and, so to speak, melting into the world's totality to its furthest width and darkest depth, the poet expands into a divinity. He has approximated at last that "greater than Socrates" invoked by Whitman in 1851; he has become that saving force which Whitman had proposed was to be the true role of the American poet. It is the divinity who speaks through Sections 39 to 51, proclaiming his divine inheritance ("Taking to myself the exact dimensions of Jehovah," etc.), performing as healer and comforter ("Let the physician and the priest go home"), exhorting every man to his supreme and unique effort. For it is a divinity who insists at every turn that he speaks but for the divine potential of all men. And, having done so, in Section 52 he departs.

Wallace Stevens, the most sophisticated among Whitman's direct poetic descendants, once specified his ancestor's recurrent and dual subject matter in the course of a resonant salute to him in "Like Decorations in a Nigger Cemetery":

> Walt Whitman walking along a ruddy shore
> . . . singing and chanting the things that are part of him
> The worlds that were and will be, death and day.

"Death and day," with its corollary "life and night," is as apt a phrase as one can think of for the extremes between which Whitman's poetry habitually alternates. "Song of Myself" is Whitman's masterpiece, and perhaps America's, in the poetry of "day"—"the song of me rising from bed and meeting the sun"—while "To Think of Time" or "Burial Poem," as Whitman once called it, belongs initially to the poetry of "death," and "The Sleepers" to the poetry of "night." But although both the latter, in their very different ways, explore in depth the dark undergrounds of experience, both return—as "Song of Myself" does—with the conviction of a sort of absolute life. "I swear I think there is nothing but immortality": so ends the meditation in "To Think of Time." And such is the determining sense everywhere in the 1855 edition; we shall shortly have occasion to contrast it with the sense of things in the edition of 1860. It may be helpful, meanwhile, to glance at the 1855 poem "There Was a Child Went Forth," to see how Whitman's characteristic psychological movement was reflected in his poetic technique—how the shifting play of his consciousness was reflected in the shifting play of his craft.

"There Was a Child Went Forth" is Whitman's most unequivocal account of the thrust toward being. It is a poem about growth, about burgeoning and sprouting; and it grows itself, quite literally, in size and thickness. The difference in the sheer physical or typographical look of the first and last stanzas is an immediate clue to the poem's thematic development. Yet what the poet enacts, on the technical side, is not an altogether uninterrupted increase in substance and vitality. The process is rather one of alternation, of enlarging and retracting, of stretching and shrinking—in which, however, the impulse toward growth is *always* dominant. The quantitatively shrunken fourth stanza, for example, is flanked by the longer eight-line stanza that precedes it and the longest, or eighteen-line stanza that follows it and completes the poem's swelling motion: giving us a process in fact of stretching-shrinking-stretching. The same process is present more artfully still within the first stanza, with its rhythmic shift from short line to longer line to still longer and back to shorter once again; but where the line that contains the quantitative shrink is nonetheless a line accentuated by the word "stretching"—"Or for many years or stretching cycles of years." The psychic stretching is thus quietly affirmed at the instant of technical shrinking; and it is the stretching impulse that triumphs and defines the poem.

The same effect is accomplished metrically. "There Was a Child Went Forth" is what is now called free verse; and no doubt the word "free" in this context would have had, had Whitman known the whole term, a political aura, and become a part of his democratic aesthetic. Whitman was the first American poet to break free from the convention of iambic pentameter as the principal and most decorous meter for poetry in English; in so doing he added to the declaration of literary independence—from England, chiefly—that had been triumphantly proclaimed for his generation in Emerson's "The American Scholar" and was the predictable artistic consequence of the political fact. Whitman's was a major gesture of technical liberation, for which every American poet after him has reason to be grateful; every such poet, as William Carlos Williams (a manifest heir of Whitman) has said, must show cause why iambic pentameter is proper for him. But it was not an act of purely negative liberation; it was emancipation with a purpose. It freed Whitman to attempt a closer approximation of metrics and the kind of experience he naturally aimed to express; and it made possible an eventual and occasional return to older and more orderly metrics—to possess them, to use them freshly, to turn them to the poet's established poetic intentions. The long uneven alternations I have been describing could hardly have been conveyed by recurring five- and four-stress lines. Whitman instinctively depended, not on the regular alternating current of the iambic, but on an irregular alternation of *rising* and of *falling* rhythms—which corresponded happily to the rise and fall of the felt life, to the flowing and ebbing—and the rising rhythm, once again, is always in command:

$$\overline{}\ \smile\ \smile\ \overline{}\acute{}\ \smile\ \overline{}$$
There was a child went forth.

And in the poem's conclusion—when a world and a child have been brought fully to interdependent life—the rhythm settles back in a line that neither rises nor falls; a line that rests in a sort of permanent stillness; a subdued iambic of almost perfectly even stress—a convention repossessed in the last long slow series of monosyllables broken only and rightly by the key words "became," "always," and "every":

These became part of that child who went forth every day, and who now goes,
and will always go forth every day.

It is not possible to invoke the imagery of stretching and shrinking without being reminded of sexual analogies, and thereby of the sexual element so prevalent in Whitman's poetry. That element was notably, even blatantly more central to the 1856 edition—it was about several poems in this edition that Thoreau, otherwise much taken with Whitman, said that "It is as if the beasts spoke"—and it operated most tellingly in 1860. Still, it was evident enough in 1855 to startle sensibilities. "Song of Myself" exhibits a degree of sexual bravado mixed with a trace of sexual nostalgia. But the sexual aspect is more apparent in the poem that inhabits the world where Freud and Jung would look for signs of the sexual impulse—the world of dreams. "The Sleepers"—or "Sleep-Chasings," according to its 1860 title—is not only a poem of night and death—"I wander all night in my visions . . . the white features of corpses"—it is a poem of profound psychic disturbance, as the speaker makes clear at once in a superb line that gained force from the 1855 typography: "Wandering and confused . . . . lost to myself . . . . ill-assorted . . . . contradictory." A portion of sexual shame contributes to the uncertainty and deepens the sense of terror—the terror, as Richard Chase has usefully hazarded, of the ego, or conscious self, confronting the id, or the unconscious, and being threatened by extinction. But, in the manner typical of the first *Leaves of Grass*, the poem moves to the discovery of solace amid fear, of pattern amid the random. Descending through the planes of night, "The Sleepers" encounters in its own heart of darkness sources of maternal comfort and spiritual revelation. Guilt is transcended and harmony restored. The adjectives of the opening stanza—"wandering and confused, lost to myself, ill-assorted, contradictory"—are matched and overcome by the adjectives of the poem's close: "sane," "relieved," "resumed," "free," "supple," "awake." There has occurred what Jung would call the "reintegration of the personality"; the ill-assorted psyche has become whole again after passing through what Jung would also call the "night journey." In "The Sleepers," Whitman displayed once more his remarkable talent for arriving by intuition at the great archetypes. And the night journey concludes in that confident recovery of day, that perfect reconciliation with night, that is the distinctive mark of the edition of 1855.

II: 1856

The second edition of *Leaves of Grass* appeared in June 1856, less than a year after the first. There had been several more printings of the latter; and, indeed, during the intervening months Whitman was mainly occupied with the new printings and with reading—and writing—reviews of his work. He still lived with his family in Brooklyn, but he had virtually given up any practical employment. He had "no business," as his mother told Bronson Alcott, "but going out and coming in to eat, drink, write and sleep." The same visitor from Concord quoted Whitman himself as saying that he only "lived to make poems." Over the months he had made twenty new ones, and included them all in the considerably expanded second edition.

Conventional norms of printing crept back a little into this edition. All the poems, old and new, were now numbered and given titles, the new poems always including the word "poem"—a word that obviously had a magical power for Whitman at the time. Among the poems added were: "Poem of Wonder at the Resurrection of Wheat"—to be known more tamely as "This Compost"; "Bunch Poem"—later "Spontaneous Me"; and "Sun-down Poem"—later "Crossing Brooklyn Ferry." The physical appearance of the poems had also become a trifle more conventional, as the eccentric but effective use of multiple dots was abandoned in favor of semicolons and commas. The poetry lost thereby its vivid impression of systole and diastole, of speech and silence, of utterance and pause, always so close to Whitman's psychic and artistic intention: for example, "I am the man . . . . I suffered . . . . I was there" gets crowded together by punctuation and contraction into "I am the man, I suffer'd, I was there." But the earlier mode of punctuation might well have become exceedingly tiresome; and Whitman, in any event, had arrived at that necessary combination of originality and convention by which the most vigorous of talents always perpetuates itself.

For the rest, the new poems dilate upon the determining theme and emotion of the first edition. There is still the awareness of evil, both general and personal: "I am he who knew what it was to be evil/ . . . Had guile, anger, lust, hot wishes I dared not speak/ . . . the wolf, the snake, the hog, not wanting in me" (an unmistakable and highly suggestive borrowing from *King Lear*, III.iv.87 ff.—Whitman drew more on literary sources than he or his critics have normally admitted). There is even a fleeting doubt of his own abilities—"The best I had done seem'd to me blank and suspicious"—a note that would become primary in the 1860 edition. But by and large the compelling emotion is one of unimpeded creative fertility, of irresistible forward-thrusting energy. It registers the enormous excitement of the discovered vocation and of its miracle-making nature: Whitman's response to the experience of having published his first volume and to the headiest of the reviews of the book. Contrary to some reports, including Whitman's forgetful old-age account, the first edition had a reasonably good sale; and among the many reviews in America and England, some were admiring, some were acutely perceptive, and one or two were downright reverential and spoke of Whitman as almost that "greater than Socrates" he had been hoping to become. Much the most stirring for Whitman, of course, was the famous letter from Emerson, which found *Leaves of Grass* "the most extraordinary piece of wit and wisdom that America has yet contributed," with "incomparable things said incomparably well in it." One sentence from this letter—

and without Emerson's permission—adorned the back cover of the 1856 edition: "I greet you at the beginning of a great career."

The tone of the new poems, consequently, was one of achieved and boundless fertility. This is the poetry of day and the poetry of unending flow. The feeling, indeed, is so large and intense as to produce a sense of profound awe: a sense, almost, of terror. That sense arises from Whitman's convinced and total association of his own fecundity ("Spontaneous Me") with that of nature at large ("This Compost"), an association itself enough to intoxicate one. It arises, too, from Whitman's startling view that the creative accomplishment—of the man-poet and of nature—issues from something superficially ugly or shameful or diseased or dead. "Spontaneous Me" mingles two kinds of poems: those that result from the artistic act and those that are involved with the physical act. The act of love, the expression of sexual energy, whether metaphorical or physical, whether heterosexual or homosexual, carries with it a sweeping sensation of shame ("the young man all color'd, red, ashamed, angry"). But the experience fulfills itself in triumph and pride, just as Whitman had deliberately expanded the erotic dimension of the new volume in triumph and pride; it leads to a great "oath of procreation," procreation in every sort; it ends in a full consciousness of wholesome abundance. In much the same way, nature, in "This Compost," reproduces life each spring out of the rotting earth: "Every spear of grass rises out of what was once a catching disease." The conduct of nature—creating life out of death, health out of sickness, beauty out of foulness, "sweet things out of such corruption"—provided Whitman with an example, an analogy to his own creative experience, so immense as to terrify him.

The terror, needless to say, did not disempower but electrified him. The most far-ranging and beautiful of the new poems, "Crossing Brooklyn Ferry," shows Whitman writing under the full force of his assurance—of his assured identification with the *élan vital* of all things. The interplay of the self and the large world it thrusts forward into is on a scale not unlike that of "Song of Myself"; the flow of the consciousness merges with the flow of reality. Every item encountered is a "dumb beautiful minister" to Whitman's responsive spirit; all the items in the universe are "glories strung like beads on my smallest sights and hearings." The complex of natural and human and created objects now forms a sort of glowing totality that is always in movement, always frolicking on. "Crossing Brooklyn Ferry" presents a vision of an entirety moving forward: a vision that is mystical in its sense of oneness but that is rendered in the most palpable and concrete language—the actual picture of the harbor is astonishingly alive and visible. And the poem goes beyond its jubilant cry of the soul—"Flow on river!"—to reach a peace that really does surpass any normal understanding. Whitman was to write poetry no less consummate; but he was never again to attain so final a peak of creative and visionary intoxication.

III: 1860

Whitman, as we have heard his mother saying, was always "going out and coming in." She meant quite literally that her son would go out of the house in the morning, often to travel on the ferry to Manhattan and to absorb the spectacle of life, and would come back into the household to eat and sleep, perhaps to write. But she unwittingly gave a nice maternal formula to the larger, recurring pattern in Whitman's career—the foray into the world and the retreat back into himself and into a creative communion with his genius. The poetry he came in to write—through the 1856 edition just examined— reflected that pattern in content and rhythm, and in a way to celebrate the commanding power of the outward and forward movement. The early poetry bore witness as well, to be sure, of the darker mode of withdrawal, the descent into the abysses of doubt, self-distrust, and the death-consciousness; but it was invariably overcome in a burst of visionary renewal. The poetry of 1855 and 1856 is the poetry of day, of flood tide.

The 1860 *Leaves of Grass*, however, gives voice to genuine desolation. In it, betimes, the self appears as shrunken, indeed as fragmented; the psyche as dying; the creative vigor as dissipated. The most striking of the new poems belong to the poetry not of day but of death. A suggestive and immediate verbal sign of the new atmosphere may be found in the difference of title between so characteristic a poem of 1855 as "There Was a Child Went Forth" and perhaps the key 1860 poem, "As I Ebb'd with the Ocean of Life." Yet the case must be put delicately and by appeal to paradox. For, in a sense, the new death poetry represents in fact Whitman's most remarkable triumph over his strongest feelings of personal and artistic defeat. There has been a scholarly debate over the precise degree of melancholy in the 1860 edition, one scholar emphasizing the note of dejection and another the occasional note of cheerfulness; but that debate is really beside the point. What we have is poetry that expresses the sense of loss so sharply and vividly that substantive loss is converted into artistic gain.

During the almost four years since June 1856, Whitman had once again gone out and come back in; but this time the withdrawal was compelled by suffering and self-distrust. Whitman's foray into the open world, beginning in the fall of 1856, took the form, first, of a brief new interest in the political scene and, second, of a return to journalism, as editor-in-chief of the Brooklyn *Daily Times* from May 1857 until June 1859. In the morning, he busied himself writing editorials and articles for the newspaper; in the afternoon, he traveled into New York, to saunter along lower Broadway and to sit watchful and silent near or amid the literati who gathered in Pfaff's popular Swiss restaurant in the same neighborhood. In the evening, he continued to write—prolifically: seventy poems, more or less, in the first year after the 1856 edition and probably a few more in the months immediately following. Then there occurred a hiatus: a blank in our knowledge of Whitman's life, and apparently a blank in his creative activity. We cannot say just when the hiatus began—sometime in 1858, one judges. It ended, anyhow, at some time before the publication in the December 1859 issue of the New York *Saturday Press* of a poem called "A Child's Reminiscence," its familiar title being "Out of the Cradle Endlessly Rocking."

On the political side, Whitman's disenchantment was even swifter than usual. The choices offered the American public in the election of 1856—Buchanan, Frémont, and Fillmore—seemed to him false, debased, and meaningless; and he called—in an unpublished pamphlet—for a president who might play the part of "Redeemer." His disappointment with the actual, in short, led as before to an appeal for some "greater than Socrates" to arise in America; and, also as before, Whitman soon turned from the political figure to the *poet*, in fact to himself, to perform the sacred function, asserting in his journal that *Leaves of Grass* was to be "the New Bible." (Not until 1866 would the two aspirations fuse in a poem—"When Lilacs Last in the Dooryard Bloom'd"—that found a new idiom of almost biblical sonority to celebrate death in the person of a Redeemer President, Abraham Lincoln.) Meanwhile, however, Whitman's private and inner life was causing him far more grief and dismay than the public life he had been observing.

A chief cause for Whitman's season of despair, according to most Whitman biographers, was a homosexual love affair during the silent months: an affair that undoubtedly took place, that was the source at once of profound joy and profound guilt, and that, when it ended, left Whitman with a desolating sense of loss. Such poems as "A Hand-Mirror" and "Hours Continuing Long, Sore and Heavy-Hearted" testify with painful clarity both to the guilt and to the subsequent misery of loneliness. At the same time, poems such as "As I Ebb'd with the Ocean of Life" and "So Long!" strike a different and perhaps deeper note of loss: a note, that is, of poetic decline, of the loss not so much of a human loved one but of creative energy—accompanied by a loss of confidence in everything that energy had previously brought into being. There had been a hint of this in "Crossing Brooklyn Ferry" in 1856—"The best I had done seem'd to me blank and suspicious"—but there self-doubt had been washed away in a flood of assurance. Now it had become central and almost resistant to hope. It may be that the fear of artistic sterility was caused by the moral guilt; but it seems no less likely that the artistic apprehension was itself at the root of the despair variously echoed in 1860. If so, the apprehension was probably due to a certain climacteric in Whitman's psychic career—what is called *la crise de quarantaine*, the psychological crisis some men pass through when they reach the age of forty. Whitman was forty in May 1859; and it was in the month after his birthday that he wrote two aggressive and, one cannot but feel, disturbed articles for the Brooklyn *Daily Times*—on prostitution and the right to unmarried sexual love—that resulted in his dismissal from the paper. Characteristically dismissed, Whitman characteristically withdrew. But no doubt the safest guess is that a conjunction of these factors—*la quarantaine*, the temporary but fearful exhaustion of talent after so long a period of fertility, the unhappy love affair—begot the new poems that gave "death and night" their prominence in the 1860 edition.

The edition of 1860 contained 154 poems: which is to say that 122 had been composed since 1856, and of these, as has been said, seventy by the summer of 1857. Most of the other fifty, it can be hazarded, were written late in 1859 and in the first six months of 1860. It can also be hazarded that among those latter fifty poems were nearly all the best of the new ones—those grouped under the title "Calamus," the name Whitman gave to his poetry of masculine love. These include "Scented Herbage," "Hours Continuing," "Whoever You Are," "City of Orgies," "A Glimpse," "I Saw in Louisiana," "Out of the Cradle," "As I Ebb'd" (published in the April 1860 issue of the *Atlantic Monthly* as "Bardic Symbols"), and "So Long!"

"A Hand-Mirror" records a feeling of self-loathing almost unequaled in English or American poetry. And it is representative of the entire volume in its emphatic reversal of an earlier work and an earlier course of feeling. In "This Compost," in 1856, Whitman was seized with a wonder verging on terror at the capacity of nature and of man to produce the beautiful out of the foul or shameful; here, in 1860, he is smitten with the dreadful conviction of having, in his own being, produced the foul and the shameful out of the potentially beautiful. "Hours Continuing Long, Sore and Heavy-Hearted" is a statement of pain so severe, so unmitigated, that Whitman deleted the poem from all subsequent editions of *Leaves of Grass*. These poems of pain are uncommonly painful to read; and yet, in the other major new poems of 1860, we find Whitman executing what might be called the grand Romantic strategy—the strategy of converting private devastation into artistic achievement; of composing poetry of high distinction out of a feeling of personal, spiritual, and almost metaphysical extinction. Keats's "Ode on a Grecian Urn" offers an example of the same, at one chronological extreme; as, at another, does Hart Crane's "The Broken Tower."

That strategy is, indeed, what the 1860 edition may be said to be about; for more than the other versions of *Leaves of Grass*, that of 1860 has a sort of plot buried in it. The plot—in a very reduced summary—consists in the discovery that "death" is the source and beginning of "poetry"; with "death" here understood to involve several kinds and sensations of loss, of suffering, of disempowering guilt, of psychic fragmentation; and "poetry" as the awakening of the power to catch and to order reality in language. What had so fundamentally changed since 1855 and 1856 was Whitman's concept of reality. In 1855, as we have seen, the thought of death led to a flat denial of it: "I swear I think there is nothing but immortality." But in "Scented Herbage" of 1860 he arrives at an opposite conclusion: "For now," as he says, "it is convey'd to me that you [death] are . . . the real reality." If Whitman's poetic faculty had formerly been quickened by his sense of the absolute life, it now finds its inspiration in the adventure of death. In "So Long!" Whitman confesses to the death of his talent: "It appears to me that I am dying. . . . My songs cease, I abandon them." Yet in "Scented Herbage" poetry is identified as the very herbage and flower of death, as Baudelaire had a few years earlier identified poetry as the flower of evil; his new poems, for Whitman, are "growing up above me above death." By 1860 Whitman had reached the perception of Wallace Stevens—in "Sunday Morning" (1923)—that "death is the mother of beauty."

Stevens' phrase might serve as motto for the 1860 edition; as it might also serve for another of the several titles for the poem that was first called "A Child's Reminiscence," then "A Word Out of the Sea," and finally (in 1871) "Out of the Cradle Endlessly Rocking." Whatever else occurs in this in every sense brilliant poem, there unmistakably occurs the discovery of poetic power, the magical power of the word, through the experience—here presented as vicarious—of the departure and loss, perhaps the death, of the loved one. It is one of the most handsomely *made* of Whitman's poems; the craft is relaxed, firm, and sure. Only an artist in virtuoso control of his technical resources would attempt a poem with such effortless alternation of narrative (or recitatif) and impassioned aria, such dazzling metrical shifts, such hypnotic exactitude of language, not to mention a narrative "point of view" of almost Jamesian complexity: the man of forty recalling the child of, say, twelve observing the calamitous love affair of two other beings, and the same man of forty projecting, one assumes, his own recent and adult bereavement into the experience of an empathic child. Whitman, by 1860, was very impressively the poet in that word's original meaning of "maker," in addition to being still the poet as inspired singer; and "Out of the Cradle Endlessly Rocking"—for all its supple play of shadows and glancing light—will bear the utmost weight of analysis. But it has perhaps been sufficiently probed elsewhere, and I will instead take a longer look at "As I Ebb'd with the Ocean of Life."

We will not be far wrong, and in any case it will illuminate the pattern of Whitman's career, if we take this poem as an almost systematic inversion of the 1855 poem "There Was a Child Went Forth," as well as an inversion of a key moment—Sections 4 and 5—in the 1855 "Song of Myself." As against that younger Whitman of morning and of spring, of the early lilacs and the red morning-glories, here is the Whitman of the decline of the day and of the year—a poet now found "musing late in the autumn day" (the phrase should be read slowly, as though the chief words were, in the older fashion, divided by dots). All the sprouts and blossoms and fruit of "There Was a Child Went Forth" are here replaced, in the poetically stunning second stanza, by:

> Chaff, straw, splinters of wood, weeds, and the sea-gluten,
> Scum, scales from shining rocks, leaves of salt-lettuce, left by the tide;

to which are added, later, "A few sands and dead leaves," "a trail of drift and debris," and finally:

> loose windrows, little corpses,
> Froth, snowy white, and bubbles,
> (See, from my dead lips the ooze exuding at last . . . .)

The poem's rhythm, instead of pulsating outward in constantly larger spirals (though it seems to try to do that occasionally), tends to fall back on itself, to fall away, almost to disintegrate; no poem of Whitman's shows a more cunning fusion of technique and content. It is here, quite properly, the falling rather than the rising rhythm that catches the ear. As against:

> There was a child went forth,

we now hear:

> Where the fierce old mother endlessly cries for her castaways

—a dying fall that conveys the shrinking away, the psychological slide toward death, the slope into oblivion that the poem is otherwise concerned with.

The major turn in the action appears in the grammatical shift from the past tense of Section 1 ("As I ebb'd," etc.) to the present tense of Section 2 ("As I wend," etc.). It is a shift from the known to the unknown, a shift indeed not so much from one moment of time to another as from the temporal to the timeless, and a shift not so much accomplished as desired. For what produces in the poet his feeling of near-death is just his conviction that neither he nor his poetry has ever known or ever touched upon the true and timeless realm of reality. The essential reality from which he now feels he has forever been cut off is rendered as "the real Me." To get the full force of the despondent confession of failure, one should place the lines about "the real Me" next to those in Sections 4 and 5 in "Song of Myself" where Whitman had exultantly recalled the exact opposite. There he had celebrated a perfect union between the actual Me and the real Me: between the here-and-now

Whitman and that timeless being, that Over-Soul or genius that he addressed as the Me myself. *That*, I suggest, was Whitman's real love affair; that was the union that was consummated in 1855 and that ended—so Whitman temporarily felt—in disunion three or four years later; "the real Me" was the loved one that departed. And now, divorced and disjoined from the real Me, the actual Me threatens to come apart, to collapse into a trail of drift and debris, with ooze exuding from dead lips. (So, by analogy, a Puritan might have felt when cut off, through sin, from the God that created him.)

Still, as Richard Chase has insisted, this poem is saved from any suggestion of whimpering self-pity by the astonishing and courageous tone of self-mockery—in the image of the real Me ridiculing the collapsing Me:

> before all my arrogant poems the real Me stands yet untouch'd, untold, altogether unreach'd,
> Withdrawn far, mocking me with mock-congratulatory signs and bows
> With peals of distant ironical laughter at every word I have written,
> Pointing in silence to these songs, and then to the sand beneath.

It is an image of immeasurable effect. And it is, so to speak, a triumph over its own content. Anyone who could construct an image of the higher power— the one he aspires toward—standing far off and mocking him with little satiric bows and gestures, comparing and consigning his verses to the sandy debris under his feet: such a person has already conquered his sense of sterility, mastered his fear of spiritual and artistic death, rediscovered his genius, and returned to the fullest poetic authority. Within the poem, Whitman identifies the land as his father and the fierce old sea as his mother; he sees himself as alienated no less from them than from the real Me, and he prays to both symbolic parents for a rejuvenation of his poetic force, a resumption of "the secret of the murmuring I envy." But the prayer is already answered in the very language in which it is uttered; Whitman never murmured more beautifully; and this is why, at the depth of his ebbing, Whitman can say, parenthetically, that the flow will return.

IV: 1867

If Whitman, by the spring of 1860, had not been "rescued" by his own internal capacity for resurgence, he would, more than likely, have been rescued anyhow by the enormous public event that began the following April with the outbreak of a national civil war. During the war years, Whitman "went forth" more strenuously than in any other period of his life, and he immersed himself more thoroughly in the activities and sufferings of his fellows. The immediate poetic fruit of the experience was a small, separately published volume of fifty-three new poems, in 1865, called *Drum-Taps*, with a

Sequel to Drum-Taps—containing "When Lilacs Last in the Dooryard Bloom'd"—tacked on to the original in 1866. Both titles were added as an Appendix to the fourth edition of *Leaves of Grass* in 1867, which otherwise contained only a handful of new poems. Several of Whitman's war poems have a certain lyric strength, either of compassion or of sheer imagistic precision; and the meditation occasioned by the death of Lincoln is among his finest artistic achievements. Nonetheless—and however remarkable and admirable his human performance was during the war—it was in this same period that Whitman the poet began to yield to Whitman the prophet, and what had been most compelling in his poetry to give way to the misrepresentation and concealment that disfigured *Leaves of Grass* over the decades to follow.

Until the last days of 1862, Whitman remained in Brooklyn, formally unemployed, making what he could out of earnings from *Leaves of Grass*, and—once the fighting had started—following the course of the war with the liveliest concern. He was initially very much on the side of the North, which he regarded as the side of freedom, justice, and human dignity. But as time went on, he came to be increasingly on the side of the nation as a whole, more anxious to heal wounds than to inflict them—and this, of course, is what he literally turned to doing in 1863. In December of the previous year, he learned that his younger brother Jeff had been wounded. Whitman journeyed south at once, found his brother recuperating satisfactorily near Falmouth, Virginia, and stayed for eight memorable days among the forward troops in the battle area. It was only eight days, but the spectacle of horror and gallantry of which he was the closest eyewitness had an enduring, almost a conversionary effect upon him. He came back north only as far as Washington; and from that moment until 1867, he spent every free moment in the military hospitals, ministering to the needs of the wounded. He became, in fact, a "wound-dresser," though a dresser primarily of spiritual wounds, bearing gifts, writing letters, comforting, sustaining, exhorting; he became, indeed, the physician-priest with whom, in "Song of Myself," he had associated the figure of the poet.

He made a living in Washington through a series of governmental jobs: as assistant to the deputy paymaster for a while; as clerk in the Indian Bureau—a position from which he was summarily dismissed when the bureau chief read *Leaves of Grass* and pronounced it unpardonably obscene; finally in the office of the Department of Interior. Here he stayed, relatively prosperous and content, until he suffered a partly paralyzing stroke in 1873. It was in the same year that, traveling north, ill and exhausted, he settled almost by accident in Camden, New Jersey, where he lived until his death in 1892.

In short, when Whitman went forth this time, or was drawn forth, into the American world of war, he was drawn not merely into New York City but into the center of the country's national life; to the actual battlefields, to the seat of the nation's political power, to the offices of government, to the hospitals, and into the presence of the men who carried on their bodies the burden of the nation's tragedy. It is not surprising that the outer and public life of the country absorbed most of his energy; it is only regrettable that, as a result, and in the course of time, the solitary singer disappeared into the public bard, into the singer of democracy, of companionship, the singer not of "this compost" but of "these States." This was the figure celebrated by William Douglas O'Connor in a book written as an angry and rhapsodic defense of Whitman at the time of his dismissal from the Indian Bureau; a book which, in its title, provided the phrase which all but smothered the genuine Whitman for almost a century: *The Good Gray Poet* (1866).

There had been a faint but ominous foreshadowing of the good gray poet in the 1860 edition: in the frontispiece, where Whitman appeared for the first time as the brooding, far-gazing prophetic figure; in the first tinkerings with and slight revisions of the earlier poems; and in the group of poems called "Chants Democratic," the volume's major blemish. The 1867 edition had no frontispiece at all; but now the process of revising, deleting, and rearranging was fully at work. A number of the "Calamus" poems on manly love, for example, were removed from *Leaves of Grass* once and for all: those which acknowledged or deplored his erotic attraction to another man—including "Hours Continuing." The sexuality of "Song of Myself" and "The Sleepers" was toned down by deleting in particular the orgasmic imagery in both of them. Much of the bizarre and the frantic was taken out of the 1856 and 1860 poetry, in the interest, as Roger Asselineau has put it, of placing "the accent on the poet-prophet rather than on the lover." In a general way, it was the intense and personal *self* of Whitman that got shaded over by the new editing—that self, in its always rhythmic and sometimes wild oscillations, that was the true source and subject of the true poetry. The private self was reshaped into the public person, and the public stage on which this person chanted and intoned became the major subject of the would-be national bard. Whitman became less and less the original artist singing by indirection of his own psychic advances and retreats; he was becoming and wanted to become the Poet of Democracy. No longer the watchful solitary, he was changing into the Poet of Comradeship.

It should not be assumed that, because these were postures, they were necessarily false or worthless; they were simply uncongenial to Whitman's kind of poetry. In the same year, 1867, that *Leaves of Grass* unveiled the prophet of the democratic culture, Whitman also published in the New York *Galaxy* a prose essay called "Democracy," where he set forth much of the evidence that, a few years later, went into the longer essay "Democratic Vistas"—as cogent and searching an account of the conditions of democracy in America, and of their relation to the life of letters, as any American has ever written. But what Whitman could do with this material in prose, he could not do effectively in verse. The democratic element in the early poems was, as has been suggested, an aesthetic element. It was part of the very stress and rhythm of the verse, implicit in the poet's way of looking at persons and things, in the principle of equality in his catalogues and the freedom of his meters, in the dynamic of his relation to his readers. Tackling democracy head on in poetry, Whitman became unpersuasive, even boring.

In the same way, Whitman's poems about the actual war were least striking when they were least personal. There is critical disagreement on this point, but in one reader's opinion, Melville wrote far more authentic war poetry because he had what Whitman did not—a powerful sense of history as allegory. In "The Conflict of Convictions," for example, Melville could suggest the thrust and scale of the struggle in a frame of grand tragedy and in a somberly prophetic mode that the aspiring prophet, Whitman, could never approach. Whitman, the man, had entered the public arena, but his muse did not follow him there; and the enduring poems culled from the war are rather of the intimate and lyrical variety—tender reminiscences or crisp little vignettes like "Cavalry Crossing a Ford," where the image is everything.

There appears among these poems, however, like an unexpected giant out of an earlier age, the work that is widely regarded as Whitman's supreme accomplishment: "When Lilacs Last in the Dooryard Bloom'd." This poem does not, in fact, have quite the artistic finality of "As I Ebb'd" or "Out of the Cradle"; or, rather, its finality is more on the surface, where it is asserted, than in the interior and self-completing pulse of the verses. But, like the other two poems just named, "When Lilacs Last in the Dooryard Bloom'd"—a string of words, D.H. Lawrence once said, that mysteriously makes the ear tingle—has to do with the relation between death and poetry. The death of Lincoln provided the occasion, and the emergent grief of an entire nation served as large but distant background. What is enacted in the foreground, however, is what so often summoned up Whitman's most genuine power: the effort to come to terms with profound sorrow by converting that sorrow into poetry. By finding the language of mourning, Whitman found the answer to the challenge of death. By focusing not on the public event but rather on the vibrations *of* that event—vibrations converted into symbols—within his private self, Whitman produced one of his masterpieces, and perhaps his last unmistakable one.

V: 1871 AND LATER

The transformation that both Whitman's figure and his work had slowly undergone was acknowledged by Whitman himself in his Preface to the fifth edition of *Leaves of Grass*, which had two identical printings in 1871 and 1872, while Whitman was still in Washington. The earlier editions, he said, had dealt with the *"Democratic Individual"* (the italics are his); in the new edition, he is concerned instead with the "Vast, composite, electric *Democratic Nationality.*" It was never clear just what the latter entity amounted to; and in any case, Whitman was not able to make it susceptible to satisfactory poetic expression. It became the subject not of poetry but of oratory and rant—elements that had always been present in Whitman's work but that, for the most part, had hitherto been sweetened by music and, as it were, liquified by verbal sea-drift.

Oratory and rant were unhappily notable even in the most interesting of the new poems added to the 1871 edition, "Passage to India." But the case of "Passage to India" is peculiar. It was stimulated by several public events (including, for one, the opening of the Suez Canal), stimuli usually dangerous for Whitman unless he could instantly personalize them, as here he could not. The poem not only bespeaks the ultimate union of all times and places and peoples but finds in that condition a universal reality; and as Richard Chase has remarked, "Whenever [Whitman] headed for the universal he was headed for trouble." The poem moves swiftly away from the tough entanglements of the concrete that were the vital strength of works as different as "Song of Myself" or "Crossing Brooklyn Ferry" or "As I Ebb'd"; and, arriving at a realm of bodiless vapor, Whitman can only utter such bodiless lines as: "the past—the infinite greatness of the past!"—which is an exclamation without content. Yet "Passage to India" is interesting, because, while providing an example of Whitman's bombast, it is also technically most accomplished. It completes a kind of parabola of Whitman's craftsmanship: from 1855, where consciousness and craft were discovering each other; through 1856 and 1860, where power and technique were very closely fused; to the later sixties, where technique almost superseded content. The technique in question is primarily a manipulation of sound patterns, something too involved to be analyzed here in detail: an extremely skillful distribution of sheer sounds, without any regard for substance. "Passage to India" is interesting too, by way of historical footnote, for the obsessive effect it was to have more than fifty years later on Hart Crane. It virtually supplied the initiating force for *The Bridge*, especially for the "Atlantis" section, the first portion of his symbolist epic that Crane composed.

Whitman spent the last nineteen years of his life in Camden, New Jersey. He made a partial recovery from the stroke of 1873, but then suffered further seizures from time to time until the one that carried him off. In between these bouts, he continued to "go out" as much as he could: to nearby Philadelphia frequently, to Baltimore and Washington, to New York, and once—in 1879—to Kansas, Colorado, and Canada. Otherwise he remained in Camden, writing short and generally trivial poems, a great amount of prose, and countless letters to friends and admirers all over the world. His old age was punctuated by a series of controversies about him in the public press: in 1876, for example, when a clamor from England to raise a subscription for Whitman was countered by a verbal assault upon him in the New York *Tribune* by Bayard Taylor. The charge was almost always obscenity; in the instance mentioned, the charge only aroused the English to greater efforts, and Whitman was so encouraged as to feel, in his own word, "saved" by the contributions—then and later—of Rossetti, Tennyson, Ruskin, Gosse, Saintsbury, and others. Longfellow and Oscar Wilde, old Dr. Holmes and Henry James, Sr., were among the visitors to his Camden home. He became the genius of the city; and his birthday became an annual celebration. It was amid such flurries of support and defamation, idolatry and contempt, that the old man—cheerful and garrulous to the end—succumbed at last to a horde of diseases that would have killed most men many years sooner.

Whitman *was*, as M. Asselineau says of him, a "heroic invalid." But it may be that his physical and psychological heroism as a man was what produced, by overcompensating for the terrible discomforts he felt, the relentless optimism of so much of his writing in the last two decades—optimism not only about himself and his condition, but about America and about history: for which and in which every disaster, every betrayal was seen by Whitman as a moment in the irresistible progress of things toward the better. The "word signs" of his poetry after 1867 became, as Whitman himself remarked in A *Backward Glance O'er Travel'd Roads* (1888), "Good Cheer, Content and Hope," along with "Comradeship for all lands." Those were also the words that fixed and froze the popular understanding of the poet.

Mention of A *Backward Glance*, however, reminds one that Whitman's most valuable work after 1867 tended to be in prose rather than in verse. The sixth edition of *Leaves of Grass*, printed in 1876 and called the "Centennial Edition" (America's centennial—America now being Whitman's subject), added almost no significant new poetry; but it did include the remarkable essay "Democratic Vistas." The latter poises a noble emphasis upon individual integrity against the moral squalor of a society that was already an impossible mixture of chaos and conformity; and in its plea for "national original archetypes in literature" that will truly "put the nation in form," it presents one of the great statements about the relation between art and culture. The next or seventh edition, that of 1881–82, contained the fine little image of the copulative collision of two eagles—an image based on a written description of such an event by Whitman's friend John Burroughs— and a poem that, with two others, gave cause for the suppression of the entire volume, following a complaint by the Society for the Prevention of Vice. But this edition was also characterized by endless revisions and expurgations and, now especially, regroupings of earlier poems: the process whereby the old man steadily buried his youth. In the same year, though, Whitman also published a separate volume of prose: *Specimen Days and Collect*. In it, along with *Specimen Days* and the several indispensable prefaces to *Leaves of Grass*, were "Democratic Vistas," Civil War reminiscences, and Whitman's annual lecture on Lincoln. *A Backward Glance* first appeared in 1888; the following year it served as the Preface to, and was the one memorable new piece of writing in, the *Leaves of Grass* of 1889.

Though it is indeed memorable and even beguiling, *A Backward Glance* is also somewhat misleading. The real motivations and the actual achievement of *Leaves of Grass* lie half-forgotten behind the comradeship, good cheer, and democratic enthusiasm of the ailing elderly bard. Like F. Scott Fitzgerald, Whitman could have said, though one cannot imagine him doing so, that he had found his proper form at a certain moment in his career, but that he had then been diverted into other forms, other endeavors less appropriate to his talent. The fact that it was in these other forms that Whitman's reputation got established makes the development more lamentable. At his best, Whitman was not really the bard of the democratic society at all; nor was he the prophet of the country's and the world's glorious future. He was, perhaps, the poet of an aesthetic and moral democracy. But he was above all the poet of the self and of the self's swaying motion—outward into a teeming world where objects were "strung like beads of glory" on his sight; backward into private communion with the "real Me." He was the poet of the self's motion downward into the abysses of darkness and guilt and pain and isolation, and upward to the creative act in which darkness was transmuted into beauty. When the self became lost to the world, Whitman was lost for poetry. But before that happened, Whitman had, in his own example, made poetry possible in America.

HAROLD BLOOM

Whitman's Image of Voice:
To the Tally of My Soul

Where does the individual accent of an American poetry begin? How, then and now, do we recognize the distinctive voice that we associate with an American Muse? Bryant, addressing some admonitory lines, in 1830, *To Cole, the Painter, Departing for Europe*, has no doubts as to what marks the American difference:

> Fair scenes shall greet thee where thou goest—fair,
> But different—everywhere the trace of men,
> To where life shrinks from the fierce Alpine air.
> Gaze on them, till the tears shall dim thy sight,
> But keep that earlier, wilder image bright.

Only the Sublime, from which life shrinks, constitutes a European escape from the trace of men. Cole will be moved by that Sublime, yet he is to keep vivid the image of priority, an American image of freedom, for which Emerson and Thoreau, like Bryant before them, will prefer the trope of "wildness." The wildness triumphs throughout Bryant, a superb poet, always and still undervalued, and one of Hart Crane's and Wallace Stevens's legitimate ancestors. The voice of an American poetry goes back before Bryant, and can be heard in Bradstreet and Freneau (not so much, I think, in Edward Taylor, who was a good English poet who happened to be living in America). Perhaps, as with all origins, the American poetic voice cannot be traced, and so I move from my first to my second opening question: how to recognize the Muse of America. Here is Bryant, in the strong opening of his poem *The Prairies*, in 1833:

These are the gardens of the Desert, these
The unshorn fields, boundless and beautiful,
For which the speech of England has no name—
The Prairies, I behold them for the first
And my heart swells, while the dilated sight
Takes in the encircling vastness. . . .

Bryant's ecstatic beholding has little to do with what he sees. His speech swells most fully as he intones "The Prairies," following on the prideful reflection that no English poet could name these grasslands. The reflection itself is a touch awkward, since the word after all is French, and not Amerindian, as Bryant knew. No matter; the beholding is still there, and truly the name is little more important than the sight. What *is* vital is the dilation of the sight, an encircling vastness more comprehensive even than the immensity being taken in, for it is only a New England hop, skip and a jump from this dilation to the most American passage that will ever be written, more American even than Huck Finn telling Aunt Polly that he lies just to keep in practice, or Ahab proclaiming that he would strike the sun if it insulted him. Reverently I march back to where I and the rest of us have been before and always must be again, crossing a bare common, in snow puddles, at twilight, under a clouded sky, in the company of our benign father, the Sage of Concord, teacher of that perfect exhilaration in which, with him, we are glad to the brink of fear:

. . . Standing on the bare ground,—my head bathed by the blithe air and uplifted into infinite space,—all mean egotism vanishes. I become a transparent eyeball; I am nothing; I see all; the currents of the Universal Being circulate through me; I am part or parcel of God. . . .

Why is this ecstasy followed directly by the assertion: "The name of the nearest friend sounds then foreign and accidental . . ."? Why does the dilation of vision to the outrageous point of becoming a transparent eyeball provoke a denaturing of even the nearest name? I hasten to enforce the obvious, which nevertheless is crucial: the name is not forgotten, but loses the sound of immediacy; it becomes foreign or out-of-doors, rather than domestic; and accidental, rather than essential. A step beyond this into the American Sublime, and you do not even forget the name; you never hear it at all:

And now at last the highest truth on this subject remains unsaid; probably cannot be said; for all that we say is the far-off remembering of the intuition. That thought by what I can now nearest approach to say it, is this. When good is near you, when you have life in yourself, it is not by any known or accustomed way; you shall not discern the footprints of any other; you shall not see the face of man; you shall not hear any name;—the way, the thought, the good, shall be wholly strange and new. . . .

"This subject" is self-reliance, and the highest truth of it would appear to be voiceless, except that Emerson's voice does speak out to tell us of the influx of the Newness, in which no footprints or faces are to be seen, and no name is to be heard. Unnaming always has been a major mode in poetry, far more than naming; perhaps there cannot be a poetic naming that is not founded upon an unnaming. I want to leap from these prose unnamings in Emerson, so problematic in their possibilities, to the poem in which, more than any other, I would seek to hear Emerson's proper voice for once in verse, a voice present triumphantly in so many hundreds of passages throughout his prose:

> Pour, Bacchus! the remembering wine;
> Retrieve the loss of me and mine!
> Vine for vine be antidote,
> And the grape requite the lote!
> Haste to cure the old despair,—
> Reason in Nature's lotus drenched,
> The memory of ages quenched;
> Give them again to shine;
> Let wine repair what this undid;
> And where the infection slid,
> A dazzling memory revive;
> Refresh the faded tints,
> Recut the aged prints,
> And write my old adventures with the pen
> Which on the first day drew,
> Upon the tablets blue,
> The dancing Pleiads and eternal men.

But why is Bacchus named here, if you shall not hear any name? My question would be wholly hilarious if we were to literalize Emerson's splendid chant. Visualize the Sage of Concord, gaunt and spare, uncorking a bottle in Dionysiac abandon, before emulating the Pleiads by breaking into a Nietzschean dance. No, the Bacchus of Ralph Waldo is rather clearly another unnaming. As for voice, it is palpably absent from this grand passage, its place taken up not even by writing, but by rewriting, by that revisionary pen which has priority, and which drew before the tablets darkened and grew small.

I am going to suggest shortly that rewriting is an invariable trope for voicing, within a poem, and that voicing and reseeing are much the same poetic process, a process reliant upon unnaming, which rhetorically means the undoing of a prior metonymy. But first I am going to leap ahead again, from Emerson to Stevens, which is to pass over the great impasse of Whitman, with whom I have identified always Hart Crane's great trope: "Oval encyclicals in canyons heaping / The impasse high with choir." Soon enough this discourse will center upon Whitman, since quite simply he *is* the

American Sublime, he *is* voice in our poetry, he *is* our answer to the Continent now, precisely as he was a century ago. Yet I am sneaking up on him, always the best way for any critic to skulk near the Sublime Walt. His revisionism, of self as of others, is very subtle; his unnamings and his voices come out of the Great Deep. Stevens's are more transparent:

> Throw away the lights, the definitions,
> And say of what you see in the dark
> That it is this or that it is that,
> But do not use the rotted names.
>
> Phoebus is dead, ephebe. But Phoebus was
> A name for something that never could be named.
> There was a project for the sun and is.
>
> There is a project for the sun. The sun
> Must bear no name, gold flourisher, but be
> In the difficulty of what it is to be.
>
> This is nothing until in a single man contained,
> Nothing until this named thing nameless is
> And is destroyed. He opens the door of his house
>
> On flames. The scholar of one candle sees
> An Arctic effulgence flaring on the frame
> Of everything he is. And he feels afraid.

What have these three unnaming passages most in common? Well, what are we doing when we give pet names to those we love, or give no names to anyone at all, as when we go apart in order to go deep into ourselves? Stevens's peculiar horror of the commonplace in names emerges in his litany of bizarre, fabulistic persons and places, but though that inventiveness works to break casual continuities, it has little in common with the true break with continuity in poets like Lewis Carroll and Edward Lear. Stevens, *pace* Hugh Kenner, is hardly the culmination of the poetics of Lear. He may *not* be the culmination of Whitman's poetics either, since that begins to seem the peculiar distinction of John Ashbery. But like Whitman, Stevens does have a link to the Lucretian Sublime, as Pater the Epicurean did, and such a Sublime demands a deeper break with commonplace continuities than is required by the evasions of nonsense and fantasy. The most authentic of literary Sublimes has the Epicurean purpose of rendering us discontented with easier pleasures in order to prepare us for the ordeal of more difficult pleasures. When Stevens unnames he follows, however unknowingly, the trinity of negative wisdom represented by Emerson, Pater and Nietzsche. Stevens himself acknowledged only Nietzsche, but the unfashionable Emerson and Pater were even stronger in him, with Emerson (and Whitman) repressedly the strongest of strains. Why not, after all, use the rotted names? If the things were things that never could be named, is not one name as bad anyway as another? Stevens's masterpiece is not named *The Somethings of Autumn*, and not only because the heroic desperation of the Emersonian scholar of one candle is not enough. Whether you call the auroras flames or an Arctic effulgence or call them by the trope now stuck into dictionaries, auroras, you are giving your momentary consent to one arbitrary substitution or another. Hence Emerson's more drastic and Bacchic ambition; write your *old* adventures, not just your new, with the Gnostic pen of our forefather and foremother, the Abyss. I circle again the problematic American desire to merge voicing and revisionism into a single entity, and turn to Whitman for a central text, which will be the supposed elegy for Lincoln, *When Lilacs Last in the Dooryard Bloom'd*. So drastic is the amalgam of voicing, unnaming and revisionism here that I take as prelude first Whitman's little motto poem, *As Adam Early in the Morning*, so as to set some of the ways for approaching what is most problematic in the great elegy, its images of voice and of voicing.

What can we mean when we speak of the *voice* of the poet, or the voice of the critic? Is there a pragmatic sense of voice, in discussing poetry and criticism, that does not depend upon the illusions of metaphysics? When poetry and criticism speak of "images of voice," what is being imaged? I think I can answer these questions usefully in the context of my critical enterprise from *The Anxiety of Influence* on, but my answers rely upon a post-philosophical pragmatism which grounds itself upon what has worked to make up an American tradition. Voice in American poetry always necessarily must include Whitman's oratory, and here I quote from it where it is most economical and persuasive, a five-line poem that centers the canon of our American verse:

> As Adam early in the morning,
> Walking forth from the bower refresh'd with sleep,
> Behold me where I pass, hear my voice, approach,
> Touch me, touch the palm of your hand to my body as I pass,
> Be not afraid of my body.

What shall we call this striding stance of the perpetually passing Walt, prophetic of Stevens's singing girl at Key West, and of Stevens's own Whitman walking along a ruddy shore, singing of death and day? Rhetorically the stance is wholly transumptive, introjecting earliness, but this is very unlike the Miltonic transuming of tradition. Walt is indeed Emerson's new Adam, American and Nietzschean, who can live as if it were morning, but though he is *as* the Biblical and Miltonic Adam, that "as" is one of Stevens's "intricate evasions of as." The Old Adam was not a savior, except in certain Gnostic traditions of Primal Man; the new, Whitmanian Adam indeed is Whitman himself, more like Christ than like Adam, and more like the Whitmanian

Christ of Lawrence's *The Man Who Died* than like the Jesus of the Gospels.

Reading Whitman's little poem is necessarily an exercise both in a kind of repression and in a kind of introjection. To read the poem strongly, to voice its stance, is to transgress the supposed boundary between reading or criticism, and writing or poetry. "As" governs the three words of origins— "Adam," "early" and "morning"—and also the outgoing movement of Whitman, walking forth refreshed from a bower (that may be also a tomb), emerging from a sleep that may have been a kind of good death. Whitman placed this poem at the close of the *Children of Adam* division of *Leaves of Grass*, thus positioning it between the defeated American pathos of *Facing West from California's Shores* and the poignant *In Paths Untrodden* that begins the homoerotic *Calamus* section. There is a hint, in this contextualization, that the astonished reader needs to cross a threshold also. Behold Whitman as Adam; do not merely regard him when he is striding past. The injunctions build from that "behold" through "hear" and "approach" to "touch," a touch then particularized to the palm, as the resurrected Walt passes, no phantom, but a risen body. "Hear my voice" is the center. As Biblical trope, it invokes Jehovah walking in Eden in the cool of the day, but in Whitman's American context it acquires a local meaning also. Hear my voice, and not just my words; *hear me as voice*. Hear me, as in my elegy for President Lincoln, I hear the hermit thrush.

Though the great elegy finds its overt emblems in the lilac-bush and the evening star, its more crucial tropes substitute for those emblems. These figures are the sprig of lilac that Whitman places on the hearse and the song of the thrush that floods the western night. Ultimately these are one trope, one image of voice, which we can follow Whitman by calling the "tally," playing also on a secondary meaning of "tally," as double or agreement. "Tally" may be Whitman's most crucial trope or ultimate image of voice. As a word, it goes back to the Latin *talea* for twig or cutting, which appears in this poem as the sprig of lilac. The word meant originally a cutting or stick upon which notches are made so as to keep count or score, but first in the English and then in the American vernacular it inevitably took on the meaning of a sexual score. The slang words "tallywoman," meaning a lady in an illicit relationship, and "tallywhack" or "tallywags," for the male genitalia, are still in circulation. "Tally" had a peculiar, composite meaning for Whitman in his poetry, which has not been noted by his critics. In the odd, rather luridly impressive death-poem *Chanting the Square Deific*, an amazing blend of Emerson and an Americanized Hegel, Whitman identifies himself with Christ, Hermes and Hercules and then writes: "All sorrow, labor, suffering, I, tallying it, absorb it in myself." My comment would be: "Precisely *how* does he tally it?" and the answer to that question, grotesque as initially it must seem, would be: "Why, first by masturbating, and then by writing poems." I am being merely accurate, rather than outrageous, and so I turn to *Song of Myself*, section 25, as first proof-text:

Dazzling and tremendous how quick the sun-rise would kill me,
If I could not now and always send sun-rise out of me.
We also ascend dazzling and tremendous as the sun,
We found our own O my soul in the calm and cool of the daybreak.
My voice goes after what my eyes cannot reach,
With the twirl of my tongue I encompass worlds and volumes of worlds.

Speech is the twin of my vision, it is unequal to measure itself,
It provokes me forever, it says sarcastically,
Walt you contain enough, why don't you let it out then?

Come now I will not be tantalized, you conceive too much of articulation,
Do you not know O speech how the buds beneath you are folded?
Waiting in gloom, protected by frost,
The dirt receding before my prophetical screams,
I underlying causes to balance them at last,
My knowledge my live parts, it keeping tally with the meaning of all things,
Happiness, (which whoever hears me let him or her set out in search of this day.)

My final merit I refuse you, I refuse putting from me what I really am,
Encompass worlds, but never try to encompass me,
I crowd your sleekest and best by simply looking toward you.

Writing and talk do not prove me,
I carry the plenum of proof and every thing else in my face,
With the hush of my lips I wholly confound the skeptic.

At this, almost the mid-point of his greatest poem, Whitman is sliding knowingly near crisis, which will come upon him in the crossing between sections 27 and 28. But here he is too strong, really too strong, and soon will pay the price of that over-strength, according to the Emersonian iron Law of Compensation, that nothing is got for nothing. Against the sun's mocking taunt: "See then whether you shall be master!" Whitman sends forth his own sunrise, which is a better, a more Emersonian answer than what Melville's Ahab threatens when he cries out, with surpassing Promethean eloquence: "I'd strike the sun if it insulted me!" As an alternative dawn, Whitman crucially identifies himself as a voice, a voice overflowing with presence, a presence that is a sexual self-knowledge: "My knowledge my live parts, it keeping tally with the meaning of all things." His knowledge and sexuality are one, and we need to ask: how does that sexual self-knowing keep tally with the meaning of all things? The answer comes in the crisis sequence of sections 26–30, where Whitman starts with listening and then regresses to touch, until he achieves both orgasm and poetic release through a Sublime yet quite literal masturbation. The sequence begins conventionally enough with bird song and human voice, passes to music, and suddenly becomes very extraordinary, in a passage critics have admired greatly but have been unable to expound:

> The orchestra whirls me wider than Uranus flies,
> It wrenches such ardors from me I did not know I possess'd them,
> It sails me, I dab with bare feet, they are lick'd by the indolent waves,
> I am cut by bitter and angry hail, I lose my breath,
> Steep'd amid honey'd morphine, my windpipe throttled in fakes of death,
> At length let up again to feel the puzzle of puzzles,
> And that we call Being.

This Sublime antithetical flight (or repression) not only takes Whitman out of nature, but makes him a new kind of god, ever-dying and ever-living, a god whose touchstone is of course voice. The ardors wrenched from him are operatic, and the cosmos becomes stage machinery, a context in which the whirling bard first loses his breath to the envious hail, then sleeps a drugged illusory death in uncharacteristic silence, and at last is let up again to sustain the enigma of Being. For this hero of voice, we expect now a triumphant ordeal by voice, but surprisingly we get an equivocal ordeal by sexual self-touching. Yet the substitution is only rhetorical, and establishes the model for the tally in the Lincoln elegy, since the sprig of lilac will represent Whitman's live parts, and the voice of the bird will represent those ardors so intense, so wrenched from Whitman, that he did not know he possessed them.

After praising his own sensitivity of touch, Whitman concludes section 27 with the highly equivocal line: "To touch my person to some one else's is about as much as I can stand." The crisis section proper, 28, centers upon demonstrating that to touch his own person is also about as much as Whitman can stand. By the time he cries out: "I went myself first to the headland, my own hands carried me there," we can understand how the whole 1855 *Song of Myself* may have grown out of an early notebook jotting on the image of the headland, a threshold stage between self-excitation and orgasm. Section 28 ends with frankly portrayed release:

> You villain touch! what are you doing? my breath is tight in its throat,
> Unclench your floodgates, you are too much for me.

The return of the image of breath and throat, of voice, is no surprise, nor will the attentive reader be startled when the lines starting section 29 take a rather more affectionate view of touch, now that the quondam villain has performed his labor:

> Blind loving wrestling touch, sheath'd hooded sharp-tooth'd touch!
> Did it make you ache so, leaving me?

Since Whitman's "rich showering rain" fructifies into a golden, masculine landscape, we can call this sequence of *Song of Myself* the most productive masturbation since the ancient Egyptian myth of a god who masturbates the world into being. I suggest now (and no Whitman scholar will welcome it) that a failed masturbation is the concealed reference in section 2 of the *Lilacs* elegy:

> O powerful western fallen star!
> O shades of night—O moody, tearful night!
> O great star disappear'd—O the black murk that hides the star!
> O cruel hands that hold me powerless—O helpless soul of me!
> O harsh surrounding cloud that will not free my soul.

The cruel hands are Whitman's own, as he vainly seeks relief from his repressed guilt, since the death of Father Abraham has rekindled the death, a decade before, of the drunken Quaker carpenter-father, Walter Whitman, Senior. Freud remarks, in *Mourning and Melancholia*, that

> . . . there is more in the content of melancholia than in that of normal grief. In melancholia the relation to the object is no simple one; it is complicated by the conflict of ambivalence. This latter is either constitutional, i.e. it is an element of every love-relation formed by this particular ego, or else it proceeds from precisely those experiences that involved a threat of losing the object. . . . Constitutional ambivalence belongs by nature to what is repressed, while traumatic experiences with the object may have stirred to activity something else that has been repressed. Thus everything to do with these conflicts of ambivalence remains excluded from consciousness, until the outcome characteristic of melancholia sets in. This, as we know, consists in the libidinal cathexis that is being menaced at last abandoning the object, only, however, to resume its occupation of that place in the ego whence it came. So by taking flight into the ego love escapes annihilation. . . .

Both conflicts of ambivalence are Whitman's in the *Lilacs* elegy, and we will see love fleeing into Whitman's image of voice, the bird's tallying chant, which is the last stance of his ego. Freud's ultimate vision of primal ambivalence emphasized its origin as being the dialectical fusion/defusion of the two drives, love and death. Whitman seems to me profounder even than Freud as a student of the interlocking of these antithetical drives that darkly combine into one Eros and its shadow of ruin, to appropriate a phrase from Shelley. Whitman mourns Lincoln, yes, but pragmatically he mourns even more intensely for the tally, the image of voice he cannot as yet rekindle into being, concealed as it is by a "harsh surrounding cloud" of impotence. The miraculous juxtaposition of the two images of the tally, sprig of lilac and song of the hermit thrush, in sections 3 and 4 following, points the possible path out of Whitman's death-in-life:

3

In the dooryard fronting an old farm-house near the white-wash'd palings,
Stands the lilac-bush tall-growing with heart-shaped leaves of rich green,
With many a pointed blossom rising delicate, with the perfume strong I love,
With every leaf a miracle—and from this bush in the dooryard,
With delicate-color'd blossoms and heart-shaped leaves of rich green,
A sprig with its flower I break.

4

In the swamp in secluded recesses,
A shy and hidden bird is warbling a song.

Solitary the thrush,
The hermit withdrawn to himself, avoiding the settlements,
Sings by himself a song.

Song of the bleeding throat,
Death's outlet song of life, (for well dear brother I know,
If thou wast not granted to sing thou would'st surely die.)

Whitman breaks the *talea*, in a context that initially suggests a ritual of castration, but the image offers more than a voluntary surrender of manhood. The broken lilac sprig is exactly analogous to the "song of the bleeding throat," and indeed the analogy explains the otherwise baffling "bleeding." For what has torn the thrush's throat? The solitary song itself, image of wounded voice, is the other *talea*, and has been broken so that the soul can take count of itself. Yet why must these images of voice be broken? Whitman's answer, a little further on in the poem, evades the "why" much as he evades the child's "What is the grass?" in *Song of Myself* 6, for the *why* like the *what* is unknowable in the context of the Epicurean-Lucretian metaphysics that Whitman accepted. Whitman's answer comes in the hyperbolic, daemonic, repressive force of his copious over-breaking of the tallies:

Here, coffin that slowly passes,
I give you my sprig of lilac.

7

(Nor for you, for one alone,
Blossoms and branches green to coffins all I bring,
For fresh as the morning, thus would I chant a song for you O sane and
    sacred death.

All over bouquets of roses,
O death, I cover you over with roses and early lilies,
But mostly and now the lilac that blooms the first,
Copious I break, I break the sprigs from the bushes,
With loaded arms I come, pouring for you,
For you and the coffins all of you O death.)

Why should we be moved that Whitman intones: "O sane and sacred death," rather than: "O insane and obscene death," which might seem to be more humanly accurate? "Death" here is a trope for the sane and sacred Father Abraham, rather than for the actual father. Whitman's profuse breaking of the tallies attempts to extend this trope, so as to make of death itself an ultimate image of voice or tally of the soul. It is the tally and not literal death, our death, that is sane and sacred. But that returns us to the figuration of the tally, which first appears in the poem as a verb, just before the carol of death:

> And the charm of the carol rapt me,
> As I held as if by their hands my comrades in the night,
> And the voice of my spirit tallied the song of the bird.

"My knowledge my live parts, it keeping tally with the meaning of all things" now transfers its knowledge from the vital order to the death-drive. I am reminded that I first became aware of Whitman's crucial trope by pondering its remarkable use by Hart Crane, when he invokes Whitman directly in the "Cape Hatteras" section of *The Bridge*:

> O Walt!—Ascensions of thee hover in me now
> As thou at junctions elegiac, there, of speed,
> With vast eternity, dost wield the rebound seed!
> The competent loam, the probable grass,—travail
> Of tides awash the pedestal of Everest, fail
> Not less than thou in pure impulse inbred
> To answer deepest soundings! O, upward from the dead
> Thou bringest tally, and a pact, new bound
> Of living brotherhood!

Crane's allusion is certainly to the *Lilacs* elegy, but his interpretation of what it means to bring tally "upward from the dead" may idealize rather too generously. That Walt's characteristic movement is ascension cannot be doubted, but the operative word in this elegy is "passing." The coffin of the martyred leader passes first, but in the sixteenth and final section it is the bard who passes, still tallying both the song of the bird and his own soul. That the tally is crucial, Crane was more than justified in emphasizing, but then Crane was a great reader as well as a great writer of poetry. Flanking the famous carol of death are two lines of the tally: "And the voice of my spirit tallied the song of the bird" preceding, and "To the tally of my soul" following. To tally the hermit thrush's carol of death *is* to tally the soul, for what is measured is the degree of sublimity, the agonistic answer to the triple question: more? less? equal? And the Sublime answer in death's carol is surely "more":

> Come lovely and soothing death,
> Undulate round the world, serenely arriving, arriving,

In the day, in the night, to all, to each,
Sooner or later delicate death.

Prais'd be the fathomless universe,
For life and joy, and for objects and knowledge curious,
And for love, sweet love—but praise! praise! praise!
For the sure-enwinding arms of cool-enfolding death.

Dark mother always gliding near with soft feet,
Have none chanted for thee a chant of fullest welcome?
Then I chant it for thee, I glorify thee above all,
I bring thee a song that when thou must indeed come, come unfalteringly.

Approach strong deliveress,
When it is so, when thou hast taken them I joyously sing the dead,
Lost in the loving floating ocean of thee,
Laved in the flood of thy bliss O death.

If this grand carol, as magnificent as the Song of Songs which is Solomon's, constitutes the tally or image of voice of the soul, then we ought now to be able to describe that image. To tally, in Whitman's sense, is at once to measure the soul's actual and potential sublimity, to overcome object-loss and grief, to gratify one's self sexually by one's self, to compose the thousand songs at random of *Leaves of Grass*, but above all, as Crane said, to bring a new covenant of brotherhood, and here that pact is new bound with the voice of the hermit thrush. The bird's carol, which invokes the oceanic mother of Whitman's *Sea-Drift* cosmos, is clearly not its tally but Whitman's own, the transgressive verbal climax of his own family romance. When, in the elegy's final section, Whitman chants himself as "Passing the song of the hermit bird and the tallying song of my soul," he prepares himself and us for his abandonment of the image of the lilac. And, in doing so, he prepares us also for his overwhelming refusal or inability to yield up similarly the darker image of the tally:

> Yet each to keep and all, retrievements out of the night,
> The song, the wondrous chant of the gray-brown bird,
> And the tallying chant, the echo arous'd in my soul. . . .

The tally is an echo, as an image of voice must be, yet truly it does not echo the carol of the hermit thrush. Rather, it echoes the earlier Whitman, of *Out of the Cradle Endlessly Rocking*, and his literary father, the Emerson of the great *Essays*. But here I require an *excursus* into poetic theory in order to explain image of voice and its relation to echo and allusion, and rather than rely upon as recondite a theorist as myself, I turn instead to a great explainer, John Hollander, who seems to me our outstanding authority upon all matters of lyrical form. Here is Hollander upon images of voice and their relation to the figurative interplay I have called "transumption," since that is what I take "tally" to be: Whitman's greatest transumption or introjection or Crossing of Identification, his magnificent overcoming both of his own earlier images of poetic origins and of Emerson's story of how poetry comes into being, particularly American poetry. First Hollander, from his forthcoming book, *The Figure of Echo*:

> ... we deal with diachronic trope all the time, and yet we have no name for it as a class.... the echoing itself makes a figure, and the interpretive or revisionary power which raises the echo even louder than the original voice is that of a trope of diachrony....
>
> I propose that we apply the name of the classical rhetoricians' trope of *transumption* (or *metalepsis* in its Greek form) to these diachronic, allusive figures....
>
> Proper reading of a metaphor demands a simultaneous appreciation of the beauty of a vehicle and the importance of its freight.... But the interpretation of a metalepsis entails the recovery of the transumed material. A transumptive style is to be distinguished radically from the kind of conceited one which we usually associate with baroque poetic, and with English seventeenth-century verse in particular. It involves an ellipsis, rather than a relentless pursuit, of further figuration....

Hollander then names transumption as the proper figure for interpretive allusion, to which I would add only the description that I gave before in *A Map of Misreading*: this is the trope-undoing trope, which seeks to reverse imagistic priorities. Milton crowds all his poetic precursors together into the space that intervenes between *himself and the truth*. Whitman also crowds poetic anteriority—Emerson and the Whitman of 1855–1860—into a little space between the carol of death and the echo aroused in the soul of the elegist of *Lilacs*. Emerson had excluded the questions of sex and death from his own images-of-voice, whether in a verse chant like *Bacchus* or a prose rhapsody like *The Poet*. The earlier Whitman had made of the deathly ocean at night his maternal image of voice, and we have heard the hermit thrush in its culmination of that erotic cry. Whitman's tally transumes the ocean's image of voice, by means of what Hollander calls an ellipsis of further figuration. The tally notches a restored Narcissism and the return to the mode of erotic self-sufficiency. The cost is high as it always is in transumption. What vanishes here in Whitman is the presence of others and of otherness, as object-libido is converted into ego-libido again. Father Abraham, the ocean as dark mother, the love of comrades, and even the daemonic *alter ego* of the hermit thrush all fade away together. But what is left is the authentic American image of voice, as the bard brings tally, alone there in the night among the fragrant pines except for his remaining comrades, the knowledge of death and the thought of death.

In 1934 Wallace Stevens, celebrating his emergence from a decade's poetic silence, boldly attempted a very different transumption of the Whitmanian images of voice:

> It was her voice that made
> The sky acutest at its vanishing.
> She measured to the hour its solitude.
> She was the single artificer of the world
> In which she sang. . . .

The tally, in *The Idea of Order at Key West*, becomes the "ghostlier demarcations, keener sounds" ending the poem. A year later, Stevens granted himself a vision of Whitman as sunset in our evening-land:

> In the far South the sun of autumn is passing
> Like Walt Whitman walking along a ruddy shore.
> He is singing and chanting the things that are part of him,
> The worlds that were and will be, death and day.
> Nothing is final, he chants. No man shall see the end.
> His beard is of fire and his staff is a leaping flame.

It is certainly the passing bard of the end of *Lilacs*, but did he chant that nothing is final? Still, this is Walt as Moses and as Aaron, leading the poetic children of Emerson through the American wilderness, and surely Whitman was always proudly provisional. Yet, the tally of his soul had to present itself as a finality, as an image of voice that had achieved a fresh priority and a perpetually ongoing strength. Was that an American Sublime, or only another American irony? Later in 1935, Stevens wrote a grim little poem called *The American Sublime* that seems to qualify severely his intense images of voice, of the singing girl and of Whitman:

> But how does one feel?
> One grows used to the weather,
> The landscape and that;
> And the sublime comes down
> To the spirit itself,
>
> The spirit and space,
> The empty spirit
> In vacant space.
> What wine does one drink?
> What bread does one eat?

The questions return us full circle to Emerson's *Bacchus*, nearly a century before:

> We buy ashes for bread;
> We buy diluted wine. . . .

This is not transumptive allusion, but a repetition of figurations, the

American baroque defeat. But that is a secondary strain in Stevens, as it was in Emerson and in Whitman. I leap ahead, past Frost and Pound, Eliot and Williams, past even Hart Crane, to conclude with a contemporary image of voice that is another strong tally, however ruefully the strength regards itself. Here is John Ashbery's *The Other Tradition*, the second poem in his 1977 volume, *Houseboat Days*:

> They all came, some wore sentiments
> Emblazoned on T-shirts, proclaiming the lateness
> Of the hour, and indeed the sun slanted its rays
> Through branches of Norfolk Island pine as though
> Politely clearing its throat, and all ideas settled
> In a fuzz of dust under trees when it's drizzling:
> The endless games of Scrabble, the boosters,
> The celebrated omelette au Cantal, and through it
> The roar of time plunging unchecked through the sluices
> Of the days, dragging every sexual moment of it
> Past the lenses: the end of something.
> Only then did you glance up from your book,
> Unable to comprehend what had been taking place, or
> Say what you had been reading. More chairs
> Were brought, and lamps were lit, but it tells
> Nothing of how all this proceeded to materialize
> Before you and the people waiting outside and in the next
> Street, repeating its name over and over, until silence
> Moved halfway up the darkened trunks,
> And the meeting was called to order.
>   I still remember
> How they found you, after a dream, in your thimble hat,
> Studious as a butterfly in a parking lot.
> The road home was nicer then. Dispersing, each of the
> Troubadours had something to say about how charity
> Had run its race and won, leaving you the ex-president
> Of the event, and how, though many of these present
> Had wished something to come of it, if only a distant
> Wisp of smoke, yet none was so deceived as to hanker
> After that cool non-being of just a few minutes before,
> Now that the idea of a forest had clamped itself
> Over the minutiae of the scene. You found this
> Charming, but turned your face fully toward night,
> Speaking into it like a megaphone, not hearing
> Or caring, although these still live and are generous
> And all ways contained, allowed to come and go
> Indefinitely in and out of the stockade
> They have so much trouble remembering, when your forgetting
> Rescues them at last, as a star absorbs the night.

I am aware that this charming poem urbanely confronts, absorbs and in some sense seeks to overthrow a critical theory, almost a critical climate, that has accorded it a canonical status. Stevens's Whitman proclaims that nothing is final and that no man shall see the end. Ashbery, a Whitman somehow more studiously casual even than Whitman, regards the prophets of belatedness and cheerfully insists that his forgetting or repression will rescue us at last, even as the Whitmanian or Stevensian evening star absorbs the night. But the price paid for this metaleptic reversal of American belatedness into a fresh earliness is the yielding up of Ashbery's tally or image of voice to a deliberate grotesquerie. Sexuality is made totally subservient to time, which is indeed "the end of something," and poetic tradition becomes an ill-organized social meeting of troubadours, leaving the canonical Ashbery as "ex-president / Of the event." As for the image of voice proper, the Whitmanian confrontation of the night now declines into: "You found this / Charming, but turned your face fully toward night, / Speaking into it like a megaphone, not hearing / Or caring." Such a megaphone is an apt image for Paul de Man's deconstructionist view of poetic tradition, which undoes tradition by suggesting that every poem is as much a random and gratuitous event as any human death is.

Ashbery's implicit interpretation of what he wants to call *The Other Tradition* mediates between this vision of poems as being totally cut off from one another and the antithetical darkness in which poems carry over-determined relationships and progress towards a final entropy. Voice in our poetry now tallies what Ashbery in his *Syringa*, a major Orphic elegy in *Houseboat Days*, calls "a record of pebbles along the way." Let us grant that the American Sublime is always also an American irony, and then turn back to Emerson and hear the voice that is great within us somehow breaking through again. This is Emerson in his journal for August 1859, on the eve of being burned out, with all his true achievement well behind him; but he gives us the true tally of his soul:

> *Beatitudes of Intellect.*—Am I not, one of these days, to write consecutively of the beatitude of intellect? It is too great for feeble souls, and they are over-excited. The wineglass shakes, and the wine is spilled. What then? The joy which will not let me sit in my chair, which brings me bolt upright to my feet, and sends me striding around my room, like a tiger in his cage, and I cannot have composure and concentration enough even to set down in English words the thought which thrills me—is not that joy a certificate of the elevation? What if I never write a book or a line? for a moment, the eyes of my eyes were opened, the affirmative experience remains, and consoles through all suffering.

PAUL ZWEIG

The Wound-Dresser

Such was Whitman's situation in December 1862 when, on a Tuesday morning, he opened the newspaper to discover that his brother George had been wounded at the battle of Fredericksburg. That afternoon he was on the train to Washington, determined to find George at all costs. It was a miserable journey. He was pickpocketed while changing trains in Philadelphia, and arrived in Washington without a cent. Once there, he went from hospital to hospital looking for his brother. It seemed hopeless to find anyone in the confusion of makeshift hospitals that surrounded the city. During his treks across the half-finished capital, Whitman ran across his former publisher, Charles Eldridge, and his Boston friend William O'Connor. Eldridge worked in the army paymaster's office, and O'Connor was a clerk for the Light House Board of the Treasury Department. When George could not be found in any of the Washington hospitals, Eldridge obtained a military pass for Whitman to go down by boat to Aquia Creek and then by train to the Virginia battlefield where the New York Fifty-first was camped. A day later, on 19 December, Whitman disembarked at Falmouth, opposite Fredericksburg, in southern Virginia. It took him half a day to find his brother in the sprawling camp. A metal sliver had pierced George's cheek, but the wound was already healing.

Until George was captured late in 1864, to spend four hellish months in a southern military prison, he would lead a charmed life during the war. He fought in a dozen arduous battles. He endured the freezing winters and the parched, dusty summers, and was promoted several times in the field. Year in year out, his companions died of cholera and typhoid as much as of southern bullets. But George, the one solidly healthy Whitman, slipped between all the dangers.

From *Walt Whitman: The Making of the Poet*. Copyright © 1984 by Basic Books.

The bond between the brothers would never be as intense as during these years of the war. In letter after letter, Whitman traced George's movements and tried to reassure his mother. In 1865, he wrote an article for the Brooklyn *Daily Union* about George's remarkable war record. The Whitman family hung on George's safety. He was their emissary to the war. The war was the one thing he and Walt would ever share. When George was captured, Whitman haunted the war office, to obtain George's exchange, and he finally succeeded.

For ten days, in December 1862, Walt shared his brother's tent at Falmouth. During the blustery gray days after the battle of Fredericksburg, he picked his way from group to group of encamped soldiers. He ate and talked with the men and filled his notebook with a vivid accumulation of names, descriptions, battle reports. The troops huddled in flimsy shelter-tents or in "shebangs" of freshly cut branches that barely cut the wind. The young soldiers, fresh from their farms and workshops, had been hardened by a year of campaigning. Death had become a casual, almost jocular companion. On the night he arrived at Falmouth, Whitman described a walk among the campfires:

> My walk out around the camp, the fires burning,—groups around—the merry song—the sitting forms—the playing light on the faces—they would tell stories—one would tell a story of a dead man sitting on the top rail of a fence—he had been shot there at sundown, mortally wounded, clung with desperate nerves and was found sitting there, dead, staring with fixed eyes in the morning.

Whitman's notebook reflects his state of mind. He has been pulled out of his "slough"—out of himself—by the grim scenes of the late battle and by the soldiers: young men like his New York stage drivers and ferryboatmen, made lean and curiously hearty by the experiences of the war. He walks along the Rappahannock River and sees Fredericksburg, "splintered, bursted, crumbled, the houses—some with their chimneys thrown down—the hospitals—the man with his mouth blown out." On a bright, freezing day, he admires a regimental inspection, the men "sifted by death, dismemberment, etc. from eleven hundred men (including recruits) to about two hundred." He sits around fireplaces improvised in holes in the ground, and is stirred by the "brightly beautiful" scene of wagon trains, encampments, locomotives, and stacked rifles, spread out over miles of battlefield. Everywhere there are graves; bodies on stretchers, covered with brown and gray blankets:

> Death is nothing here. As you step out in the morning from your tent to wash your face you see before you on a stretcher a shapeless extended object, and over it is thrown a dark grey blanket—it is the corpse of some wounded or sick soldier of the reg't who died in the hospital tent during the night—

perhaps there is a row of three or four of these corpses lying covered over. No one makes an ado. There is a detail of men made to bury them; all useless ceremony is omitted. (The stern realities of the marches and many battles of a long campaign make the old etiquets a cumber and a nuisance.)

There is a terse, terrible clarity in these notes that is already stirring toward poetry. But a poetry that is new for Whitman, quieter, more pictorial, as if the powerful scenes of the war could almost speak for themselves. The poet needed only open his eyes and report the casual truths that lay about him, dense with unspoken, unspeakable meanings. The row of bodies in front of the hospital tent would become the subject of one of Whitman's finest poems:

> A sight in camp in the daybreak gray and dim,
> As from my tent I emerge so early sleepless,
> As slow I walk in the cool fresh air the path near by the hospital tent,
> Three forms I see on stretchers lying, brought out there untended lying,
> Over each a blanket spread, ample brownish woolen blanket,
> Gray and heavy blanket, folding, covering all.
>
> Curious I halt and silent stand,
> Then with light fingers I from the face of the nearest the first just lift the blanket;
> Who are you my dear comrade?
> Then to the second I step—and who are you my child and darling?
> Who are you sweet boy with cheeks yet blooming?
>
> Then to the third—a face nor child nor old, very calm, as of beautiful
> yellow-white ivory;
> Young man I think I know you—I think this face is the face of the
> Christ himself,
> Dead and divine and brother of all, and here again he lies.

These were days that changed Whitman's life. The previous summer, he had been oppressed by the war and by his own aimlessness. New York had weighed on him. He had written a handful of blustering war poems and sentimental fables. But his feelings were best captured in a fragmentary poem he culled from his notebooks:

> Year that trembled and reel'd beneath me!
> Your summer wind was warm enough, yet the air I breathed froze me,
> A thick gloom fell through the sunshine and darken'd me,
> Must I change my triumphant songs? said I to myself,
> Must I indeed learn to chant the cold dirges of the baffled?
> And sullen hymns of defeat?

Now, only a few months later, in freezing Virginia, among men collecting themselves after the battle for further battle, among new sights and new feelings, Whitman was renewed. Already, a remarkable handful of poems is germing that will form the core of "Drum-Taps." They are short, casual poems; the poet is hardly present in them. F.O. Mathiessen compared them to certain Dutch and Flemish genre paintings: understated and precise; realistic in the way that Stephen Crane would be realistic in *The Red Badge of Courage*. The poems register a stripping down, a setting aside of personality, which Whitman had praised in his great early poems, where nakedness and the open road had been figures for self-renewal—had praised, but not practiced, for his naked self had caroused, more like a gigantic opera singer than a simplified seer.

The men told him about their forced marches; they described the eerie scenes of wounded and dead; and Whitman, caught by the passion of these young men, saw with their eyes, felt with their bodies. When he wrote, his voice—which had been floridly his own—became transparent, almost humble:

> A march in the ranks hard-prest, and the road unknown,
> A route through a heavy wood with muffled steps in the darkness,
> Our army foil'd with loss severe, and the sullen remnant retreating,
> Till after midnight glimmer upon us the lights of a dim-lighted building,
> We come to an open space in the woods, and halt by the dim-lighted building,
> 'Tis a large old church at the crossing roads, now an impromptu hospital,
> Entering but for a minute I see a sight beyond all the pictures and poems
>   ever made,
> Shadows of deepest, deepest black, just lit by moving candles and lamps,
> And by one great pitchy torch stationary with wild red flame and
>   clouds of smoke,
> By these, crowds, groups of forms vaguely I see on the floor, some in the
>   pews laid down,
> At my feet more distinctly a soldier, a mere lad, in danger of bleeding
>   to death, (he is shot in the abdomen,)
> I stanch the blood temporarily, (the youngster's face is white as a lily,). . . .

Whitman heard this story from a Maine soldier who had been at the battle of White Oaks Church in Virginia. By the time he wrote the poem, he had seen plenty of war hospitals. Already at Falmouth, he visited hospital tents where men lay on the ground or on mattresses of pine boughs. One of the first things he noticed in camp, he wrote his mother, "was a heap of feet, arms, legs, etc., under a tree in front of a hospital, the Lacey House," where the worst cases were brought. Whitman would see plenty of amputated limbs during the next three years. Doctors sawed arms and legs off from morning till night. Stories were told of soldiers who saved their limbs by taking a pistol with them to the operating room, and leveling it at the surgeon.

At the Lacey House, Whitman wrote letters for the wounded soldiers. He gave a Confederate captain a newspaper, and he talked to whomever seemed lonely or needy. Men died while he watched. ("Death is nothing here.") It was an upheaval, an overthrowing of all his feelings. For a decade he had written poem-sermons on the health and youth of the flesh. The poems had reverberated with a kind of invulnerability. Yes, there had been a dark side, culminating in the "death death death death death" of "Out of the Cradle," but it had been romantic and songlike. Death had been a nervous tune, edging around his song of health. But here were actual men dying; here were bodies ripped open by shrapnel, drained by disease. "Now that I have lived for 8 or 9 days amid such scenes as the camps furnish," he wrote his mother, ". . . really nothing we call trouble seems worth talking about."

On 29 December, 1862 Whitman returned to Washington. The ten days at Falmouth had washed New York out of his life, and he was determined to stay as close to the war as possible. That meant staying in Washington which, as virtually a Union enclave in the Confederacy, was filled with constant troop movements in case of surprise raids by General Lee's mobile army. On the day Whitman arrived back in Washington, he wrote to Emerson asking for help in procuring a government job; and the letter gives us a notion of Whitman's mood:

> Dear Friend,
> Breaking up a few weeks since, and for good, my New York stagnation—wandering since through camp and battle scenes—I fetch up here in harsh and superb plight—wretchedly poor, excellent well, (my only torment, family matters)—realizing at last that it is necessary for me to fall for the time in the wise old way, to push my fortune, to be brazen, and get employment, and have an income—determined to do it, (at any rate until I get out of horrible sloughs).

Whitman was penniless and had only a few friends in Washington; he had no idea how he was going to make a living. But he had decided to stay. He was not always "cautious"; sometimes, in the upsurge of new feelings, he leaped first and considered later. So he had gone to New Orleans, fourteen years before. And now he was in Washington, determined, somehow, to settle there.

Within days, Eldridge had gotten Whitman a part-time job as a copyist for an army paymaster, Major Hapgood. Whitman found himself a "weary little bedroom," in a roominghouse on L Street where the O'Connors also lived. A few days later, sitting in Major Hapgood's office on the top floor of a tall house on Fifteenth and F streets, with a view of the Potomac and Georgetown to the south, and the houses of Washington spread around, Whitman wrote his sister-in-law Martha about his first few days in Washington. Every day, crowds of "poor sick pale tattered soldiers" climbed the stairs to the paymaster's office, only to find they were in the wrong place or had the wrong papers, and were forced to leave, disappointed and tired. It was awful. The day before, he had gone out to the Campbell Hospital to visit two Brooklyn boys from George's regiment:

> Yesterday I went out to the Campbell Hospital to see a couple of Brooklyn

boys, of the 51st. They knew I was in Washington, and sent me a note, to come to see them. O my dear sister, how your heart would ache to go through the rows of wounded young men, as I did—and stop to speak a comforting word to them. There was about 100 in one long room, just a long shed neatly whitewashed inside. One young man was very much prostrated, and groaning with pain. I stopt and tried to comfort him. He was very sick. I found he had not had any medical attention since he was brought there— among so many he had been overlooked. So I sent for the doctor, and he made an examination of him—the doctor behaved very well—seemed to be anxious to do right—said that the young man would recover—he had been brought pretty low with diarrhea, and now had bronchitis, but not so serious as to be dangerous. I talked to him some time—he seemed to have entirely give up, and lost heart—he had not a cent of money—not a friend or acquaintance—I wrote a letter from him to his sister—his name was John A. Holmes, Campbello, Plymouth county, Mass. I gave him a little change I had—he said he would buy a drink of milk, when the woman came through with milk. Trifling as this was, he was overcome and began to cry. Then there were many, many others. I mention the one, as a specimen. My Brooklyn boys were John Losery, shot at Fredericksburgh, and lost his left forearm, and Amos H. Vliet—Jeff knows the latter—he has his feet frozen, and is doing well. The 100 are in a ward (6)—and there are, I should think, eight or ten or twelve such wards in the Campbell Hospital—indeed a real village. Then there are some 38 more Hospitals here in Washington, some of them much larger.

The next day, and the next, Whitman went back to the Campbell Hospital. He stopped at the bedsides of the wounded soldiers; he talked with the doctors and brought whatever he could afford—some writing paper, fruit juices, a little tobacco—to cheer up the young men, many of whom had been brought up by boat and then ridden in brutally jolting army wagons, half dead from their wounds or from diarrhea. The scenes in the hospitals overwhelmed Whitman. So many suffering young men, so much loneliness and need. Within days, he knew that he was not on the fringes of the war any longer, but at its heart. His job hunting was forgotten. In mid-January 1863, Emerson wrote him letters of recommendation for Salmon P. Chase, the Secretary of the Treasury, and William Seward, the Secretary of State; but Whitman did not use them for more than a year. His whole being was absorbed by these young men who haunted his days and his nights: the farmers' sons and the young factory workers, most of them away from home for the first time in their lives. Now they lay in the whitewashed buildings that had been thrown up on empty land around the city to house the Union wounded.

For years, Whitman had made a habit of talking with strangers; and his life, as I have said, had been a form of street theater. Now the theater had come indoors into the long hospital sheds. He still talked with strangers; he gave of himself, as a man throws a buoy to someone who is drowning.

Suddenly the "health" and "magnetism" Whitman had celebrated in his poems, or radiated playfully on his walks along Broadway, were no longer sources of egotistical pride: they were a medicine; they helped men live.

Whitman's Washington existence organized itself almost immediately. For several hours each day, he worked in Major Hapgood's office and then went to one of the dozens of hospitals that surrounded Washington. We see him looking out over the city and the Potomac from Major Hapgood's high window—the panoramas of snow or rain; the clear days and the dusty parched days, all curiously peaceful and still, even in the midst of the war; and we see him, for hours and days at a time, going from bedside to bedside in the hospitals. Sometimes he sat down to write a letter for a wounded boy, or give a small gift, or help dress a wound. Sometimes he simply stopped and talked for a while. It quickly appeared that he was a born nurse. As a poet, he had the ability to lose himself in what he saw, to see it from its own point of view, so to speak. Now, as a hospital nurse, he seemed to feel the boys' needs as if they were his own.

For the first time in fourteen years, Whitman was on his own. He supported himself meagerly by writing "letters" to New York newspapers and by copying for Major Hapgood. His room on L Street was little more than a place to sleep: four bare walls, a bed, and a coal stove; almost a monk's cell, or an urban Walden, as Justin Kaplan has called it. It was a precarious existence, but Whitman was not thinking about his comforts. "It doesn't seem to me it makes so much difference about worldly successes," he wrote to his brother Jeff in April, "(beyond just enough to eat and drink, and shelter, in the moderatest limits) any more, since the last four months of my life especially, and that merely to *live*, and have one fair meal a day, is *enough.*"

In January, he had asked Jeff to help him raise money for his hospital visits, and Jeff's colleagues at the Brooklyn Water Works had contributed a few dollars each. They and other friends would continue to send Whitman money for most of the war. Whitman spent the money on small items— peaches, raspberry syrup, tobacco, a little brandy—which he distributed on his visits. When a soldier was destitute, Whitman gave him some money. His notebooks are filled now with the names of soldiers, their regiments, their wounds and illnesses, what they want him to bring on his next visit: some preserves maybe, or peppermints, a Bible or a newspaper. Sometimes there is more:

Ward K bed 47, Oscar F. Wilber co G 54th N.Y. talked with him July 22nd '63 afternoon—asked me to read a chapter in the New Testament—I complied asking him what, "make your own choice" said he. I opened at the close of one of the books of the evangelists in the first part testament describing the latter hours and crucifiction of Christ—he asked me to read the following chapter how he rose again. It pleased him very much, the tears were in his eyes—asked me if I "enjoyed religion," I said "probably not my dear in the way you mean"—he said it was his main reliance, he smiled sweetly said he did not fear death—I said "Why Oscar don't you think you will get well" He said I may but it is not probable—he then told me his condition—his wound was very bad, it discharged much—he had also for quite a long time diarroeha altogether prostrating him—he behaved very manly calm and sweet, spoke slow and low, had large fine eyes very eloquent.

For months, and then years, Whitman's life centered on the hospitals. Although he apparently received an authorizing letter from a church organization called the Christian Commission, he had no use for official visitors who were often cold and distant and looked as though they were simply doing a job. The soldiers shrank from them, Whitman observed. Whitman was not doing a job. There was an exaltation in his work, a flush of love and horror with which he often had to struggle to keep his bearings.

In February 1863, the Government Patent Office was transformed into a hospital, and Whitman noted the irony of the setting. "Rows of sick, badly wounded and dying soldiers," were jammed between "high and ponderous glass cases, crowded with models in miniature of every kind of utensil, machine or invention it ever entered the mind of man to conceive." The Patent Office had been America's temple of "progress." But here was the undersong of progress: these hurt bodies and suppurating wounds and cries of pain. Two years later, Whitman again walked through the halls of the Patent Office, just before Lincoln's second inaugural ball was to be held there, and reflected on the contrast: "To-night, beautiful women, perfumes, the violin's sweetness, the polka and the waltz; then the amputations, the blue face, the groans, the glassy eye of the dying, the clotted rag, the odor of wounds and blood, and many a mother's son amid strangers, passing away untended there."

Whitman eventually recorded his hospital visits in *Memoranda during the War*, which became a section of *Specimen Days*. He scattered further notations in *November Boughs* (1888). It all came from the smudged, penciled notes he took day after day, as he walked between the rows of beds, stopping here and there with his little gifts and his inspiriting presence. He gave expert care, sensed what the soldiers needed: here were the "delicate hands guiding the cart." Over and over again, in letters and in his notes, Whitman described his days in the hospitals. It was an unvarying routine, and yet not a routine, because the unshielded presence of the dying was all around him:

Thursday, Jan. 21.—Devoted the main part of the day to Armory—Square hospital; went pretty thoroughly through wards F, G, H, and I; some fifty cases in each ward. In ward F supplied the men throughout with writing paper and stamp'd envelope each; distributed in small portions, to proper subjects, a large jar of first-rate preserv'd berries, which had been donated to me by a lady—her own cooking. Found several cases I thought good subject for small sums of money, which I furnish'd. (The wounded men often come up broke, and it helps their spirits to have even the small sum I give them.) My paper and envelopes all gone; but distributed a good lot of amusing reading matter; also, as I thought judicious, tobacco, oranges, apples, etc. Interesting cases in ward I; Charles Miller, bed 19, company D, 53d Pennsylvania, is only sixteen years of age, very bright, courageous boy, left leg amputated below the knee; next bed to him, another young lad very sick; gave each appropriate gifts. In the bed above, also, amputation of the left leg; gave him a little jar of raspberries; bed 1, this ward, gave a small sum; also to a soldier on crutches, sitting on his bed near. . . . (I am more and more surprised at the very great proportion of youngsters from fifteen to twenty-one in the army. I afterwards found a still greater proportion among the southerners.)

Evening, same day, went to see D.F.R., before alluded to; found him remarkably changed for the better; up and dress'd—quite a triumph; he afterwards got well, and went back to his regiment. Distributed in the wards a quantity of note-paper, and forty or fifty stamp'd envelopes, of which I had recruited my stock, and the men were much in need.

The hospital wards were Whitman's setting now. He was no longer the nimble-footed poet of Manahatta, as in his early poem, "Pictures," or the rough, splendid workingman waving to passers-by from the top of a Broadway stage. He was a mother-man distributing his care among hundreds and thousands of helpless young men who filled the hospital sheds and the tent cities, which multiplied as the war's toll grew:

During those three years in hospital, camp or field, I made over six hundred visits or tours, and went, as I estimate, counting all, among from eighty thousand to a hundred thousand of the wounded and sick, as sustainer of spirit and body in some degree, in time of need. These visits varied from an hour or two, to all day or night; for with clear or critical cases I generally watch'd all night. Sometimes I took up my quarters in the hospital, and slept or watch'd there several nights in succession.

Almost from the first, Whitman thought about collecting his notes into a book. He would give America a view of her own suffering soul; he would make the invisible visible: the hospitals, those forgotten places where the débris of war had been cast up—a débris of living young men suffering from the grotesque wounds of war. A boy with a pierced bladder dribbles urine through his wound. Another boy gives off a smell of rot from a gangrenous leg. Another, dying of a stomach wound, looks untouched and peaceful, sleeping the sleep of youth that degenerates day by day into a fever-ridden anguish and then death. After only a few weeks in Washington, Whitman wrote to Emerson:

I desire and intend to write a little book out of this phase of America, her masculine young manhood, its conduct under most trying of and highest of all exigency, which she, as by lifting a corner in a curtain, has vouchsafed me to see America, already brought to Hospital in her fair youth—brought and deposited here in this great, whited sepulchre of Washington itself— (this union Capital without the first bit of cohesion—this collect of proofs how low and swift a good stock can deteriorate—) Capital to which these deputies most strange arrive from every quarter, concentrating here, well-drest, rotten, meagre, nimble and impotent, full of gab, full always of their thrice-accursed party—arrive and skip into the seats of mightiest legislation, and take the seats of judges and high executive seats—while by quaint Providence come also sailed and wagoned hither this other freight of helpless worn and wounded youth, genuine of the soil, of darlings and true heirs to me the first unquestioned and convincing western crop, prophetic of the future, proofs undeniable to all men's ken of perfect beauty, tenderness and pluck that never race yet rivalled. . . .

As I took temporary memoranda of names, items, etc. of one thing and another, commissioned to get or do for the men—what they wished and what their cases required from outside, etc.—these memoranda grow bulky, and suggest something to me—so I now make fuller notes, or a sort of journal, (not a mere dry journal though, I hope)—This thing I will record—it belongs to the time, and to all the States—(and perhaps it belongs to me).

The distance between the hospitals and the brightly lit magnificence of the Capitol building, with its domed chambers, frescoes, and gold leaf, enraged Whitman. And the rabble of office seekers, the swarming politicians, the never-ending rhetoric of Congress. It was a circus enclosed in a ring of terrible truth; an incarnation of the trivial neighboring with the awful simplicity of the war's direst result. By October 1863, Whitman's book was all but written. It is a miscellany of observations; a pell-mell heaping of journal entries, battle scenes told to Whitman by wounded soldiers, hospital visitings, reports of living and dying, longer accounts of special cases. The book is Whitman's notebook amplified; it is Teufelsdröckh's bag of scraps, recounting the biography not of the poet but of the hospitals and, in Whitman's view, of the war itself: America's soul-making ordeal. Whitman wrote to his Boston friend James Redpath, who earlier that year had published Louisa May Alcott's *Hospital Sketches*:

My idea is a book of the time, worthy the time—something considerably beyond mere hospital sketches—a book for sale perhaps in a larger American market—the premises or skeleton memoranda of incidents, persons, places, sights, the past year (mostly jotted down either on the spot or in the spirit of seeing or hearing what is narrated). . . .

I have much to say of hospitals, the immense national hospitals—in them too most radical changes of premises are demanded—(the air, the spirit of a thing is every thing, the details follow & adjust themselves). I have many hospital incidents, [that] will take with the general reader—I ventilate my general democracy with details very largely & with reference to the future—bringing in persons, the President, Seward, Congress, the Capitol, Washington City, many of the actors of the drama—have something to say of the great trunk America, the West etc etc—do not hesitate to diffuse myself—the book is very rapid—is a book that can be read by the five or ten minutes at (being full of small parts, pieces, paragraphs with their dates, incidents etc)—I should think two or three thousand sale ought to be certainly depended on here in hospitals in Washington, among departments etc.

It was to be an inexpensive book, selling for one dollar at most, and ready for the holiday season. But Redpath had his doubts, and Whitman's book did not see the day until, as usual, he published it himself a dozen years later. Whitman's belief in the order of disorder, the random heaping of notes reflecting a deeper order of actual experience, was not more acceptable to literary minds of his day than was his sexual frankness. For the time being, Whitman's trunk would hold onto its miscellaneous treasure.

Neither *Memoranda during the War* nor *Specimen Days* hints at the troubled intensity of Whitman's fascination with the hospitals. This world of dying young men stirred emotions he had never fully allowed himself to feel before. It was as if his fugitive lists of names—a glance, the invitation of a passing face—had materialized and become inescapable. He went back every day, living the role of healer and life giver he had imagined in "Song of Myself" seven years before:

> To any one dying. . . thither I speed and twist the knob of the door,
> Turn the bedclothes toward the foot of the bed,
> Let the physician and the priest go home.
> I seize the descending man. . . . I raise him with resistless will.

In the hospitals, Whitman saw himself lifting the wounded from their beds by the force of his sympathy and loving care. Every day, he peered and watched, like his night wanderer in "The Sleepers"; and as he went through the wards, the beds became a miniature of the country at large, a geography of America's young men, with whom he exchanged vows of love, more potent, in his eyes, than any medicine:

> O what a sweet unwonted love (those good American boys, of good stock, decent, clean, well raised boys, so near to me)—what an attachment grows up between us, started from hospital cots, where pale young faces lie & wounded or sick bodies. My brave young American soldiers—now for so many months I have gone around among them, where they lie. I have long discarded all stiff conventions (they & I are too near to each other, there is no time to lose, & death & anguish dissipate ceremony here between my

lads & me)—I pet them, some of them it does so much good, they are so faint & lonesome—at parting at night sometimes I kiss them right & left—The doctors tell me I supply the patients with a medicine which all their drugs & bottles & powders are helpless to yield.

In his letters to his mother and friends, Whitman seems awed by the bond that grew up between him and the boys he visited. It is a sweet, brooding feeling, thriving on desperation, on the need of frightened young men for reassurance and tender care. In the crude hospital sheds, surrounded by dying and hopeless strangers, the soldiers must have grasped at this large, friendly man, with his easy manner, who entered their lives as if he had known them for a long time. Whitman had rehearsed this role, too, in his poems. In "Calamus," he had distributed tokens of love and sympathy to young men: the sprigs of lilac, moss, pinks, and laurel leaves had stood for his best self, his poems. Now the tokens changed: they were candies, tobacco, slices of cake, and peaches cut up in some cream; they were sheets of letter paper, stamps, and a few coins of money. The young men took them—small comfort in a dire place—knowing that they stood for more—for the intense, at times puzzling feelings of this bearded man who came to visit them in high boots, thick jacket, and hat. He still smelled of soap, for he had scrupulously bathed before coming out to whatever cluster of buildings he chose for his visit each day.

Amid the "butcher sights" of the hospitals Whitman felt himself flooded with love for the young soldiers. He kissed and fondled them as if they were his sons: "I never before had my feelings so thoroughly and (so far) permanently absorbed, to the very roots, as by these huge swarms of dear, wounded, sick, dying boys." It was not unusual for him to spend half the night going from bed to bed spooning out jam or stewed fruit from a pot.

> Yet after all this succoring of the stomach (which is of course most welcome & indispensible) I should say that I believe my profoundest help to these sick and dying men is probably the soothing invigoration I steadily bear in mind, to infuse in them through affection, cheering love, & the like, between them and me. It has saved more than one life. There is a strange influence here. I have formed attachments in hospital, that I shall keep to my dying day, & they will the same, without doubt.

It is clear that the hospitals were vital places for Whitman. During four years, he rarely missed a day, with his knapsack full of gifts and his florid fatherliness. Even when the war was over, and the country labored to forget its four years' ordeal, Whitman went on visiting the chronic cases that lingered in a few outlying hospitals. He thrived as a bringer of comfort. For once, his "doubts" about "appearances," the undertone of meaninglessness that had dogged the larger-than-life voice of his poems, were laid to rest. For the hospitals were a field of action beyond all doubting. In his poems, he had invited his readers to an adventure of self-change, full of danger and erotic delight. But it had been a lonely activity, with uncertain results. The suspicion of failure was never far. In the hospitals, Whitman set aside his metaphors, in order to live them. His poet had been a bringer of health; his poet's world had been an "open road," and the poet had opened his mind to embrace whatever came his way. Now the hospitals were his open road. As he went up and down the wards, it seemed to him that all of America was at his feet, represented by this gathering of the sick and the dying, these young men from all over the country, whom Whitman had once imagined as citizens in his republic of comrades or as his companions in the aromatic springtime of "Calamus" love:

> While I was with wounded and sick in thousands of cases from the New England States, and from New York, New Jersey, and Pennsylvania, and from Michigan, Wisconsin, Ohio, Indiana, Illinois, and all the Western States, I was with more or less from all the States, North and South, without exception. I was with many from the border States, especially from Maryland and Virginia, and found, during those lurid years 1862–63, far more Union southerners, especially Tennesseans, than is supposed. I was with many rebel officers and men among our wounded, and gave them always what I had, and tried to cheer them the same as any. I was among the army teamsters considerably, and, indeed, always found myself drawn to them. Among the black soldiers, wounded or sick, and in the contraband camps, I also took my way whenever in their neighborhood, and did what I could for them.

In the wards, Whitman tried to save the boys' lives, and sometimes he succeeded. Often he had to watch them die, and there were days when he felt overwhelmed by the destructive rage of the war. But he knew that the hospitals gave him something, too. In the hospitals, the coy play of Cupid and Psyche—the "indirections" that gave his poems their suggestive weaving of themes—was replaced by frank and open acts of love. Here his homosexual ardor was not suspicious or shameful: it was a medicine; it buoyed up the sick and the dying. There was no need to veil it in euphemisms or to project it in grand notions of comradeship and democracy. There was no need even to make poetry out of it. Whitman could simply hug, and kiss, and hold hands. He could let his emotions flow "without check, with original energy."

The hospitals were a release for Whitman. They were a way around the self-censoring and the Victorian self-accusations that erupted even amid his strongest "Calamus" poems. We see the terrible extremes of the hospitals in all of his letters. In one, he describes "wounds full of crawling corruption," and the "dreadful" sadness of the suffering men—this was his heavy refrain in the letters—while also exalting in the new-found release of his deepest desires:

> In the hospitals among these American young men, I could not describe to you what mutual attachments & how passing deep & tender these boys— some have died, but the love for them lives as long as I draw breath—those soldiers know how to love too when once they have the right person & the right love offered them. It is wonderful.

It was wonderful. And also terrible. And Whitman swung between the extremes, in a tension that sometimes exhausted him. By 1864, his health had begun to suffer, and a slow slide into sickness began. He had bouts of prolonged weakness and dizziness. On hot sunny days, he walked around Washington with an umbrella, for fear of sunstroke. Late in the year, he had to return to Brooklyn to rest and regain his strength. In the light of his weakening health, the humorous descriptions he gives of himself in the letters—he is always fat, red-faced, and hearty—become ominous. The red face was probably a sign of vascular problems and hypertension, fed by his exhausting involvement in the hospitals. The stroke that disabled Whitman in 1873 was apparently already brewing in his system.

Sometimes, in the emotionally heated atmosphere of the hospitals, Whitman became reckless and poignant. There are sad beautiful letters in which he takes chances, expresses his homosexual longings with troubled directness. In the spring of 1863, he fell in love with a young soldier, Thomas Sawyer, who had been a patient at the Armory Square Hospital. When Sawyer got better and went back to his regiment, Whitman bought some underwear and a shirt for him, but Sawyer forgot to stop by Whitman's room to pick them up. Whitman wrote Sawyer letters that must have puzzled him, they are so tense with emotion:

> I was sorry you did not come up to my room to get the shirt & other things you promised to accept from me and take when you went away. I got them all ready, a good strong blue shirt, a pair of drawers & socks, and it would have been a satisfaction to me if you had accepted them. I should have often thought now Tom may be wearing around his body something from me. . . .
> My dearest comrade, I cannot, though I attempt it, put in a letter the feelings of my heart—I suppose my letters sound strange & unusual to you as it is, but as I am only expressing the truth in them, I do not trouble myself on that account.

In another letter, he embroidered a fantasy for the future: he and Sawyer, and maybe another hospital friend, Lew Brown, whose leg was amputated later in the year, would live together after the war and share everything and never be lonely again.

One more time after the war was over, Whitman laid himself bare in his long, troubled love for the streetcar conductor, Peter Doyle. But it was in the hospitals that Whitman opened his emotions for the first time. To John Trowbridge he had confessed that he was surprised, in reading his poems, at his ability to feel so much. The poems lived an open life, apart from the furtive inwardness of the poet, who strove to become his book and yet, in this matter of full, spontaneous feelings, had not succeeded. But now he had truly become his poems. His fantasy of comradeship was now expressed not in a book but in a letter to a young friend.

The hospitals aroused Whitman in every way. It was there that his extravagant idea of the 1850s was unexpectedly realized. He had wanted to write poems that poured from his enlarged life. He had dreamed of a kind of omnipresence: the "voice of Walt Whitman" would penetrate every corner of America; the "travelling soul" of his poems would enter everywhere, see everything, establishing a web of relationships, like his "patient spider," spinning out "filament, filament" into the surrounding emptiness. The dream was wild; and by the end of the decade, it had palpably failed. But now the dream had become unexpectedly true. Whitman's experience in the hospitals had been written out first in his book; his book had been a program, and now, against all hope, he was building it in his acts and feelings.

This man-myth of the 1860 *Leaves of Grass* had made of the hospitals a "found poem" to live within. Yet how terrible that found poem was! Here was the tragedy for Whitman: his dream of love was inextricably tangled up with death, as it had been in his poems. The refrain of "Out of the Cradle"—"death death death death death"—had become ugly and concrete. The boy in the poem singing of lost love was now a man finding love all around him in the hospital wards, but the refrain had become deafening.

The hospitals were the culmination of Whitman's years of experiment. He had produced a book, and now he had produced a self; and it was all perched on a precarious edge. In many respects, his book appeared to be a failure, its greatness barely glimpsed by a handful of friends. Even Emerson had become remote and cool. Whitman's self, bathed in the erotic, fed on suffering; it lived off the helplessness of a dying generation. No wonder then that these "contradictions" tore him apart and finally helped to make him sick. By the war's end, he had retreated from the vitality of his ten-year experiment. For the war was not only an ending, but a beginning: it was the beginning of his old age; the beginning of his public legend, and his stiffened, defensive stance as the "good grey poet," a subtly pious bard who stood for wholesome religious feelings and progress. This was the Whitman whom William Rossetti helped to make famous in England, making possible the grudging acceptance of Whitman in America in his last decades. It was the Whitman we have all come to know, with his grizzled beard and his frozen optimism.

Chronology

1819	Birth of Walter Whitman, on May 31 near Huntington, Long Island, to Louisa Van Velsor and Walter Whitman, a carpenter and builder of houses, each descended from the earliest settlers on Long Island, and each a follower of the radical Quaker circuit rider, Elias Hicks. The poet was the second born of eight Whitman children who grew beyond infancy, at least four of whom were disturbed or psychotic.
1823	Movement of Whitman family to Brooklyn, where the boy attends public school until 1830.
1830–31	Office boy to lawyers and to a doctor.
1831–35	Apprenticed as printer's devil on the Democratic newspaper *Patriot* and then the *Star*.
1835–36	Works as printer in New York City.
1836–38	Schoolteaching in various Long Island towns.
1838–39	Publishes and edits a new weekly, *Long-Islander*, from Huntington, then works on Jamaica *Democrat*. Early poems and sketches.
1840–41	Active in campaign of Martin Van Buren, and then returns to schoolteaching.
1841	From May on, he lives in New York City, working as compositor for *New World*, and is active in Democratic party.
1842–45	Works in New York City for several newspapers, and publishes stories and sketches, as well as the "temperance novel," *Franklin Evans*.
1845–48	Works in Brooklyn again for *Star*, and then the *Daily Eagle*.
1848	Brief sojourn in New Orleans as newspaper editor.
1848–49	Edits *Brooklyn Freeman*, as part of the Free Soil movement.
1849–54	The crucial years of return to his family; the notebooks of 1853–54 are the embryo of *Leaves of Grass*.
1855	Self-publication of first edition of *Leaves of Grass* in early July, followed by death of his father on July 11. On July 21 Ralph Waldo Emerson mails the magnificent letter hailing *Leaves of Grass* and its poet. The twelve untitled poems include what later will be titled "Song of Myself" and "The Sleepers."

1856   Second edition of *Leaves of Grass*, the new poems including what will come to be titled "Crossing Brooklyn Ferry." The volume includes Emerson's letter, and Whitman's extraordinary reply to it. Thoreau and Bronson Alcott visit Whitman in Brooklyn.

1857–59   Edits Brooklyn *Times*. Undergoes desolate period in late 1858 lasting well into 1859, presumably centering upon a homo-erotic relationship about which we can only surmise.

1860   Publication of third edition of *Leaves of Grass* in Boston by Thayer and Eldridge. In Boston to read proof, Whitman visits Emerson. Third edition includes "Calamus" poems and what will later be titled "Out of the Cradle Endlessly Rocking" and "As I Ebb'd with the Ocean of Life."

1861–62   Returns to journalism, while visiting the sick and war-wounded at New York Hospital. Departs for Virginia battle front in December 1862 to seek out his wounded brother George.

1863–64   The "Wound-Dresser" years in Washington, D.C., visiting wounded soldiers in the military hospitals.

1865   Dismissed from clerkship at Department of the Interior, perhaps because of the scandal of the third edition of *Leaves of Grass*. Composes "When Lilacs Last in the Dooryard Bloom'd" during the summer, in reaction to the martyrdom of Abraham Lincoln. The elegy is published in October, in *Drum-Taps and Sequel*. First meeting with Peter Doyle, then aged eighteen.

1867   Fourth edition of *Leaves of Grass*.

1870   Fifth edition of *Leaves of Grass*; *Democratic Vistas*.

1873   Paralytic stroke in January; death of mother in May; moves to brother George's house in Camden, New Jersey, in June.

1879   Travels in American West.

1880   Travels in Canada.

1881   Final meeting with Emerson, in Concord.

1882   Is visited by Oscar Wilde in Camden. *Leaves of Grass* is banned in Boston, but is reprinted in Philadelphia, where *Specimen Days and Collect* is published.

1884   Moves to own house in Camden.

1888   Severe paralytic stroke.

1891   Publishes *Good-Bye my Fancy* and final edition of *Leaves of Grass*.

1892   Death on March 26 in Camden.

Contributors

HAROLD BLOOM, Sterling Professor of the Humanities at Yale University, is the author of *The Anxiety of Influence, Poetry and Repression* and many other volumes of literary criticism. His forthcoming study, *Freud: Transference and Authority*, attempts a full-scale reading of all of Freud's major writings. He is the general editor of *The Chelsea House Library of Literary Criticism*.

D. H. LAWRENCE was equally powerful as novelist, poet and visionary polemicist. His poetry, at its later best, is profoundly Whitmanian, as are his greatest novels, *The Rainbow* and *Women in Love*. He died in 1930, aged only forty-five.

KENNETH BURKE is the most eminent of living American literary theorists and critics. His crucial books are *A Grammar of Motives* and *The Rhetoric of Religion*.

RICHARD CHASE taught at Columbia, and is remembered for his writings on American literature, particularly his *The American Novel and its Tradition*.

ROY HARVEY PEARCE is Professor of English at the University of California, San Diego. His books include *The Continuity of American Poetry*, probably the best general study of its subject.

The late JAMES WRIGHT was one of the principal American poets of his generation, particularly in his *The Branch Will Not Break* and *Shall We Gather at the River?*

R. W. B. LEWIS is Professor of English and American Literature at Yale. His books include *The American Adam*, and distinguished studies of Hart Crane and Edith Wharton.

The late PAUL ZWEIG was Professor of Comparative Literature at Queens College. His books include *The Heresy of Self-Love* and *The Adventurer*.

Bibliography

Allen, Gay Wilson. *The Solitary Singer*. New York: New York University Press, 1967.
_____. *The New Walt Whitman Handbook*. New York: New York University Press, 1975.
Allen, Gay Wilson, and Bradley, S., eds. *The Collected Writings of Walt Whitman*. New York: New York University Press, 1963–.
Arvin, Newton. *Whitman*. New York: The Macmillan Company, 1938.
Asselineau, Roger. *The Evolution .of Walt Whitman*. 2 vols. Cambridge, Mass.: Harvard University Press, Belknap Press, 1960 and 1962.
Black, Stephen. *Whitman's Journey into Chaos*. Princeton: Princeton University Press, 1975.
Blodgett, H.W., ed. *Walt Whitman: An 1855–56 Notebook Toward the Second Edition of Leaves of Grass*. Carbondale: Southern Illinois University Press, 1959.
Blodgett, H.W., and Bradley, S., eds. *Leaves of Grass: Comprehensive Reader's Edition*. New York: Norton, 1968.
Bloom, Harold. *A Map of Misreading*. New York: Oxford University Press, 1975.
_____. *Poetry and Repression*. New Haven: Yale University Press, 1976.
Borges, Jorge Luis. "The Achievements of Walt Whitman." *Texas Quarterly* 5 (1962): 43–48.
Bowers, F., ed. *Whitman's Manuscripts: Leaves of Grass (1860): A Parallel Text*. Chicago: University of Chicago Press, 1955.
Bradley, S.; Blodgett, A.; Golden, A.; and White, W., eds. *Leaves of Grass: A Textual Variorum of the Printed Poems*. New York: New York University Press, 1980.
Bucke, R.M., ed. *Notes and Fragments*. London, Canada: A. Talbot & Co., 1899.
Bucke, R.M.; Harned, T.H.; and Traubel, H.L., eds. *The Complete Writings*. New York and London: G.P. Putnam's Sons, 1902.
Burke, Kenneth. *Attitudes Toward History*. 2d ed., rev. Los Altos, Calif.: Hermes Publications, 1959.
Carlisle, E.G. *The Uncertain Self: Whitman's Drama of Identity*. East Lansing: Michigan State University Press, 1973.
Chase, Richard. *Walt Whitman Reconsidered*. New York: William Sloane Associates, 1955.
Coffman, Stanley. "'Crossing Brooklyn Ferry': A Note on the Catalog Technique in Whitman's Poetry." *Modern Philology* 2 (1954): 225–32.
_____. "Form and Meaning in Whitman's 'Passage to India.'" *Publications of the Modern Language Association* 70 (1955): 337–49.

Crawley, Thomas. *The Structure of Leaves of Grass*. Austin: University of Texas Press, 1970.

Furness, C., ed. *Walt Whitman's Workshop*. New York: Russell & Russell, 1964.

Golden, A., ed. *Walt Whitman's Blue Book*. New York: New York Public Library, 1968.

Griffith, Clark. "Sex and Death: the Significance of Whitman's 'Calamus' Themes." *Philological Quarterly* 39 (1960): 18–38.

Hindus, Milton, ed. *Walt Whitman: The Critical Heritage*. New York: Barnes and Noble, 1971.

————. *Leaves of Grass: One Hundred Years After*. Stanford, Calif.: Stanford University Press, 1955.

Kaplan, Justin. *Walt Whitman: A Life*. New York: Simon and Schuster, 1980.

Lewis, R. W. B., ed. *The Presence of Walt Whitman*. New York: Columbia University Press, 1962.

Loving, Jerome. *Emerson, Whitman and the American Muse*. Chapel Hill: University of North Carolina Press, 1982.

Matthiessen, F. O. *American Renaissance*. New York: Oxford University Press, 1941.

Miller, Edwin Haviland. *Walt Whitman's Poetry: A Psychological Journey*. New York: New York University Press, 1969.

————, ed. *A Century of Whitman Criticism*. Bloomington: Indiana University Press, 1969.

Miller, James E., Jr. *The American Quest for a Supreme Fiction: Whitman's Legacy in the Personal Epic*. Chicago: University of Chicago Press, 1979.

————. *A Critical Guide to "Leaves of Grass."* Chicago: University of Chicago Press, 1957.

————. *Walt Whitman*. New York: Twayne Publishers, 1962.

————. *Whitman's "Song of Myself": Origin, Growth, Meaning*. New York: Dodd, Mead, 1964.

Murphy, Francis, ed. *Walt Whitman*. Harmondsworth: Penguin, 1969.

Musgrave, S. *T.S. Eliot and Walt Whitman*. Wellington: New Zealand University Press, 1952.

Pearce, Roy Harvey. *The Continuity of American Poetry*. Princeton: Princeton University Press, 1961.

————, ed. *Whitman*. Englewood Cliffs, N.J.: Prentice-Hall, 1962.

————, ed. *Leaves of Grass (Facsimile Edition of the 1860 Text)*. Ithaca, N.Y.: Great Seal Books, 1961.

Rubin, Joseph Jay. *The Historic Whitman*. University Park, Penns.: Pennsylvania State University Press, 1973.

Stovall, Floyd. *The Foreground of Leaves of Grass*. Charlottesville: University Press of Virginia, 1974.

Strom, Susan. "'Face to Face': Whitman's Biblical References in 'Crossing Brooklyn Ferry.'" *Walt Whitman Review* 24 (1978): 7–16

Symonds, John Addington. *Walt Whitman: A Study*. New York: AMS Press, 1968.

Trilling, Lionel. "Sermon on a Text from Whitman." *Nation* 160 (1945): 215–20.

Waskow, Howard. *Whitman: Explorations in Form.* Chicago: University of Chicago Press, 1966.

White, William, ed. *Daybooks and Notebooks.* 3 vols. New York: New York University Press, 1978.

Zweig, Paul. *Walt Whitman: The Making of the Poet.* New York: Basic Books, 1984.

Acknowledgments

"Walt Whitman: The Real Me" by Harold Bloom from *The New York Review of Books*, copyright © 1984 by *The New York Review of Books*. Reprinted by permission.

"Whitman" by D.H. Lawrence from *Studies in Classic American Literature* by D.H. Lawrence, copyright © 1923 by Thomas Seltzer, Inc., 1951 by Frieda Lawrence. Reprinted by permission.

"Policy Made Personal" by Kenneth Burke from *Leaves of Grass One Hundred Years After* edited by Milton Hindus, copyright © 1955 by Stanford University Press. Reprinted by permission.

"The Theory of America" by Richard Chase from *Walt Whitman Reconsidered* by Richard Chase, copyright © 1955 by Richard Chase. Reprinted by permission of William Sloane Associates, Inc., Publishers.

"Whitman Justified: The Poet in 1860" by Roy Harvey Pearce from *Historicism Once More* by Roy Harvey Pearce, copyright © 1969 by Princeton University Press. Reprinted by permission.

"The Delicacy of Walt Whitman" by James A. Wright from *The Presence of Walt Whitman* edited by R.W.B. Lewis, copyright © 1962 by Columbia University Press. Reprinted by permission.

"Always Going Out and Coming In" by R.W.B. Lewis from *Trials of the Word* by R.W.B. Lewis, copyright © 1965 by R.W.B. Lewis. Reprinted by permission of Harcourt, Brace, Jovanovich.

"Whitman's Image of Voice: To the Tally of My Soul" by Harold Bloom from *Agon* by Harold Bloom, copyright © 1982 by Oxford University Press. Reprinted by permission.

"The Wound-Dresser" by Paul Zweig from *Walt Whitman: The Making of the Poet* by Paul Zweig, copyright © 1984 by Basic Books. Reprinted by permission.

Index

A
Abrams, Meyer H., 71
Adam, 131
Adonais, 8
aesthetics, 96, 106, 125
    Whitman's philosophy, 69, 107, 110,
        122
"After Trying a Certain Book," 92
age
    views of Whitman, 40
Alastor, 7
Alcott, Bronson, 111
Alcott, Louisa May, 152
Allen, Gay Wilson, 7, 74, 95
"Always Going Out and Coming In," 99–
    125
American literature, 128, 140, 142
    analyzed by Whitman, 122, 124
    contrast with European literature,
        90
    influence on Whitman, 105
    influenced by Whitman, 1, 7, 94, 99,
        106, 130, 131, 157
    moral foundations, 18
    progenitors, 127
    social responsibility, 60, 61
    Whitman's stature, 4, 112
American poetry, 127, 139
    form, 97
    influenced by Whitman, 7, 88, 92,
        100, 108, 109, 110, 125, 130, 131
    Whitman's stature, 4
American Primer, 72
"American Scholar, The," 110
"American Sublime, The," 140
"Among the Multitude," 40
anancoluthon, 41
anarchy, 57
antithesis, 27, 28
Anxiety of Influence, The, 131
archetype, 61, 62, 108, 111, 124
Aristotle, 27
Arnold, Matthew, 56, 57, 58

art, 114–16, 119
    creative act, 100
    function, 79
    humanism, 80
    imagination, 92
    moral basis, 18
    philosophy, 48, 49
    relation to culture, 124
    symbolism, 50
    Whitman's philosophy, 69, 105, 106,
        113
"Art and Artists," 105
"As I Ebb'd with the Ocean of Life," 8,
        75, 84, 85, 114–19, 122, 123
    poetic identity, 6, 7
    theme of singleness, 59
"As Adam Early in the Morning," 131
Ashbery, John, 7, 130, 141, 142
Asselineau, Roger, 74, 121, 124
Atlantic Monthly, 116
autobiography, 73, 74, 77, 105
    Whitman's style, 84
auto–eroticism, *see* masturbation

B
"Bacchus," 129, 131–41
Backward Glance, A, 66, 69, 104, 106,
        124, 125
ballad, 46
"Bardic Symbols," 116
"Base of All Metaphysics," 85
bathos, 77
Baudelaire, Charles, 71, 117
"beat" poetry, 100
beauty, 117
Beckett, Samuel, 8
Benét, Stephen Vincent, 62
bird
    symbolism, 46, 47, 49–51, 53, 132,
        134–38
blade
    symbolism, 39
Blake, William, 67, 68

blood
motif in Whitman, 37
Bloom, Harold, 127–42
body
associated qualities, 27
celebration by Whitman, 46
relationship to soul, 22
symbolism in Whitman's poetry, 35
Borges, Jorge Luis, 8
"Boston Ballad, A," 104
Bradstreet, Anne, 127
Breton, Andre, 8
Bridge, The, 123, 137
influenced by Whitman, 7
"British Literature," 91
"Broadway Pageant, A," 47
Brodkey, Harold
influenced by Whitman, 7
"Broken Tower, The," 116
Brown, Lew, 156
Bryant, William Cullen, 105, 127, 128
admired by Whitman, 89
"Bunch poem," 112
"Burial," 79
"Burial Poem," 109
Burke, Kenneth, 25–54
Burroughs, John, 124
"By Blue Ontario's Shore," 3, 75
symbolism, 38, 39

C
"Calamus" poems, 78, 80, 85, 132, 154, 155
autobiographical elements, 74
celebration of equality, 40
masculine love, 15, 46, 116
poetic identity, 6
revisions, 121
sexual motifs, 35
structure, 41
symbolism, 38, 47, 48
theme, 50
Camden, N.J., 120, 123, 124
Campion, Thomas, 91
Carlyle, Thomas, 56, 101, 104
Carroll, Lewis, 130
"Cavalry Crossing a Ford," 122
"Chanting the Square Deific," 132
"Chants Democratic," 65, 75, 80, 121
charity, 19, 20, 22
Chase, Richard, 55–63, 111, 119, 123
Chevy-Chase, 46

childhood, 81, 82
"Children of Adam" poems, 78, 80, 84, 132
poetic identity, 6
"Child's Reminiscence, A," 80, 115, 117
Christianity
limitations, 20
viewed by Whitman and Emerson, 1
"City of Orgies," 116
Civil War, U.S.
effect on Whitman, 45, 46, 52, 63, 120
reflected in Whitman's poetry, 119, 122
Whitman's participation, 4, 87, 143–57
Cole, Thomas, 127
community, 57, 62
compassion
Whitman's philosophy, 21
comradeship
political goal, 62
theme in Whitman's poetry, 16, 17, 30, 41, 58, 121, 124, 155, 157
"Conflict of Convictions, The," 122
consciousness, 111
conservatism, 58
Constitution, 25, 58
Conversations with Eckermann, 89
Cowley, Malcolm, 72
Cox, James M., 87
Crane, Hart, 116, 123, 127, 129, 137, 138
influenced by Whitman, 7, 100
Crane, Stephen, 61, 146
Crescent, 103
criticism, literary, 131, 132
"Crossing Brooklyn Ferry," 8, 72, 78, 112, 113, 115, 123
motherhood theme, 42
poetic identity, 7
temporal sequence, 40
culture, 28
relation to art, 124
Whitman's philosophy, 72
Culture and Anarchy, 56, 58

D
Daily Times, 114, 116
Daily Union, 144
de Man, Paul, 142
death, 135, 137, 144
poetic relationship to love, 50

relation to poetry, 122
theme in Whitman's poetry, 16–18, 20, 23, 34, 41, 43, 46–49, 52, 53, 80, 82, 83, 109, 114, 117, 139, 147, 157
"Death Carol," 52
"Death of Longfellow," 89
Declaration of Independence, 25, 58
"Delicacy of Walt Whitman, The," 87–97
"Democracy," 121
democracy, 57
    aesthetics, 106, 107, 110
    archetypes, 61
    association with comradeship, 35
    compared to European governments, 28
    espousal by Whitman, 41, 44, 45, 59, 62, 99, 121, 122, 125, 155
    founding philosophy of U.S., 25
    historical importance, 58
    idealism of Whitman, 26, 30
    individualism, 29
    paradox of U.S. expansionism, 31
    philosophical ideal, 23
    political corruption, 32
    relationship to literature, 60, 66
    relationship to nature and science, 27
    theme in Whitman's poetry, 16, 17, 42, 48, 49
    Whitman's philosophy, 22, 55, 56, 63
"Democratic Vistas," 36, 121, 124, 125
    literary views, 66
    political views, 25–32, 55–59, 61–63
    prophetic poetry, 68
dialectic process, 44, 56
Dickinson, Emily, 3, 4
diction, 93
    Whitman's style, 94, 95
diversity
    theme in Whitman's work, 34
Doyle, Peter, 156
dream, 111
Drum Taps, 93
    realism, 61
    theme of comradeship, 16
    Whitman's Civil War experiences, 4, 46, 119, 145

E
Eagle, 103, 104
"Earth, My Likeness," 41
east

characterized by Whitman, 31
ego, 2, 111, 135
élan vital, 108, 113
Eldridge, Charles, 143, 147
elegy, 131, 132, 134
    contributions of Whitman, 7, 8
Eliot, T.S., 61
    influenced by Whitman, 7, 9, 100
Emerson, Ralph Waldo, 4, 104, 106, 107, 110, 127–33, 138–42, 151, 157
    admired by Whitman, 89
    aid to Whitman, 147, 148
    comparison with Whitman, 45
    influence on Robert Frost, 7
    influence on Whitman, 8, 56, 73, 101
    moral emphasis, 18
    praise of Whitman, 9, 112, 113
    views on nature, 27
    views on religion, 1
    views on poets, 70
"Enfants d'Adam" poems, *see* "Children of Adam" poems
English language
    poetic possibilities, 92
English literature
    influenced by Whitman, 110
epic, 106
Epicureanism, 130
equality, 62
eroticism
    element of Whitman's style, 5
Essays, 138
"Ethiopia Saluting the Colors," 91
"Europe," 78
"Europe: The 72d and 73d Year of These States," 104
"Evangeline," 90
expansionism, 31

F
"Facing West from California's Shores," 132
"Faith Poem," 76
feudalism
    compared to democracy, 2, 7, 28
Figure of Echo, The, 139
Fitzgerald, F. Scott, 125
flag
    symbolism, 36
Flaubert, Gustave, 21
form, poetic, 95–97, 106, 107
Fredericksburg, battle of, 143, 144

free trade, 55
free verse, 110
freedom
    as requisite of the soul, 18–20, 22
    concept in American letters, 127
    relationship to poetry, 72, 76
    Whitman's philosophy, 21, 23, 57, 110
Freeman, 103
Free–Soil Party, 103
Freneau, Philip Morin, 127
Freud, Sigmund, 2, 111, 135
Frost, Robert, 4, 61
    influenced by Emerson, 7
Fugitive Slave Law, 103
"Full of Life Now," 78

G
Galaxy, 121
García Lorca, Federico, 78
Gilded Age, 56
Ginsberg, Allen, 8, 65, 72
"Glimpse, A," 116
God
    symbolism, 50
Goethe, Johann Wolfgang von, 70, 89, 104
Good Gray Poet, The, 121, 157
Gosse, Edmund William, 124
grammar, 96
Grant, Ulysses S., 56, 57
grass
    symbolism, 36, 37, 39
"Great Are the Myths," 75

H
"Hand–Mirror, A," 115, 116
Hapgood, Major, 147, 149
Hawthorne, Nathaniel
    moral emphasis, 18
Hegel, Georg Wilhelm Friedrich, 44, 56, 132
Hemingway, Ernest
    influenced by Whitman, 7
Henley, William Ernest, 20
hero
    Whitman's concept of artist, 105, 106
Herrick, Robert, 91
history, 57
    importance of democracy, 58
    Whitman's philosophy, 28, 56, 63
Hollander, John, 138, 139

Holloway, John, 70
Holmes, Oliver Wendell, Sr., 124
Holy Spirit
    symbolism, 50
homosexuality
    theme in Whitman's work, 35, 115, 121, 155, 156
Hospital Sketches, 152
"Hours Continuing Long, Sore and Heavy–Hearted," 115, 116, 121
Houseboat Days, 141, 142
Howells, William Dean, 61
Huckleberry Finn, 61, 128
    influence on Hemingway, 7
humanism
    element of Whitman's art, 66, 70, 79, 80
hypertension, 156

I
"I Hear America Singing," 75
"I Saw in Louisiana," 116
"I Sing the Body Electric," 37
"I Was Looking A Long While," 75
iambic meter, 90–92, 97
iambic pentameter, 91, 110
id, 2, 111
"Idea of Order at Key West, The," 140
idealism, 57
    Whitman's style, 63
identity,
    theme in Whitman's poetry, 14, 17, 34, 40
imagination
    relationship to art, 92
    relationship to poetic form, 97
imagism, 100
"In Cabin'd Ships at Sea," 48
In Memoriam, 8
"In Paths Untrodden," 132
Indian Bureau, 120, 121
individuality
    espousal by Whitman, 13, 14, 29, 55, 57, 59–61, 63, 121
"Inscription," 32
Isaiah, 39

J
James, Henry, Sr., 124
Jarrell, Randall, 92, 93
Jesus Christ, 131, 132
    symbolism, 50

journalism, 103
Jung, Carl, 108, 111

K
Kafka, Franz, 8
Kahler, Erich, 72
Kaplan, Justin, 7, 149
Keats, John, 80, 116
Kenner, Hugh, 130
King Lear, 8, 112
"Kosmos," 79

L
Laforgue, Jules, 97
language, 42
    poetic usage, 69–71, 76, 82, 92, 117
    style, 95
    usage and innovations, 73
    Whitman's philosophy, 72
    Whitman's style, 93, 94, 122
Lawrence, D. H., 11–23, 84, 122, 132
    praise of Whitman, 9
"Leaf of Faces, A," 78
Lear, Edward, 130
leaves,
    symbolism, 37–39, 53
Leaves of Grass, 66, 75, 80, 132, 138, 157
    assessment of Paul Zweig, 8
    autobiographical elements, 77
    innovations in language, 70
    personalization of history, 25
    political philosophy, 32–45
    praised by Emerson, 9
    preface, 88
    prophetic poetry, 68
    publication, 6
    revisions, 69, 79–86, 99–125
        early editions, 72
        edition of 1855, 10–11
        edition of 1856, 111–14
        edition of 1860, 73, 74, 114–19
        edition of 1867, 119–22
        editions of 1871 and later, 122–25
        edition of 1876 ("Centennial Edition"), 124
        edition of 1892 ("Deathbed" edition), 96
    utopianism, 65
Lee, Robert E., 147
Lewis, R. W. B., 99–125
liberalism, 29

"Like Decorations in a Nigger Cemetery," 109
lilac
    symbolism, 46–53, 132, 134–36, 138
Lincoln, Abraham
    admired by Whitman, 4, 6, 46, 47, 50, 115, 120, 122, 125, 131, 132, 135, 150
literary criticism, 131, 132
literature
    influenced by Whitman, 100
    moral function, 30
    political force, 60
    realism, 61
    role in society, 57, 59, 62, 66
    traditions and conventions, 8
    Whitman's philosophy, 32
literature, American, *see* American literature
Longfellow, Henry Wadsworth, 105, 124
    admired by Whitman, 89
    comparison with Whitman, 90, 94
    moral emphasis, 18
    poetic forms, 92
love, 19, 135
    limitations, 20
    philosophical ideal, 23, 30
    symbolism, 50
    theme in Whitman's poetry, 16, 17, 46, 157

M
Man Who Died, The, 132
"March in the Ranks Hard–prest, A," 93, 146
masturbation, 5, 6, 133–35
materialism, 57
    U.S. political milieu, 25–27
Mathiessen, F. O., 145
"Me Imperturbe," 75
melancholia, 135
Melville, Herman, 23, 106, 108, 133
    comparison with Whitman, 122
    moral emphasis, 18
Memoranda during the War, 150, 153
men, 15, 16
    ideals of Whitman, 30
metalepsis, 139
metaphor, 139
metaphysics, 60
middle class, 57
Mill, John Stuart, 56

Miller, Henry, 8
Miller, James, 72
Milton, John, 91, 104, 139
mind
    relationship to soul, 22
"Miracles," 76
Mirror and the Lamp, The, 71
Moby Dick, 73, 128, 133
morality
    American literature, 18
    basis of literature, 30
    structural presentation in poetry, 43
    Whitman's philosophy, 19
motherhood, 28
    theme in Whitman's work, 40, 42,
        47–49, 52
Mourning and Melancholia, 135
"My Tribute to Four Poets," 89
"Myself and Mine," 76
mysticism, 105

N
nativity
    theme in Whitman's work, 34, 40
naturalism, 61
"Nature," 27
nature
    relationship to poetry, 66
    theme in Whitman's poetry, 27, 104,
        106, 113, 116
negation
    structure of Whitman's poetry, 42,
        43
neo–romanticism, 100
New Orleans, 103, 147
New York City
    reflected in Whitman's work, 102
Nietzsche, Friedrich, 87, 88, 92, 130
Norris, Frank, 61
north
    characterized by Whitman, 31
"Not Heaving from My Ribb'd Breast
        Only," 41
November Boughs, 150

O
"O Captain! My Captain!," 91
O'Connor, William Douglas, 121, 143,
        147
Octopus, The, 61
"Ode on a Grecian Urn," 116

"Other Tradition, The," 141, 142
"Our Old Feuillage," 39
"Out of the Cradle Endlessly Rocking,"
        33, 51, 69, 77, 83, 115–17, 122,
        138, 147, 157
    poetic identity, 7
    motherhood theme, 42, 47
    singleness theme, 59

P
parallelism, 96, 97
"Passage to India," 66, 67, 99, 105, 123
Patent Office, U.S., 150
Pater, Walter, 130
Pearce, Roy Harvey, 65–86
Perry, Bliss, 7
personalism
    espousal by Whitman, 55, 57, 59–61
philosophy, political
    Whitman's ideas, 55
"Pictures," 104, 151
Poe, Edgar Allan
    moral emphasis, 18
"Poem of Joys," 78, 80
"Poem of Wonder at the Resurrection of
        Wheat," 112
"Poet, The," 70, 73, 106, 139
poetic form, *see* form, poetic
poetry, 114, 119, 121, 122, 129, 132, 139
    allusions, 8
    archetypes, 61
    audience and publication, 78
    autobiographical elements, 74
    deconstructionism, 142
    form, 96, 97
    importance of language, 117
    influenced by Whitman, 17, 73, 82,
        83, 90, 94, 100, 110, 125
    meaning, 93
    personal grief and artistic achieve-
        ment, 116
    philosophy, 65, 138
    purpose, 79, 80, 88, 115
    relationship and contrast with
        prophecy, 67, 68, 120
    social force, 57, 66
    source of power, 75, 76
    style, 95
    symbolism, 71
    traditions of the past, 89
    typography, 102

Whitman's philosophy, 69, 70, 72, 81, 92, 105–08, 113
poetry, American, *see* American poetry
"Poets to Come," 3, 65
"Policy Made Personal," 25–54
political philosophy
    Whitman's ideas, 55
Pound, Ezra, 73
    influenced by Whitman, 100
power, 50
"Prairies, The," 127, 128
praise
    use by Whitman, 52
"Preface of 1855," 88, 91, 92, 95, 103, 105, 107
prophecy
    contrast with poetry, 120
    relationship to poetry, 67, 68
    Whitman's style, 58, 59, 66, 84
prosody, 88
    innovations of Whitman, 90–92, 110
"Proto–Leaf," 74
Psalms, 39
punctuation, 112

Q
"Quadroon Girl," 90

R
Ransom, J.C., 35
realism, 57, 61, 76, 146
"Reconciliation," 91
Red Badge of Courage, The, 61, 146
Redpath, James, 152, 153
religion
    relationship to poetry, 71
    Whitman's philosophy, 28, 65, 66, 70, 80, 105
"Reminiscence," 81
Representative Men, 70
repression, 135
"Respondez! Respondez!," 44, 45
"Reversals," 45
Rhetoric, 27
rhythm, 53
"Rock, The"
    influenced by Whitman, 7
romanticism, 71, 106, 116
    view of the poet, 7
Rossetti, William, 124, 157

Rubin, Joseph Jay, 7
Ruskin, John, 124

S
Saintsbury, George Edward Bateman, 124
Salut au Monde!, 33, 78, 80
salvation
    limitations, 19
    Christian view, 20
Sand, George, 102, 104
Saturday Press, 115
Saturnalia, 44
Sawyer, Thomas, 156
Scarlet Letter, The, 18
"Scented Herbage of My Breast," 38, 116, 117
    symbolism, 39
Schyberg, Frederik, 74
science
    relationship to democracy and nature, 27
sea
    symbolism, 81, 82
self–reliance, 129
sentimentalism, 77
Sequel to Drum-Taps, 120
sex
    theme in Whitman's work, 34, 35, 37, 42, 43, 110, 111, 113, 121, 133, 134, 139
Shakespeare, William, 28, 104
Shapiro, Karl, 72
Shelley, Percy Bysshe, 8, 61, 135
    view of the poet's role, 7
slavery, 21
"Sleep–Chasings," 79, 111
"Sleepers, The," 35, 72, 79, 109, 111, 121, 153
    search for identity, 6
smell, 39, 47
"So Long!," 79, 115–17
social reform, 55
"Song for Occupations," 75
"Song of Myself," 38, 105, 113, 123, 133–36, 153
    autobiographical elements, 101
    democratic aesthetic, 107
    divinity of poet, 108
    place in American poetry, 109
    poetic identity, 2, 3, 7

political philosophy, 56, 59
prophetic elements, 120
revisions, 72, 75, 118, 121
sexual imagery, 5, 35, 111
structure, 41, 106
symbolism, 36, 37, 48, 51
"Song of Prudence," 75
Song of Songs, 138
"Song of the Answerer," 75, 76
"Song of the Broad–Axe," 27, 53, 75
"Song of the Exposition," 33
"Song of the Open Road," 40, 44
"Song of the Redwood–Tree," 27
soul, 137, 138
    need for freedom, 20, 22
    philosophical ideal, 23
    poetic identity, 2
    principle of comradeship, 16
    relationship to literature, 30
    requirements, 19
    Whitman's liberating view, 18, 21
Sound and the Fury, The, 61
south
    characterized by Whitman, 31, 32
Specimen Days, 58, 92, 125, 150, 153
    Whitman's respect for early U.S.
        poets, 89
Spinoza, Benedict, 43
spirit
    compared to physical world, 27
Whitman's political philosophy, 26
"Spontaneous Me," 35, 113
star
    symbolism, 46, 47, 49–51, 53, 132
"Starting from Paumanok," 38, 47, 74
    structure, 42, 43
Stevens, Wallace, 4, 61, 117, 127, 129–
    31, 139, 141, 142
    influenced by Whitman, 2, 7, 9, 100,
        109
Strachey, Lytton, 89
stream–of–consciousness, 106
succession, 28
Sun Also Rises, The, 61
"Sunday Morning," 117
"Sun–Down Poem," 72
superego, 2
"Supermarket in California, A," 65
symbolism, 71, 100
sympathy
    Whitman's philosophy, 19–22
"Syringia," 142

T
talea, 132, 136
tally
    symbolism, 132, 135–39
Taylor, Bayard, 124
Taylor, Edward, 127
Tennyson, Alfred Lord, 124
    comparison with Whitman, 8
"Theory of America, The," 55–63
"There Was a Child Went Forth," 76,
    101, 109, 110, 114, 118
"These I Singing in Spring," 39
"This Compost," 75, 112, 113, 116
Thoreau, Henry David, 111, 127
Thus Spake Zarathustra, 92
"To Zole, the Painter, Departing for
    Europe," 127
"To the Leaven'd Soil They Trod," 31
"To Think of Time," 79, 109
Tocqueville, Alexis de, 56, 58
transcendentalism
    influence on Whitman, 55
transumption, 138, 139
Tribune, 104, 124
Trinity, Holy
    symbolism, 50
trope, 132, 137, 139
Trowbridge, John, 156
typography, 111
    effect on Whitman's poetry, 102, 105

U
unconscious, 111
United States
    celebrated by Whitman,
        99
    Civil War, 150–52, 155
    compared to European political de-
        velopment, 19, 28
    cultural milieu, 88
    expansionism, 31
    founding philosophy, 25, 58, 62
    literature, 60
    materialistic ethos, 90
    political development, 26, 27
    pre–Civil War politics, 115
    social milieu, 57, 59
    viewed by Whitman, 29, 30, 32, 55,
        124, 153
universalism
    theme in Whitman's work, 14, 29,
        34, 44, 108, 123

V
Victorian Age, 89
Victorian Sage, 70
visionary poetry, 67, 68
voice in literature, 131, 135, 137, 138

W
Walden, 73
"Walt Whitman," (poem), 74, 75, 80
Washington, D.C., 147–49, 152
Waste Land, The
    influenced by Whitman, 7
Wave, The
    influenced by Whitman, 7
west
    characterized by Whitman, 31
"When Lilacs Last in the Dooryard
    Bloom'd," 8, 32, 122, 131, 139,
    140
    celebration of Lincoln, 115
    color associations, 35
    elegy for Lincoln, 120
    personalization of history, 25
    poetic identity, 7
    political philosophy, 45–53
    portrayal of women, 31
    symbolism, 36, 132, 134, 135, 137,
    138
    Whitman's sense of failure, 5
"Whitman" (essay), 11–23
Whitman, George, 143, 144
Whitman, Jeff, 148, 149
Whitman, Martha, 147

"Whitman Justified: The Poet in 1860,"
    65–86
"Whitman's Image of Voice: To the Tally
    of My Soul," 127–42
Whittier, John Greenleaf
    admired by Whitman, 89
"Whoever You Are," 116
Wilde, Oscar, 124
wildness
    theme in American literature, 127
Williams, William Carlos, 110
wisdom, 50
"With Antecedents," 40
"Witnesses," 90
women, 15, 16, 47
    idealism of Whitman, 30, 31
word
    usage and innovations, 72
"Word out of the Sea, A," 69, 76–81, 83,
    117
"Wound–Dresser, The," 143–57
    Whitman's Civil War experiences, 4
Wright, James A., 87–97
Wyatt, Thomas, 91

Y
Yeats, William Butler, 67, 68

Z
Zweig, Paul, 143–57
    assessment of Whitman's work, 7, 8
    biography of Whitman, 4, 5, 9